S0-BST-938

American Heat

Studies in Social, Political, and Legal Philosophy
Series Editor: James P. Sterba, University of Notre Dame

This series analyzes and evaluates critically the major political, social, and legal ideals, institutions, and practices of our time. The analysis may be historical or problem-centered; the evaluation may focus on theoretical underpinnings or practical implications. Among the recent titles in the series are:

American Heat

Ethical Problems with the United States' Response to Global Warming

Donald A. Brown

ROWMAN & LITTLEFIELD PUBLISHERS, INC.
Lanham • Boulder • New York • Oxford

CABRINI COLLEGE LIBRARY
610 KING OF PRUSSIA ROAD
RADNOR, PA 19087

48966505

ROWMAN & LITTLEFIELD PUBLISHERS, INC.

Published in the United States of America
by Rowman & Littlefield Publishers, Inc.
4720 Boston Way, Lanham, Maryland 20706
www.rowmanlittlefield.com

12 Hid's Copse Road
Cumnor Hill, Oxford OX2 9JJ, England

Copyright © 2002 by Rowman & Littlefield Publishers, Inc.

All rights reserved. No part of this publication may be reproduced, stored
in a retrieval system, or transmitted in any form or by any means, electronic,
mechanical, photocopying, recording, or otherwise, without the prior permission
of the publisher.

British Library Cataloguing in Publication Information Available

Library of Congress Cataloging-in-Publication Data

Brown, Donald A., 1944–
    American heat : ethical problems with the United States' response
to global warming / Donald A. Brown.
        p. cm. — (Studies in social, political, and legal philosophy)
    Includes bibliographical references and index.
    ISBN 0-7425-1295-9 (cloth : alk. paper) — ISBN 0-7425-1296-7 (pbk. : alk. paper)
    1. Global warming—Government policy—Moral and ethical aspects—United
States. 2. Environmental ethics—United States. I. Title. II. Series.
    QC981.8.G56 B75 2002
    179'.1—dc21   2002001798

Printed in the United States of America

⊗™ The paper used in this publication meets the minimum requirements of American
National Standard for Information Sciences—Permanence of Paper for Printed Library
Materials, ANSI/NISO Z39.48-1992.

Contents

Foreword:
Political Power and Moral Authority

POLITICAL POWER AND MORAL AUTHORITY

Political power and moral authority are not the same thing. The current worldwide policy debates on global environmental change make this dramatically apparent. While individual nation-states exercise considerable international power, these same nations experience a corresponding decline in moral authority on the world stage.

What accounts for this apparent paradox? How is it that the statements of political leaders sound more and more hollow, lacking the moral authority to inspire respect, even within their own constituencies? The answer is quite simple: Moral authority cannot be commanded; it can only be acknowledged. Moreover, to be acknowledged, it must be earned. Moral authority cannot, in this sense, emanate from the top downward in any social structure. Instead, it must of necessity emerge from the bottom up. This is so because moral authority rests ultimately on a widely shared and mutually accepted sense of legitimacy. People, communities, nations, and international groups attribute moral authority to particular spokesmen or representatives of power only to the extent that they acknowledge their legitimacy and become convinced of their moral vision.

Sources of power are clearly identifiable, but legitimacy is far more difficult to identify and to sustain—especially in global affairs. Recent street clashes between government authority and civil society in country after country make this clear. In the Philippines, in the former Yugoslavia, and in Peru, sudden changes in the character of political regimes have occurred because, in the eyes of individuals and the institutions of civil society, political figures have lost their legitimacy and moral authority to govern. When legitimacy collapses, those in power can continue to rule only with the increasing use of force, and this effort further undermines their moral authority.

On a global scale, this process is now made manifest in the escalating street protests that accompany each successive meeting of the G-8 countries— ostensibly the most powerful political regimes in the world. These repeated clashes underscore that political power and moral authority are not the same thing. No amount of political, economic, or military power can, on its own, establish legitimacy in the hearts and minds of the world's peoples who feel that their needs are not being met.

If moral authority and legitimacy—on which it is based—are not located automatically within the structures of power, where can they be found? How can we locate them? How does moral authority come to be recognized, acknowledged, and strengthened? What role, if any, can moral authority play in formulating public policy on a local, national, or global scale? These are troubling questions, but they demand answers.

In the following pages, Donald Brown explores these issues in great depth in light of the moral shortcomings of the official bargaining positions of the United States on global warming. It is his belief that these moral shortcomings are not widely discussed or understood by the American public. Further, he argues that if these ethical failures were more widely understood by the American public, a large portion of the public would react to the morally indefensible stance of the American government. Brown suggests that—just as it did in the days of antislavery and civil rights campaigns—a fully informed public would react by demanding that its government abandon its unethical bargaining positions and devise a more morally acceptable approach to global warming issues.

THE NATURE OF MORALITY AND ETHICS

Morality and ethics have to do with the tension between the way the world *is* and the way it *ought to be*. In everyday experience, we all recognize moral injunctions when people say things like, "This is what *ought to* happen," "There *ought to* be a law," or "I think they *should*." Each of these statements rests on an implied morality or embedded ethic. In reality, all propositions about how we should behave or how public policy should be formulated rest on an implicit ethic and implied morality.

Where do these systems of morality come from? How do we acquire them? On one level, it is apparent that concepts of morality are derived from the world's great religious traditions. All the world's religions have developed norms of morally acceptable behavior. To a large degree, these can be recognized as deontological—or rule based—systems of ethics, emphasizing "thou shalt" or "thou shalt not." In these instances, norms about how we ought to behave individually and collectively are linked very explicitly to particular understandings of how the world is constructed, what animates it, and what gives human life and the created order meaning and purpose.

The world's great religious traditions, however, are not the only origin of ethical reasoning. Philosophers have long discussed moral systems as a feature of the universal human capacity for making reasoned judgments and exercising choice. In addition, anthropologists have documented the fact that systems of ethical reasoning are present in all cultures. In fact, "ethics"—like culture itself—can be said to be a human universal. No known culture exists without an ethic of some sort, just as no known culture exists without the phenomenon of language.

This is not to say that there currently exists an easily identifiable uniform or universal ethic. To affirm this would be like asserting that there is a universal language, and this is manifestly absurd in the face of the evidence of the enormous variety of languages across human cultures. Nevertheless, although a universal language does not exist, the tools of linguistics allow us to look comparatively at different languages and discern the grammar of each one respectively. When this is done, additional statements can be made on a more general level about the nature of language, grammar, and the human capacity for understanding beyond any one instance of these things in a particular language. Similarly, ethicists can help us understand the moral logic in any particular culture, and they can help us view this ethic comparatively across different cultures.

It is important to understand that this kind of analysis does not focus on explicit statements of morality or formal statements of belief. These can be quite misleading. What people say they are doing and what they actually do can be quite distinct. Behavior, not intention, is the focal point of this kind of ethical analysis.

The analogy to the study of language is useful. When descriptive linguists study the grammar of a living language, they do not look up rules in a book. On the contrary, they study the unconscious patterns and implicit rules that speakers of that language use collectively in everyday speech. In a similar manner, ethicists can reveal the implicit ethic in any culture by examining its behavior and recording the implicit rationale for that behavior.

In this book, Donald Brown guides the reader to examine the implicit morality of the U.S. position on global warming. He does this by analyzing the specific stance that the American government has taken repeatedly in global climate negotiations. The ethic of the American administration is rarely—if ever—stated directly, but it is nevertheless manifest implicitly in the manner in which the administration frames the problem and has chosen to act or not act. The strength of this book is that it analyzes the implicit morality of U.S. government behavior.

THE SCALE AND SCOPE OF ETHICAL ANALYSIS

Some might argue that considering the ethics or morality of the official U.S. position on global warming is an ill-conceived exercise from the outset. The United States, so the argument might go, has done nothing illegal. There is no authoritative international convention or treaty approved by the U.S. Senate that the government is violating. Voters elect politicians, not statesmen, and political leaders inevitably represent the perceived self-interest of the constituency that brings them to power. The world cannot reasonably expect the U.S. government to act other than it has.

Strictly speaking, this may well be so. Much of what the United States has said officially in the global warming talks may be ill informed or ill advised, but it is not proposing anything illegal.

The problem with this stance, however, is that it sidesteps the essential character of moral analysis. The question is not what behavior is *legal* but what behavior is *morally defensible*. Legality and morality are not the same thing. A discussion of ethics begins where legality leaves off. There may not yet be laws that forbid or command specific activities, but there are nonetheless widely acknowledged principles that, it can be argued, should govern behavior in the absence of explicit laws. These principles are in the realm of what is often called "soft law"—that is, law not yet codified into statutes—but they are principles that have demonstrated growing acceptance within and among states and a growing recognition in practice.

For example, what might be called the "affected-party-participation principle" would emphasize that those affected by a particular decision should have a means of participating in making that decision. This broad principle is a general statement of the kind of particular principle that America's founding fathers insisted on and were willing to go to war to defend—"no taxation without representation." In addition, the "innocent-party-indemnification principle" is widely acknowledged in practice. It suggests that if innocent individuals or groups are hurt or suffer damages from the actions of another group or individual through no fault of their own, it is reasonable to expect that they should receive some measure of compensation. Similarly, the "polluter-pays principle" is widely understood and acknowledged as fair and equitable in environmental affairs. It holds simply that those who cause pollution should pay for its abatement and mitigation. Although specific laws may be passed to enact aspects of these broad principles, the principles themselves exist whether or not statues have been formulated to encapsulate them.

The importance of these principles of soft law is especially pronounced in global environmental matters. As a human community, we are confronted with a series of global ecological crises, engendered in part by patterns of human behavior. These circumstances are systemwide and involve the biogeochemical processes in an ecosystem that transcends all national borders. This is our current dilemma. Global institutions with sufficient authority and control do not yet exist to match the global character of the crisis that the human community confronts. In this respect, our tools do not match the task. We face a global crisis, yet our response is international, often collapsing into conflicts of self-interest between contending nation-states. As Donald Brown amply illustrates in this book, this kind of myopic squabbling is fundamentally misplaced. It should be—and would be if the public were widely aware of it—a major source of American shame.

The only way out of this self-defeating mismatch between the crisis and the tools that we have used to respond to it is for national leaders to begin to act as global statesmen. This challenge requires moving beyond existing law, drawing instead on sound principles for ethical behavior in a complex ecosystem. For this to occur, there needs to be a realignment of power and authority in the global governance system. New laws will have to be forged on both the national and the international level in response to the ethical imperatives of human survival in the global ecosystem.

To be effective, these laws will need to derive their authority not simply from the power of the states that enact them but rather from the authority of the moral and ethical principles on which they rest. Donald Brown's thorough study of the global warming position of the United States is a crucial first step in this process. It enables us to grasp the scale and scope of the ethical analysis that we will need to undertake to overcome the collapse of America's moral on this pressing issue before the human community.

Tim C. Weiskel
Director, Harvard Seminar on Environmental Values

Preface

This book examines the positions that the United States has taken in global warming negotiations through an ethical lens. Lamentably, the book's conclusions are often harshly critical of the U.S. responses to global warming over the past decade and a half. In fact, the book concludes that many of the U.S. positions in global climate change negotiations are ethically bankrupt no matter what ethical theory is used to make an ethical analysis. Because there is so much at stake in global warming, because the poorest people around the world are likely to suffer most from human-induced climate change, and because the United States is the largest producer of greenhouse gases and has been the least willing country to reverse the global warming threat, the U.S. response to global warming is an American shame.

The book's strong criticisms of the United States on global warming are made reluctantly. As a U.S. citizen, I enjoy the freedom of speech that allows me to make these strong criticisms without fear of serious government retribution. As a citizen of the United States who has frequently traveled abroad, I am also aware that many of the protections given to U.S. citizens by due process of law and other civil liberties are among the world's best. In addition, an American can be particularly proud of the many achievements of the United States in the fields of environmental protection, human rights, and the struggles for justice that have taken place in the country, including but not limited to the fight for civil rights. Without doubt, U.S. citizens can feel safe because of the protection given them by several constitutionally based rights and freedoms that do not shield billions of others around the world. Ironically, therefore, I draw these harsh judgments about a country that allows such conclusions to be made publicly.

Most of this book was completed before September 11, 2001, the day on which the United States experienced horrific terrorist attacks. This event also has made me acutely aware of the good fortune I have had in being born in a country that protects each person's right to practice his or her religion or to seek ultimate meaning in any way that is compelling. The U.S. Constitution's guarantee of separation of church and state is a bulwark against the fanaticism that appears to be the animating passion of the religious extremists responsible for recent terrorist attacks on the United States.

These zealots are neither advocates of religious tolerance nor supporters of the democratic freedoms that U.S. citizens can take for granted. Holy wars waged in the name of religion are often a reaction to the universalizing tendencies of democracies that work to keep religion separate from government so that no religious belief becomes an entitlement to a higher class of democratic rights. Religious extremists are no friends of broad-based democracy.

Yet the history of the global warming debate recounted in this book leads to the conclusion that tactics often employed by large economic interests are another threat to democratic ideals. Democracies are undermined when economic interests organize to prevent government from intervening in the market economy even when necessary to ensure just and ethical outcomes. One cannot examine the role played by the fossil fuel industry in the global warming debate in the United States without being stunned by how it has been successful in keeping the public confused. Therefore, both religious zealots and powerful economic interests can be enemies of democracy.

Potent economic interests can undermine democratic ideals in a number of obvious ways, including everything from direct corruption of government officials to unfair campaign financing that guarantees that only candidates who can raise huge amounts of money from those who have it have any chance of being competitive in elections. Yet the history of the global warming debate in the United States demonstrates a subtler but perhaps even more insidious way in which large economic interests can control and distort public debate on issues vital to democracies. Although economic consequences of proposed government actions should inform decision making in democratic institutions, if profit maximization considerations are allowed to obscure other vital concerns, democracy suffers. Complex technical matters like global warming are particularly vulnerable to manipulation by large economic interests because of the unavoidable need to rely on well-paid experts to analyze the scientific need for and economic consequences of government involvement in the market. The mixture of the unavoidable need for well-paid experts and huge amounts of money in the hands of a few potentially affected interests is a witch's brew that democracies cannot avoid drinking.

Surely, investors have a right to hire experts to protect investments from unnecessary government interference, yet this book will demonstrate how well-paid experts have been used over and over again to make arguments on behalf of economic interests that obscure the ethical dimensions of global warming issues. The history of global warming policy in the last twenty years reveals how powerful economic interests can frustrate the implementation of the democratic ideal of open public debate, if these interests can hide controversial ethical and social assumptions in the dense thicket of scientific and economic arguments that are made on their behalf by well-paid experts and public relations firms.

This book will show how economic interests have made arguments against global warming programs in the United States through the use of "value-neutral" scientific and economic analyses that contain numerous hidden but ethically dubious assumptions. For this reason, to implement the democratic ideal of open public debate on vital issues, citizens must demand that the ethical dimensions of scientific and economics arguments made in opposition to public policy initiatives be made explicit. Only then will the dream of a vibrant American democracy have a chance. That is, in our dream of a just democracy, we cannot forget about the immense power of well-financed experts to confuse the people. The global warming policy debate in the United States from 1980 to the present is a remarkable example of economic interests' ability to frame the very questions under consideration in public fora. Yet, in the United States, unlike many other parts of the world, democracy is always at least a possibility.

However, as a former liaison of the U.S. Environmental Protection Agency to the United Nations from 1995 to 1998, a member of several U.S. delegations to UN negotiations on environmental and development issues, and a long-term observer of the U.S. role in international environmental issues, I feel that I have a special responsibility to speak out if I see my country acting in a particularly irresponsible and dangerous way. As someone who directly participated in international sustainable development negotiations at the United Nations that included climate change issues, I often witnessed the United States mindlessly blocking solutions to environmental problems that had strong support by many in the rest of the world while offering no meaningful American counterproposals. My experience has led me to conclude that on a host of international environmental issues, the United States has allowed itself to be transformed in the past decade and a half from leader to obstructionist. I therefore reluctantly write this book because I have been in a position that has allowed me to witness up close the irresponsibility of the United States on a growing number of international environmental and sustainable development issues. With knowledge comes responsibility. Citizens in a country that allows a high degree of free speech have no excuse for remaining quiet if they conclude that decisions being made in their name are inconsistent with ethically responsible behavior. If the international community is to be guided by ethical norms rather than narrow national interest, citizens in countries that protect speech have a special duty to speak out.

I write this book as someone who has great love for a country that does not always follow its most inspirational ideals for justice. The United States is particularly challenged by the conflict entailed by pursuing its economic self-interest while building a just and ethical international global order. Even great nations can lose sight of the need to sometimes restrain national interest for the sake of international justice and fairness. In the words of the second verse of "America the Beautiful" by Katherine Lee Bates, we as American citizens have a duty to restrain America's excesses in such cases:

> America! America!
> God mend thine ev'ry flaw,
> Confirm thy soul in self-control,
> Thy liberty in law!

When the world began to wake up to the global environmental crisis in the 1970s, the United States was the undisputed leader on environmental policy. This widely recognized leadership role lasted at least until the early 1980s, and on some environmental problems the United States still has the strongest laws in the world. Yet on an unsettling number of international environmental issues, including global warming, the United States has not only forfeited its leadership role but has too often become the major barrier to protecting the global environment. Because of the seriousness of the emerging global environmental problems and because the United States is the world's greatest superpower, the world urgently needs the United States to reemerge as an environmental leader.

This book is strongly critical of the U.S. government for failing to live up to its ethical responsibilities for global warming. Although the Carter administration showed some early signs of being willing to accept U.S. obligations for this problem, both Democrats and Republicans in the U.S. Congress and all presidential administrations since Jimmy Carter's share some of the blame for the American failure and irresponsibility. Although the Clinton administration was more interested in global warming than either Reagan's or the elder George Bush's administration, President Clinton exhibited strong interest in this problem only toward the second half of his second term. In fact, at the United Nations' June 1997 five-year review of the 1992 Earth Summit, President Clinton admitted that he had not done enough to educate the American people about this problem. Thereafter, the Clinton administration made several serious attempts to increase the American public's understanding of global warming and the U.S. special responsibility for its solution. Yet even then President Clinton failed to significantly raise the visibility of this enormous problem.

When he ran for president, Al Gore rarely mentioned global warming despite the fact that he clearly understood its profoundly troubling import for the United States. Of course, during this time both Clinton and Gore faced a Congress that was very hostile to taking any steps on global warming that might entail costs for the United States.

Among strong congressional opponents to global warming programs were both Democrats and Republicans. In the mid-1990s, a global warming program blocking coalition formed in Congress, comprised of both Democrats representing their traditional political base, that is, labor unions, and Republicans speaking on behalf of their core constituency, namely, corporate interests. For this reason, both Democrats and Republicans are responsible for the ethical failure of the United States on global warming.

I also write this book because I believe that most U.S. citizens are generous and will eventually support equitably based international environmental treaties once they understand why the U.S. positions are often ethically bankrupt. That is, I write this book because I believe that Americans will do the right thing once the smoke is cleared. Therefore, inspiring this book is a belief that the United States will lead the world to a fair and equitable sharing of the burdens and benefits of protecting the global environment once its citizens understand what is ethically troublesome with current U.S. positions. The United States will lead the world to a just international environmental order as soon as the cries for equity and justice become stronger than the political power of certain potent economic interests in the United States. Although I have great faith that U.S. citizens eventually will respond appropriately to the ethical problems described in this book, I have growing pessimism about the ability of strong but narrow economic interests in the United States to cloud the lens through which U.S. citizens must view their ethical responsibilities. This book will demonstrate, for example, how fossil fuel interests and several energy-intensive industries in the United States have continued to make arguments that have obscured the ethical dimensions of the global warming problem. Until the United States finds a way to reduce the vast power of these narrow economic interests to distort public discourse about environmental policy, it will continue to be an arduous struggle to help U.S. citizens understand their responsibilities for emerging global environmental problems. Therefore, this book has also been written to help make the ethical dimensions of global warming more visible to U.S. citizens than they have been in recent global warming debates in the United States.

This book has also been written in the belief that an ethical focus on global environmental matters is key to achieving a globally acceptable solution. That is, solutions to many of the most serious global environmental problems that the world is now facing will not be agreed to unless nations around the world feel that they are being treated fairly. Along this line, on issue after issue, international environmental negotiations have been stalemated over fights between the

· rich and poor nations—over questions of international equity and distributive justice that have arisen in the past twenty years. Because international environmental problems need global solutions and because poorer nations will not agree to participate in global responses unless they feel that they are being treated fairly, the United States needs to support the creation of equitably grounded global solutions to environmental problems. Unfortunately, the United States recently has mostly chosen to largely ignore the ethical and equitable dimensions of global environmental problems at the same time that poorer nations are increasing the intensity and volume of their complaints about the failure of proposed international environmental solutions to consider questions of distributive justice.

Although quite happily this book is written at a time both when the number of environmental ethics courses taught in U.S. universities has been growing and when religious attention to environmental matters has been increasing, this book is also written in the belief that neither most of our ecologically engaged philosophers nor our environmentally concerned theologians are paying near enough attention to the ethical dimensions of arguments being made by nations in international negotiations. Too many, although not all, of those interested in environmental ethics have been focused on abstract questions while missing obvious ethical questions arising in international environmental negotiations. For this reason, some of the most important ethical questions entailed by the growing global environmental crisis remain largely unexamined, even by those who have great interest in environmental ethics. In addition to the fact that important ethical questions embedded in international environmental issues are being ignored, even those who follow international environmental negotiations miss some important ethical questions because they are often hidden in the scientific, economic, and legal discourses that structure the international environmental political debate. This book seeks to help identify the obvious ethical questions that are arising in issues now largely debated by the scientists and economists that are engaged in international negotiations.

Many environmental ethicists are focused on issues that are not connected to crucial and pressing environmental ethical questions. That is, the focus of many environmental ethicists and theologians has been directed largely at such metaethical questions as whether humans have duties to animals and plants and what is the nature and source of a religious environmental ethic. Although these are important questions and are very relevant to some practical issues, as this book demonstrates, they have little to do with many of the environmental controversies that are unfolding right in front of us at this moment in history. For this reason, extraordinarily important ethical issues are being overlooked by many of our most concerned philosophers and theologians. This book has also been written, therefore, to help those concerned about the ethical dimensions of global warming understand where battles need to be engaged if ethical and values concerns are to be addressed at all. A first-order challenge is to identify the ethical issues embedded in the policy debate. Only then can there be a meaningful discussion of the ethical dimensions of emerging issues.

Some of the ethical conclusions that I make in this book seem to me to be unassailable. For instance, I believe that the use of scientific uncertainty and cost-benefit analyses that focus only on domestic issues to block serious U.S. responses to the threat of global warming is ethically unjustifiable no matter what ethical approach is taken. Other conclusions are made more tentatively, including my analysis of the Kyoto trading mechanisms. Although I feel quite confident in ethically condemning many positions that the United States has taken on global warming, on others I desire to invite ethical reflection. I am amazed at the lack of ethical concern over some of the U.S. positions on global warming, particularly on how it has approached the Kyoto trading mechanisms and its approach to an equitable sharing of national targets. For this reason, it is my hope to stimulate more ethical attention to some of these issues rather than to draw final ethical conclusions at this moment in history.

Acknowledgments

There are a number of people to whom I am indebted for their insightful comments on draft chapters of this book. I particularly want to thank Jim Sterba, who has been very supportive of this endeavor and who made many valuable comments. I also want to thank Will Aiken, Paul Baer, Linda Brown, Paul Carrick, John Dernbach, John Lemons, Dave Reed, Adam Rose, Ed Wells, and Laura Westra for their valuable comments on sections of the book. Ralph Lehman was very helpful in keeping me up to date on breaking scientific issues. I am indebted to my brother George Brown, who has provided me with invaluable computer support.

The cartoons throughout this book have been reprinted with permission of the Centre for Science and the Environment, New Delhi, India. They have been included because they brilliantly summarize the ethical dissatisfaction with many U.S. positions on global warming that is growing around the world. They also brilliantly sum up a number of complex ideas about fairness and justice.

Part I

PRELIMINARY MATTERS

Chapter One

Absence of Ethical Concern

A two-inch high headline of the December 18, 1998, *New York Times* roared, "House to Debate Impeachment Today as U.S. Continues Air Assault on Iraq." Buried back on page 23 was a story that raised much deeper ethical questions for U.S. society than the Monica Lewinsky affair and clearly more ominous long-term U.S. foreign policy problems than the bombing of Iraq. The caption of the story on page 23 ironically understated the significance of the story's contents. It announced, "Earth Temperature in 1998 Is Reported at Record High." A quick reading of this caption would lead the reader to think that this story was simply about one new global temperature record being set. Yet a close reading of the story revealed the following:

1. The year 1998 was the warmest "by far" than any year since at least 1860 and probably in the past 2,000 years.
2. New monthly high-temperature records were set in each of the eighteen consecutive months ending in October 1998.
3. The year 1998 was the twentieth consecutive year for above-average global surface temperatures.
4. The year 1998 was the third record-breaking year since 1995.

The article also quoted Dr. Phillip D. Jones, a climatologist at the University of East Anglia, who stated that the 1998 temperature average was "amazing." "As new global high-level temperatures records have been set in the 1990s, they usually exceed old ones by a mere hundredths of a degree, but 1998 was likely to top the previous record of 1997 by a full quarter of a degree."

This new temperature information is just the most recent evidence in a stream of disturbing facts that have been recently flowing in that support climate models that predict that the world will heat up because of human

3

emission of greenhouse gases. Oceans are rising, ice caps and glaciers are melting, disease-infected mosquitoes are being seen at higher elevations, animals are changing migration patterns, more intense storms (e.g., Hurricane Mitch) are more frequently killing people and destroying communities around the world, and both droughts and flooding are increasing as the climate models predict they should. Yet there is no strong political support for corrective action in the United States. Nor do most Americans see or understand the extraordinary ethical failure of the U.S. response to global warming. Very few Americans are aware of the obstructionist role that the United States has consistently played for over a decade in international negotiations on climate change.

In the September 4, 1999, *New York Times,* Bill McKibben, in an op-ed piece titled "Indifferent to Planet Pain," said,

> I used to wonder why my parents' generation had been so blind to the wrongness of segregation; they were people of good conscience, so why had inertia ruled so long? Now I think I understand better. It took the emotional shock of seeing police dogs rip the flesh of protestors for white people to really understand the day-to-day corrosiveness of Jim Crow. . . . We need that same gut understanding of our environmental situation if we are to take the giant steps we must take soon.

Yet there is little evidence that awareness of the urgency of the climate change problem is being felt at a gut level in the United States. There is even less evidence that Americans see the gross ethical failure entailed by the U.S. response to global warming that will be examined in this book. There are several reasons why there is as yet no moral outcry in the United States on climate change.

Unlike the brutal television images of dogs and police attacking defenseless civil rights marchers that galvanized the public in the early 1960s, there is little direct visible evidence that demonstrates how human suffering is being caused in the rest of the world by the use of sports utility vehicles in the United States. To understand the climate change problem well enough to trigger distress at the unethical behavior of those who are causing it, one must understand things that are not immediately evident to the naked eye, such as how the burning of fossil fuels in the United States may affect people who are separated by great time and distance.

Most ethical systems and our intuitive ethical sensitivity are focused on one's responsibilities to people who are close by and who can be directly affected by one's actions. The technical power that humans now have to adversely affect people separated by time and space is a great new challenge to ethical reasoning. Yet because human-induced climate change will most hurt the poorest on the planet, seriously reduce the quality of life for future generations, and threaten plants and animals around the world, climate change and other emerging global environmental problems must be understood to raise very serious ethical issues.

In addition to these difficulties in seeing our ethical obligations caused by our separation from the impacts in time and space, this failure to see the ethical dimensions entailed by the climate change problem has at least several additional causes. First, as is discussed throughout this book, representatives of the fossil fuel industry and some heavy industry in the United States have successfully controlled the articulation of climate change issues in ways that have deflected our attention away from the ethical dimensions of the global warming problem. That is, these economically interested parties have successfully made certain issues the central focus of debate in the United States on climate change, issues that appear on their surface to be "value-neutral" disputes about scientific and economic "facts." These issues include questions of scientific uncertainty of climate change impacts, whether cost-benefit analyses justify government action to reduce greenhouse gases, and other issues that tend to deflect public scrutiny from the ethical questions entailed by human-induced global warming. Like the magician who tricks his audience to pay attention to someplace other than where the rabbit is being put into the hat, this book demonstrates how these economic interests have over and over again deflected public attention from an ethical framing of human-induced climate change issues.

ECONOMICALLY INTERESTED PARTIES HAVE SHIFTED ATTENTION FROM THE ETHICAL DIMENSIONS OF GLOBAL WARMING

This book shows how economically interested parties have been successful in making political debate focus on what appear to be factual questions in a way that ignores hidden ethical issues entailed by the vested interests' positions. This book also argues that to make progress on climate change, we need to make explicit the ethical premises of arguments about what we should do about global warming.

For instance, a purely scientific framing of questions surrounding the science of climate change would ask questions about the quality of scientific proof. Because scientists are taught to be silent unless there is a certain amount of statistical confirmation of a null hypothesis, the scientists will often be reluctant to acknowledge potential harm until the scientific proof is in. In environmental disputes, where science is often uncertain, scientists on either side of an issue usually fight each other by attacking their opponents on the quality of their science, not on the unstated ethical assumptions. Those scientists who do not stick to the scientifically proven "facts" are charged with doing "bad" or "junk" science. Newspapers continually report such disputes as matters on which the scientists do not agree rather than as matters on which some scientists disagree on certain unstated ethical premises, such as who should have the burden of proof. Moreover, the journalistic ethic requires that "both sides" of a story be told about any public dispute. For this reason, almost every newspaper article on global warming has reported "both sides" of the global warming science story even though the vast majority of atmospheric scientists have concluded that the earth is warming because of human influences. As a result, even those paying attention to the climate change debate are likely to be confused by press accounts of the global warming story. This is so because those few newspapers that have been following the global warming story often read as if scientists are evenly split about whether this problem is worthy of being worried about. Yet, as we will see, much of climate science is not in serious dispute while economically interested parties have been successful in getting the public to focus on those issues about which there is some uncertainty.

An ethical framing of climate change scientific questions would ask a different question than a scientific framing alone would. That is, an ethical framing of questions of uncertainty would ask whether there is enough scientific information (a scientific question) about potentially serious and irreversible environmental impacts, coupled with not enough time to resolve scientific uncertainties before harm occurs, to trigger an ethical responsibility to act now. This is not only an ethical question; it is also a question capable of generating feelings of responsibility in ways that a discussion of scientific "facts" alone cannot. An ethical framing of the climate science questions includes scientific elements; that is, what do we know for sure, and what is uncertain that many in the general public would not feel competent to comment about? Yet once the scientific uncertainties are identified, many would not be shy in voicing an opinion about whether responsibility to act exists. For this reason, only an ethically framed question about the science of climate change has the potential to motivate U.S. citizens to see their responsibility to act now in the face of some scientific uncertainty about the timing and magnitude of climate change impacts. Therefore, an ethical framing of questions relating to scientific uncertainty about global warming is both practically important to harness political energy and needed to help society do the right thing.

Those who point to scientific uncertainty about climate change as a basis for their position that the United States should not take action are making an argument that appears to be a dispute about "facts," but their position actually contains a hidden ethical position. That position, for instance, might be that government should assume a strong burden of proof to show that a problem exists before it takes action that might affect private economic interests. Yet not until the hidden ethical element is made express can the unstated ethical assumption be critically examined.

For the same reason, other controversies surrounding climate change policy need to be examined through an ethical lens to allow critical reflection on many hidden ethical assumptions. This book therefore examines several of the arguments most frequently made in opposition to U.S. action on global warming through an ethical lens.

This book also identifies other important ethical questions entailed by global warming that the United States needs to face in the not-too-distant future.

THIS BOOK'S THESIS AND ORGANIZATION

This book's thesis is a triple one. First, the U.S. response to global warming thus far is ethically unsupportable. Second, making the ethical dimensions of climate change more explicit is the key to moving forward on this enormous threat. Third, there are a number of important ethical issues that the United States needs to face in global warming negotiations in the years ahead. To achieve these objectives, this book examines arguments most frequently made in opposition to U.S. action on global warming and other important barriers to international progress through an ethical lens.

The United States is by far the most important actor in ongoing international climate negotiations. It both emits far more greenhouse gases and exerts more power than any other nation. It is also better situated financially to do something about global warming than most nations. Because understanding the ethical issues entailed by global warming is a key to moving forward in international negotiations, the book seeks to point the way to more effective international negotiations.

The book is comprised of three sections. The first section examines some preliminary matters that need to be understood to examine ethical issues entailed by global warming that are the focus of the second and third sections. Because the global warming problem has been the subject of international negotiations since the early 1990s, chapter 2 reviews the role that the United States has played in these negotiations. Understanding the historical position of the United States on global warming creates a necessary context for evaluating the ethical dimensions of the country's responsibility for climate change discussed throughout this book. The positions that the United States has taken in climate change negotiations thus far will be shown to be, more often than not, a consistent barrier to reducing the great threat of global warming.

Chapter 3 introduces basic environmental ethical concepts and issues that will be mentioned throughout the book. This chapter draws certain distinctions between environmental ethics and environmental science and reviews the basic elements of the most common ethical approaches to environmental affairs. Because this chapter attempts to provide a basic grounding in environmental ethics, those with a good background in environmental ethics may choose to skip this chapter.

Reaching a global solution to the climate change problems will not be easy. The ethical issues created by the global warming problem are shown in chapter 4 to create serious challenges to traditional ways of conducting foreign policy. Chapter 4 begins with a discussion of why foreign policy establishments that follow traditional approaches to foreign policy are not likely to focus on the ethical dimensions of human-induced climate change. The chapter also explains why blindness to the ethical dimensions of the global warming problem in international negotiations is likely to continue to create barriers to reaching international consensus on how to stabilize greenhouse gases below dangerous levels. Chapter 4 also discusses the role of environmental ethics in international affairs and argues that an ethical prism is a key to making progress in negotiations on many, if not all, global warming issues. This chapter also argues that global warming not only is the most serious environmental problem of the twenty-first century but also will be the most troubling foreign policy problem for the United States in the next decade.

Chapter 5 describes what is at stake in human-induced climate change. This chapter examines the significance of climate to nations in general terms, the specific climate change impacts that are predicted, and how the poorest nations are likely to be most severely affected by climate change. In this chapter, global warming is shown to be an extraordinarily serious threat to human health and the environment with profound potential adverse impacts on many nations. It is also a problem of immense global historical significance that raises difficult questions of international distributive justice.

Because there admittedly is some scientific uncertainty about the consequences of human-induced climate change, chapter 6 examines what we know about global warming and what is uncertain. The chapter explains the limits in general circulation models that are being used to predict global warming impacts and why, despite scientific uncertainty, global warming has been viewed for some time as a real problem by most scientists around the world.

The second section of the book is the beginning of a more focused ethical analysis of recent U.S. positions on global warming. Opponents of U.S. action on climate change often make four arguments against U.S. global warming programs.

First, a group of scientists skeptical about the proof of human-induced climate change argue that the U.S. government should not take action until the scientific uncertainties are resolved. This argument is examined from an ethical perspective in chapter 7. This chapter also introduces the concept of the "precautionary principle" adopted in the UN Framework Convention on Climate Change and explains why this principle, along with other ethical considerations, establishes a strong ethical responsibility by the United States to act now to reduce threats from global warming, notwithstanding some scientific uncertainty about magnitude and timing of climate change impacts.

Chapter 7 demonstrates why it is inconceivable that any ethical system would condone the status quo on greenhouse gas emissions in the United States even after recognition of some scientific uncertainty about the timing and magnitude of climate change impacts. That is, no ethical analysis would condone the behavior of the United States on global warming given what is not in dispute in climate change science, the extraordinary seriousness of global warming impacts, the fact that the poorest nations are likely to suffer most, the reality that great harm will happen before all scientific uncertainties are resolved, and the special responsibility of the United States for the historical buildup of greenhouse gases and projected future emissions.

The second argument most often heard against government global warming action in the United States is that the United States should not take action unless the developing world commits to reduce its emissions because the developing world is becoming a larger and larger part of the global problem. The ethical issues raised by this argument are critically considered in chapter 8.

A third argument frequently heard in opposition to U.S. action is that government reduction of greenhouse gases is not supported by cost-benefit analyses. An ethical critique of this argument is made in chapter 9.

The fourth argument against U.S. action on climate change is based on the premise that the United States could significantly reduce the costs of lowering emissions if it were allowed to invest in emission reduction projects anywhere in the world where low-cost projects could be found. This argument holds that the United States should not reduce greenhouse gases until the world agrees to a complex trading scheme in greenhouse gas reductions that would allow the United States to obtain credit from U.S.-financed foreign projects. The ethical problems with this argument are examined in chapter 10.

Having concluded the examination of the ethical merits of excuses made by the United States for not taking action on global warming, the third section of the book examines additional important ethical issues that the United States will need to face in the years ahead.

Chapter 11 explores the ethical controversies entailed by what is likely to be the most contentious question that needs to be faced to reach a global solution.

That is, on what equitable basis should national targets for reducing green-house gases be set, given the variations in historical and cumulative emissions, current total and per capita emissions, and other differences between nations? This chapter examines the approach of the United States thus far to questions of equitable allocation of national responsibility and shows the U.S. position to be ethically problematic as well as inconsistent with positions that the United States has taken on other issues.

Chapter 12 examines the issue of the level at which humans should attempt to stabilize greenhouse gases given that humans have already changed the climate system in ways that make return to preindustrial concentrations of greenhouse gases in the atmosphere virtually impossible for hundreds of years. This chapter argues that the level at which nations will need to agree to attempt to stabilize greenhouse gases should be understood to raise important but as yet little considered ethical questions.

Chapter 13 draws certain conclusions after identifying other ethical questions that need to be faced by the international community. These issues are the following:

- What is a fair allocation of costs for damages caused by warming that cannot reasonably be avoided?
- To what extent should future population increases be included in considering equitable allocation of burdens for reducing greenhouse gases?

These ethical issues, along with those already considered in previous chapters of this book, are likely to be at the heart of climate change policy controversies in the next decade. For this reason, the ethical dimensions of climate change must be faced to achieve the desperately needed global solution. The world needs the United States to face these issues if we are going to avoid serious damage to the planet and particularly serious harm to the poorest people around the world as well as the plants and animals that we share the earth with. Chapter 13 also includes a summary of the major arguments made in this book. The chapter argues why the United States has a particular responsibility to recognize the ethical dimensions of human-induced climate change.

In developing global warming policy, there are three reasons why the United States must focus on the ethical dimensions of the global warming problem:

- The failure to consider the ethical dimensions of global warming will mean that the United States will act unethically by destroying environmental entities that should be protected as the common heritage of humankind, hurt people who have no say in the development of U.S. policy, and make life brutish for some members of future generations.

* An ethical focus is key to moving forward in international negotiations that are currently stalled over disputes between the rich and poor nations about issues of equity.
* An ethical focus is needed to develop the political support in the United States to boldly move forward.

On this last point, as is demonstrated in various parts of this book, economic interests have successfully deflected public attention from ethical issues to what appear to be on their surface "value-neutral," "factual" questions about science and cost-benefit calculations and other economic matters. This shift in focus from ethical to "value-neutral" issues robs public debate of its potential to harness and mobilize feelings of responsibility.

The lack of moral concern over climate change in the United States referred to by Bill McKibben is not only culturally curious but also a phenomenon that points to several strategically important issues that must be faced to move forward on climate change policy issues in the United States. As was the case with the civil rights movement once the moral dimensions of segregation became nationally apparent in the mid-1960s, when U.S. citizens understand the moral dimensions of the climate change problem, they will get behind strong public policy to correct ethically unsupportable behavior.

The United States is now one of the world leaders on civil rights law, although real racial problems still remain. Improvement on racial issues has been rapid in the United States as the ethical dubiousness of racial discrimination became understood and internalized. This book was written in the belief that once Americans understand the wrongness of past and current U.S. positions on human-induced climate change, they will lead the world in moving to ethically benign energy use. To get there, this book argues, we must make ethical analysis a central focus of the global warming debate.

Some of the ethical conclusions made about the behavior of the United States in this analysis are made quite strongly. Others are much more tentative. In addition, some of the ethical analyses made in this book are not much more than an attempt to identify the ethical issues that need to be faced by the United States. Accordingly, this book should be understood not only as a strong ethical condemnation of the U.S. positions on some global warming issues but also as a plea to encourage a conversation about the ethical dimensions of the U.S. positions on global warming. Along this line, this book should be understood as a strong entreaty to pay particular attention to the ethical issues embedded in economic and scientific arguments about environmental policy. That is where many of the most important ethical issues often arise in practical environmental policymaking, but these issues are at the same time hidden from public scrutiny because many scientists and economists act as if their analyses are ethically neutral. It is hoped that this book demonstrates why we need to fully integrate ethical considerations into the policy languages of science, economics, and law on important environmental issues.

Chapter Two

History of U.S. Participation in Global Warming Negotiations

Although the United States has been a leader on many international issues since World War II, this chapter describes how the United States has consistently been a barrier that has blocked a variety of approaches to reducing global greenhouse emissions for at least the past decade and a half. Although the Clinton administration was much more engaged in solving the global warming problem than either the Reagan or the first Bush administration, this chapter sets the stage for explaining why even more recent U.S. positions in global warming negotiations or the reasons given by the U.S. Congress for lack of support of Clinton administration positions have continued to raise serious ethical questions. Because recent pronouncements of the George W. Bush administration signal a return of U.S. global warming policy to positions reminiscent of the Reagan and elder George Bush presidencies, this chapter sets out the factual basis for a strong ethical critique of positions of the George W. Bush administration that will be made in later chapters. This chapter also shows that those who have opposed U.S. action to reduce greenhouse gas emissions have made certain recurring arguments year in and year out. Later chapters of this book examine these arguments from an ethical perspective.

1824 TO THE BEGINNING OF CLIMATE CHANGE TREATY NEGOTIATIONS IN 1990

During the first 150 years of climate change science, as a nation the United States was not officially engaged in discussion of the potential human causes of global warming. Yet in the early nineteenth century, scientists began discussing the way in which atmospheric gases make the planet warmer. In

1824, Gene-Baptiste-Joseph Fourier published a paper that concluded that the atmosphere absorbs some of the sun's heat, which would otherwise escape back into space, and then reradiates this heat back to earth.[1] In so doing, certain naturally occurring atmospheric gases make our planet warmer than it would be in the absence of these gases.[2] The atmosphere's role in trapping heat would become known as the "greenhouse effect."

The first relatively successful calculation of how much the human use of fossil fuel could warm the planet was published in a paper in 1896 by Svante Arrhenius, a Swedish Nobel Prize–winning chemist.[3] Knowing that two gases, carbon dioxide and water vapor, are responsible for the natural warming of the atmosphere and heating the planet, Arrhenius calculated that a doubling of carbon dioxide would increase the earth's temperature by 4 to 6°C, only a few degrees more than what the most sophisticated computers would predict ninety years later.[4] Arrhenius was not worried about the potential ability of humans to change the climate because he believed that it would take several thousand years for humans to release enough greenhouse gases to cause a doubling of natural levels of carbon dioxide. Yet this would prove to be an erroneous assumption that would begin to become evident about fifty years later. Arrhenius did not foresee the enormous worldwide increase in the use of fossil fuels that would take place after World War II.

In the late 1930s, G. S. Callendar, an English chemist, argued that human activities were causing an increase in atmospheric carbon dioxide and that this might have already started global warming.[5] Despite Callendar's concern, and although the scientific community has known about the potential of human-induced warming to raise the earth's temperature since the early nineteenth century, global warming received little attention from the scientific community during the first half of the twentieth century. Apathy about global warming prevailed during this time because scientists did not see the tremendous growth in fossil fuel use that really took off after World War II. Moreover, in the early part of the twentieth century, many in the scientific community who understood the potential of human actions to change the global climate were not very concerned because they believed that the oceans would absorb much of the carbon being emitted by human activities.

In 1957, two scientists with the Scripps Institute of Oceanography, Roger Revelle and Hans Suess, found that much of the carbon dioxide emitted to the earth's atmosphere is not absorbed by the oceans, as some had assumed, leaving significant amounts in the atmosphere that could eventually warm the earth.[6]

The nations of the world began to wake up from their global warming slumber with the establishment of a carbon dioxide measuring station in 1958 at Mauna Loa, Hawaii. This first reliable station for measuring global carbon dioxide levels was established by an American, Charles Keeling.[7] By the late 1960s, the data from Mauna Loa and other stations had established that carbon dioxide was steadily building up in the atmosphere in proportion to human use of fossil fuels (see fig. 2.1).[8]

It was not, however, until the 1970s that widespread concern over global warming arose with the improvements in the general circulation models— that is, complex computer models that attempt to mathematically describe the earth's climate system.[9] With these computer models, scientists could look at reasonable potential impacts of the human use of fossil fuels and other greenhouse gases. By 1979, a report by the National Academy of Sciences, taking advantage of the computer models, concluded that "a wait-and-see policy [on global warming] may mean waiting until it is too late."[10]

In February 1979, the UN Environment Program (UNEP), the World Meteorological Organization (WMO), and the International Council of Scientific Unions (ICUN) sponsored the First World Climate Conference in Geneva, Switzerland. This conference examined the scientific basis for climate change.[11]

By the early 1980s, concern over global warming was growing rapidly in the international scientific community.[12] At the end of the Carter administration in 1980, a report by the President's Council on Environmental Quality

Figure 2.1 Atmospheric concentration of carbon dioxide, 900 to 2000.

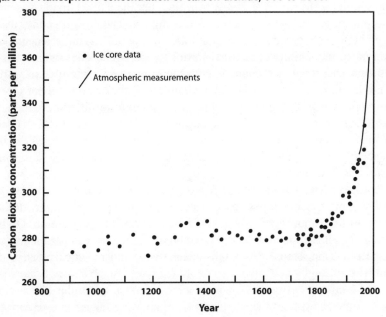

Source: United Nations Environment Programme and World Meteorological Program.

concluded that "the responsibility of the carbon-dioxide problem is ours and we should accept it and act in a way that recognizes our role as trustee for future generations."[13] The Reagan administration, however, showed little interest in accepting responsibility for global warming.

In 1985, UNEP and WMO sponsored the Second World Conference in Villace, Austria. Scientists from twenty-nine countries came to this conference and concluded that "some warming of climate now appears inevitable."[14] The participants at this conference also agreed that in the first half of the twenty-first century, a rise in global mean scale temperature could occur that would be greater than any in human history.[15]

In the late 1980s, a number of European countries began to press for concerted international action to begin to reduce greenhouse gas emissions, while the United States, first in the Reagan and then in the Bush administration, emphasized scientific uncertainty and the unacceptable costs of action.

In 1988, partly in response to the call by the United States for more scientific research before taking global warming action, UNEP and WMO, in accordance with a resolution of the UN General Assembly, established the Intergovernmental Panel on Climate Change (IPCC). The IPCC's mission was to analyze the evidence on the global warming problem and give advice on its potential solutions to the international community.

As early as 1988, some nations wanted to take internationally coordinated action to reduce the threat of global warming, but the United States was worried about the effect that such action could have on its domestic economy. As is explained in chapter 5, by this time much of the underlying science about the threat of human-induced global warming was not in question; however, significant uncertainties remained about the timing and magnitude of warming. By this time, there was growing recognition of the fact that the longer the world waited to take action, the more damage could result from human releases of greenhouse gases into the atmosphere, if the underlying scientific concern would be proven to be valid. Yet the United States stressed the importance of reducing the scientific uncertainties before taking action to avoid costs to the U.S. economy.

The United States acted as if harm to the domestic economy, should the global warming theory prove to be false, was of much greater concern than damage to the atmosphere, which could be avoided by early action. During this time, fossil fuel interests and, in particular, some coal and petroleum lobbies were waging intense campaigns against government action by stressing scientific uncertainty and adverse economic impacts to the United States. The views of coal and petroleum interests were remarkably similar to the positions that the Reagan and Bush administrations were taking in international negotiations.

In April 1988, a joint UNEP/WMO report warned that the pace of climate change is increasing at a rate to which natural systems cannot adapt. This report advised that actions should be taken to reduce the emission of greenhouse gases. It also outlined issues to be considered at the then-forthcoming Toronto conference on global change.[16]

This conference, "The Changing Atmosphere: Implications for Global Security," was held in Toronto, Canada, in June 1988 and included both government and citizen participants. This conference called for a reduction in carbon dioxide emissions by about 20 percent of current levels by the year 2005. This conference is widely viewed to be responsible for mobilizing support for the initiation of international negotiations on a climate treaty.

Testifying before the U.S. Senate Energy Committee on June 23, 1988, James Hansen, a U.S. government scientist, announced that he was "ninety-nine percent confident" that the recent warming was not a random event but a real indication of global climate change:

> Global warming is now sufficiently large that we can ascribe with a high degree of confidence a cause and effect relationship to the greenhouse effect. . . . Extreme events such as summer heat waves and heat wave/drought occurrences in the Southeast and Midwest United States may be more frequent in the next decade.[17]

Hansen's remarks sparked a great controversy among some scientists and many Congress members. He was vigorously attacked by fossil fuel interests for jumping the gun on concluding that human-induced global warming could be observed.

In the late summer of 1988, presidential candidate George Bush spoke about what would be his approach to global warming when he said, "Those who think we are powerless to do anything about the greenhouse effect are forgetting about the White House effect. As president I intend to do something about it."[18] Like his son thirteen years later, this campaign promise would prove to be arguably misleading.

The first meeting of the newly created IPCC convened in November 1988 in Geneva. The plenary meeting of the IPCC included some thirty-five nations, including the United States, the Soviet Union, several other foreign governments, and international governmental and nongovernmental organizations.[19] As a result of this meeting, the IPCC was charged to prepare an integrated state-of-the-art report on the science, impacts, and responses to global climate change by September 1990.[20]

Two weeks before the inauguration of George Bush in January 1989, the National Academy of Sciences (NAS) recommended to the president-elect that global warming be placed high on his agenda. NAS warned that "the future welfare of human society" is at risk.[21]

On March 11, 1989, an "environmental summit" was held at The Hague, Netherlands, that brought together presidents, prime ministers, and heads of state from seventeen nations and other government officials from seven other nations. The group recommended the creation of a new agency within the United Nations to "be responsible for combating any further global warming of the atmosphere."[22] The United States coldly greeted this proposal, and as a result it went nowhere.

In 1989, twenty-two countries, including France, Japan, Italy, and Canada, called for negotiations on a global warming treaty.[23] The United States, led by White House Chief of Staff John Sununu, initially resisted the growing international call to begin negotiating a treaty because, according to the United States, too little was known about the economic impacts of a treaty on the United States. Following a public flap created in early May 1989 when the White House attempted to dilute congressional testimony of government scientist Jim Hansen about the seriousness of global warming, the United States announced that it would support negotiations of a framework convention on climate change.[24]

In 1989, the United States established the national Global Change Research Program pursuant to the Global Change Research Act (P.L. 100–606), a program that would spend considerable money over the next decade supporting research on global warming issues but would not lead to real reductions in U.S. greenhouse emissions.

The United States joined the climate change negotiations by hosting a conference on global warming on April 17–18, 1990, in Washington, D.C. At this conference, President Bush again called for further study on the problem while representatives from the European Economic Community argued that "gaps in knowledge must not be used as an excuse for inaction" and that "Americans are falling behind on this, and . . . the time for action has come."[25]

In November 1990, more than 130 nations met in Geneva for the Second World Climate Conference. The conference declaration called for all nations to begin setting targets or establishing programs for reducing the emission of greenhouse gases. Yet the setting of specific targets was strongly opposed by the United States and the Soviet Union.[26] Nevertheless, this conference provided the political and policy mandate that allowed the UN General Assembly to authorize the negotiation of a framework convention on climate.[27]

In November 1990, the IPCC issued the First Scientific Assessment of Climate Change, the most comprehensive scientific study on climate change up to that time.[28] The IPCC report concluded that global warming was a real problem and that it was caused at least in part by human activities. This first IPCC assessment reported that if states continued to pursue "business as usual," the global average temperature would rise by an average of 0.3°C per decade, a rate of change unprecedented in human history.[29] Yet despite the fact that the IPCC creation had been strongly supported by the United States to resolve issues of scientific uncertainty, the IPCC's conclusions did not convince the United States that it should make serious enforceable commitments to reduce greenhouse gas emissions. The United States wanted more study, implicitly rejecting the advice of the very institution it helped create to make recommendations on global warming science.

In response to strong calls for action on global warming coming mostly out of Europe, on December 21, 1990, the United Nations created the Intergovernmental Negotiating Committee (INC), the body responsible for negotiating a global warming convention.

NEGOTIATIONS ON THE CLIMATE CHANGE CONVENTION

Negotiations leading up to what would become the UN Framework Convention on Climate Change (UNFCCC) took place in five meetings that started in early 1991 and ended just before the UN Conference on Environment and Development, usually referred to as the Earth Summit, held in Rio de Janeiro in June 1992. The United States hosted the first INC meeting in Chantilly, Virginia, in February 1991.[30] Additional INC sessions were held in Geneva on June 19–29, 1991 (INC-2); in Nairobi, Kenya, on September 9–10, 1991 (INC-3); in Geneva on December 9–20, 1991 (INC-4); and in New York on April 29–May 8, 1992 (INC-V).[31]

During these negotiations, several important contentious issues were at the center of most discussions. On these issues, the United States would continue to be in the middle of the controversy, often resisting proposals that had the support of many nations. The controversial issues included the following:

• The desirability of establishing targets and timetables to reduce greenhouse gas emissions
• The responsibility of the developed nations to take the lead in reducing greenhouse gases
• The responsibility of the developed nations to provide financial assistance to the poor nations for reductions in greenhouse gas emissions in the South

Even before the start of these negotiations, the United States took certain clear-cut positions and was not afraid to often stand alone.[32] Although many nations had concluded by 1990 that it was time to enter into a treaty that would limit world emission of greenhouse gases, the United States, often isolated from the rest of the world with the exception of a few oil exporting nations, strongly resisted proposals to negotiate enforceable targets and timetables for reducing global greenhouse gas emissions throughout the negotiations on the climate change convention. The United States took the most consistently hard-line position throughout these negotiations and argued for a much less ambitious approach to the global warming problem than proposals of other nations on the basis of scientific uncertainty about climate change impacts and potential adverse impacts on the U.S. economy of a convention with enforceable emission reduction targets.

Probably the most contentious issue in negotiations leading up to the climate convention was the issue of whether the treaty should include enforceable emissions targets for each nation. One commentator summed up the approaches of the parties to the convention negotiations as follows:

> At the time it began, the climate negotiations could be presented in simplified fashion as representing a test of strength among three groups of participants. Defending the concept of an extremely general Framework Convention, the United States argued that there was an overriding need for further scientific research and a better assessment of the economic costs and benefits of the different possible options (including adaptation) before discussing the adoption of quantitative targets and timetables. . . . The United States was joined by Saudi Arabia and Kuwait which sought to avoid any binding commitments to specific quantitative reductions in carbon emissions to a fixed date. . . . The European Commission adopted the position of stabilizing regional CO_2 emissions in the year 2000 at the 1990 level. This objective was presented as a first phase target en route to subsequent reductions. . . . A small number of developing countries played a large role in the negotiations. The small island states, the Sub-Saharan African countries, and some of the countries with large, exposed deltaic plains, pressed aggressively for an action-oriented convention that would address both adaptation and abatement issues.[33]

During the early negotiations, the developing nations generally took the position that, since the developed nations were mainly responsible for the climate change problem, the developed nations should be responsible for the solution.[34] In contrast, the United States took the position that any nation's responsibility to reduce greenhouse gas emissions should be based on the ability of each nation to respond, not on the proportional responsibility of each nation for causing the global problem.[35] For this reason, the United States resisted a formula that would assign responsibility for the amount of greenhouse gas reductions on the basis of a nation's historical share of global emissions.

This issue of equity in describing national obligations among nations was a major issue during negotiations leading up to the climate conventions.[36] The developing nations were willing to commit to reductions in greenhouse gas emissions provided that the developed nations were willing to commit "new and additional" financial resources to cover the full incremental costs in implementing these measures.[37] In other words, the developing nations were interested only in committing to reductions that were financed by those nations that they believed had caused the problem. During the negotiations, the United States consistently opposed convention provisions creating these new financial commitments. One commentator has summed up the U.S. position on equitable commitments as follows:

> During most of the Bush administration, United States' policy toward international fairness and equity, and fair and equitable burden sharing regarding climate change in particular, was one of disinterest and opposition . . . especially when that was interpreted to mean "targets and timetables" for United States' greenhouse gas emissions or downward adjustment to consumption patterns in the United States.[38]

During the treaty negotiations, it became increasingly clear that global warming issues were a priority of the North but of less urgency to the South, where governments were driven to address more urgent problems of development and basic human needs.[39] Yet it became increasingly clear to the South, that is, to the world's poorest nations, that climate change convention could have far-reaching economic implications on all nations. As one commentator from the South has noted,

> A climate change convention would therefore affect levels and patterns of energy use. It would have implications for energy generation, transmission and utilization, for industry and transportation. Moreover since forests act as carbon sinks, a convention would also have a major impact on land use patterns. Efforts to control emissions of other greenhouse gases would also have similar implications, though on a less extensive scale. Methane emissions, for example, are associated with agriculture and animal husbandry. In short, a climate convention could constitute a major multilateral economic agreement. The sharing of costs and benefits implied in the convention could significantly alter economic destinies in individual countries.[40]

Although the southern nations became increasingly involved in the negotiations as they went forward, generally speaking the developing nations took the position that since the developed countries were mainly responsible for causing climate change, it was their responsibility to take measures for a solution.[41] In stark contrast, the United States opposed this view.[42] The United States, therefore, wanted the developing nations to accept responsibility to take action but reluctantly was willing to acknowledge "differentiated responsibilities" for national obligations. "Differentiated responsibilities" was a term that was understood to mean that not every nation had the same responsibility to reduce its greenhouse gas emissions. Yet the United States pressed for the developing nations to accept commitments that were not based on the negligible historic contributions of the South.[43] The term "differentiated responsibilities," agreed to in the abstract in the lead-up to the Earth Summit, would continue to generate conflict between the United States and the developing nations in negotiations in the years ahead.

From early in the climate negotiations, the United States also made it clear that the global warming negotiating text documents being negotiated at the Earth Summit should not contain rhetoric about the "guilt" or "crimes" of the developed nations.[44] The United States also fought hard against any language that could be construed as assigning responsibility based on a nation's proportional share of greenhouse gases that have been emitted into the atmosphere.

Several contentious controversies between the developed and developing nations arose in early convention negotiations around how projects to reduce greenhouse gases in the developing nations would be financed. The first was whether the developed nations should pay the "full" cost or "agreed incremental" costs of developing world projects to reduce greenhouse gases. In other words, if a developing world nation proposed to put in a power plant that would reduce greenhouse emissions because it used greenhouse-friendly technologies, such as solar power, a question in contention between the developed and developing worlds was whether the developed world would pay for the full cost of the power plant or the difference in cost between a more conventional power plant and the solar energy plant. The United States insisted that only agreed incremental costs should be paid for by the developed nations.

Another hotly contested financial issue between the North and the South was the institutional mechanism through which developing-world global warming projects would be funded. The developing world wanted a new climate fund to be created, while the developed nations pushed for the financing mechanism to be housed in the already established Global Environment Facility (GEF) located in the World Bank. The developing world strongly opposed the GEF as the institution to finance its climate change projects because, as a unit in the World Bank, the GEF was seen to be under the control of the United States and other developed nations. This was so because decision making in the World Bank was based on the amount any nation contributes to the bank. For this reason, the large donor nations to the World Bank, especially the United States, controlled its decisions. Long before this issue arose of where to house the financing mechanism for climate change projects in the poor nations, the developing world had often criticized the World Bank for its failure to include developing-world participation in decision making.

The identification of the GEF as the financing mechanism was also opposed by many environmental nongovernmental organizations (NGOs) because the World Bank had acquired a very bad environmental reputation in the 1980s and early 1990s for financing large, environmentally destructive development projects in the developing world. For these reasons, the identification of the GEF as the financing mechanism was a lightning-rod issue in negotiations leading up to the Rio Earth Summit. During the Earth Summit, the GEF's information booth was attacked and burned, allegedly by environmental and developing-world NGOs in protest of the North's insistence that the financing mechanism would be housed in the World Bank.

Progress toward the final convention was very slow in the first four INC meetings in 1991.[45] When it became clear that the United States would not accept definitive targets and timetables, that the developed nations would insist on the GEF in the World Bank as the financing mechanism, and that the developing world would not accept any commitments, delegations finally got down to hard work, but not until the last INC in May 1992.[46] Many participants in the negotiations have acknowledged that rapid progress was finally made on the convention text because the parties were facing a deadline of submitting a convention to the then already much publicized Earth Summit that would take place in the last two weeks of June 1992. As the negotiations got closer to the June 1992 Earth Summit, the U.S. positions on several issues hardened to the point that many questioned whether President Bush would attend the Rio conference.[47] In defending the positions taken by the United States in the negotiations and explaining why he might not go to the Earth Summit, President Bush stated that the American lifestyle was not negotiable.

In the waning hours of the May 1992 INC, the global warming treaty text was finally agreed to.[48] Soon thereafter, President Bush announced that he would go to Rio.

The United States, having stood virtually alone on most of the most contentious issues, finally achieved its major negotiating goals in the final convention text.[49] The convention contained no enforceable targets and timetables for greenhouse gases and in particular made no concessions in this respect based on the historical role of the United States in greenhouse gas buildup in the atmosphere. The United States also prevailed on its major positions with respect to financing. First, for projects in the developing world that would reduce greenhouse gases, the developed world had made no commitment for "new and additional" development assistance. Second, the UNFCCC made the GEF the interim financial mechanism for those projects that were "agreed" to by GEF, although the convention conceded to one concern of the developing nations in regard to increasing the role of the developing-world participation in the GEF. The United States did finally agree to provide $50 million for core GEF projects (which included but was not limited to climate change projects) and $25 million to provide assistance to developing nations to conduct studies on how greenhouse gases were being used within developing nations. The United States also finally agreed to purposely ambiguous and unenforceable language about the goal of the UNFCCC and the need to stabilize greenhouse gas emissions by 2000 at 1990 levels. This specific language, in relevant part, is as follows:

> The ultimate objective of this Convention and any related legal instruments that the Conference of the Parties may adopt is to achieve, in accordance with the relevant provisions of the Convention, *stabilization of greenhouse gas concentrations in the atmosphere at a level that would prevent dangerous anthropogenic interference with the climate system.* Such a level should be achieved within a time frame sufficient to allow ecosystems to adapt naturally to climate change, to ensure that food production is not threatened and to enable economic development to proceed in a sustainable manner.[50]
>
> The developed country parties . . . commit themselves specifically as provided for in the following: . . . Each of these Parties shall adopt national policies and take corresponding measures on the mitigation of climate change, by limiting its anthropogenic emissions of greenhouse gases and protecting and enhancing its greenhouse gas sinks and reservoirs. These policies and measures will demonstrate that developed countries are taking the lead in modifying longer-term trends in anthropogenic emissions consistent with the objective of the Convention, *recognizing that the return by the end of the present decade to earlier levels of anthropogenic emissions of carbon dioxide and other greenhouse gases not controlled by the Montreal Protocol would contribute to such modification.*[51]
>
> In order to promote progress to this end, each of these Parties shall communicate detailed information on its policies and measures . . . *as well as on its resulting projected anthropogenic emissions by sources and removals by sinks of greenhouse gases not controlled by the Montreal Protocol for the period referred to in subparagraph (a), with the aim of returning individually or jointly to their 1990 levels these anthropogenic emissions of carbon dioxide and other greenhouse gases not controlled by the Montreal Protocol.*[52] (italics added)

In agreeing to this language, the United States agreed to make a good-faith effort to reduce its greenhouse gas emissions to 1990 levels by 2000. As we will see, many Americans have ignored the fact that the United States agreed in a binding treaty to try to reduce its emissions to 1990 levels, although this promise is not enforceable in an international court.

To get its way on the major issues, the United States also agreed to the inclusion of Article 3 of the UNFCCC on principles, a section that had been pushed by the developing nations and initially resisted by the United States. As we will see later in this book, several of the UNFCCC's principles found in Article 3 have often been ignored by opponents to climate change action in the United States. In fact, as we will see, Congress has acted recently as if these principles have never been agreed to despite the fact that the convention was ratified by the United States shortly after the 1992 Rio conference. Relevant language included in the principles section of the UNFCCC about the duties of the developed world to take action before the developing world includes the following:

> The Parties should protect the climate system for the benefit of present and future generations of humankind, on the basis of *equity* and in accordance with their *common but differentiated responsibilities* and respective capabilities. Accordingly, the *developed country Parties should take the lead* in combating climate change and the adverse effects thereof.[53] (italics added)

Even though the United States has agreed to this language, which requires the developed nations to make progress on reducing greenhouse gas emissions before the commitments are expected from the developing nations, many in Congress have continued to insist that this provision be ignored and that the developing nations make commitments before the United States takes steps to reduce its emissions.

Also agreed to in the principles section of the convention is language dealing with scientific uncertainty that has also often been ignored by opponents to U.S. climate change action. The specific language, which as we will see is usually referred to as the "precautionary principle," is as follows:

> The Parties should take precautionary measures to anticipate, prevent or minimize the causes of climate change and mitigate its adverse effects. Where there are threats of serious or irreversible damage, *lack of full scientific certainty should not be used as a reason for postponing such measures,* taking into account that policies and measures to deal with climate change should be cost-effective so as to ensure global benefits at the lowest possible cost.[54] (italics added)

Except for these UNFCCC principles, which the United States has often ignored in recent years, the United States mostly got what it wanted on issues most important to it. For the most part, the world's only superpower, the United States, had succeeded, with help from Saudi Arabia and Kuwait, five months after Operation Desert Storm, in blocking a convention that would bind the nations of the world to reducing their growing greenhouse emissions.

As we will see in chapter 5, some nations more than others are threatened by global warming. For these nations, the United States was willing to gamble on a bet that climate change might not be great. The United States was willing to take this bet to avoid economic costs to the United States, where the stakes included potentially significant damage to human health and the environment for other nations. In other words, the United States was willing to put other nations at risk to protect its economic interests.

One hundred and fifty-four countries finally agreed to the UNFCCC shortly before the Earth Summit in Rio in June 1992. The Bush administration, having achieved its major objectives in the text of the convention, signed the UNFCCC in Rio and successfully got the Senate to ratify it quickly in October 1992, just four months after the Rio conference.

A remarkably revealing insider's view of the U.S. positions in negotiations leading up to the UNFCCC has been written by William A. Nitze.[55] Nitze was deputy assistant secretary of state for oceans and international environment and scientific affairs and head of the U.S. delegation to the INC meetings and to the IPCC. Nitze has acknowledged that it was the U.S. strategy from the beginning of the negotiations to avoid binding commitments to hold U.S. carbon dioxide emissions below a specified level by a date certain.[56] Nitze has stated that it was the U.S. strategy to avoid committing to enforceable reduction targets despite the fact that many in the U.S. government believed that holding U.S. emissions to 1990 levels by 2000 would not have harmed the U.S. economy.[57] Nitze has further acknowledged that the U.S. position was not based on "a rational assessment of the national interest" but rather was the result of the ideology and politics of a small circle of White House advisers led by Chief of Staff John Sununu.[58] According to Nitze, who was at the very center of U.S. policymaking on climate change, this political ideology was in part based on the power of coal and oil industries in states needed by President Bush in future elections.[59]

Nitze also acknowledged that the hard-line position of the United States on refusing to agree on targets and timetables for greenhouse gases also was the cause of failure to agree on other issues that could have been resolved in the UNFCCC. These additional missed opportunities, according to Nitze, included agreements on the following:

- An infrastructure for inventorying and monitoring greenhouse gas sources and sinks, particularly in developing countries
- The process for forming national strategies, including internal policy and reforms
- A mechanism for financing projects to implement national strategies that leverage other public funds
- A process for setting longer-term greenhouse gas reduction goals and allocating responsibility for achieving those goals[60]

Therefore, the U.S. positions in negotiations on a climate convention resulted in significant lost opportunities to put mechanisms in place that would help nations avoid damage from the global warming problem, according to one of the lead negotiators of the United States, William Nitze. If the United

States had agreed to be bound by the target to stabilize greenhouse gas emissions at 1990 levels by the year 2000 (the proposal that had been strongly but ultimately unsuccessfully pushed by many of the European nations), it would have emitted 1,632.1 million tons of carbon, yet by 1997, the year in which the Kyoto Protocol was negotiated, the United States emitted 1,813.6 million tons of carbon, an increase of over 11 percent from the 1990 level.[61]

The United States also, according to Nitze, did little in climate negotiations to diffuse growing mistrust between the rich and poor nations on three issues, a problem that continues to haunt climate negotiations to this day. The three issues are the following:

- The developing nations perceive the rich nations' efforts to get the poor nations to reduce their greenhouse gas emissions as a device to gain control over their development and a threat to their sovereignty—a form of eco-colonialism.
- The developing nations see the climate change problem as a pretext for the rich nations to divert development assistance funds from something that is important to poor nations to something that is important to the rich nations.
- The developing nations interpret the behavior of the rich nations on climate change as attempts to shift the responsibility of the rich nations that have caused the problem to the poor nations.[62]

FROM RIO TO KYOTO

The Clinton administration came into existence in January 1993, just seven months after the Earth Summit. From the beginning, the Clinton administration took a much more engaged approach to global warming than either the Reagan or the Bush administration. While campaigning for the White House, then Senator Al Gore acknowledged that the developed nations would have to act to reduce the high level of carbon emissions before the developing nations.[63]

Just a month after he took office, President Clinton unveiled a BTU tax, which was designed to raise $72 billion over five years while both cutting the federal deficit and cutting greenhouse gas emissions.[64] The Senate quickly made it clear that this tax would not become law. Congress also made it clear that it would not support serious programs to lower U.S. greenhouse gas emissions. Although the U.S. executive branch was willing to move cautiously to accept its responsibilities to reduce greenhouse gas emissions, Congress resisted and followed the positions of the fossil fuel industry and other opponents of global warming programs.

In April 1993, President Clinton announced voluntary measures to stabilize U.S. greenhouse gas emissions after being snubbed on the BTU tax.[65] The U.S. Climate Action Plan was comprised of fifty new or expanded programs, largely voluntary, that sought to promote energy efficiency among commercial, residential, and industrial users; promote the use of natural gas and other cleaner fuels; increase the efficiency of hydroelectric and other energy production; and reduce emissions of chlorofluorocarbons (CFCs) and other greenhouse gases.[66] Although these voluntary measures would somewhat slow the growth of U.S. emissions, they utterly failed to reverse overall trends of increasing U.S. greenhouse gas emissions. The very mild voluntary programs adopted by the Clinton administration did little to reverse growing energy consumption trends both because the voluntary programs were too weak and because the United States was in the middle of an energy binge, caused by a new appetite for large sports utility vehicles and a host of electronic devices, including rapid increase in the use of computers. In fact, rather than stabilizing greenhouse gases at 1990 levels by 2000, the United States would find its greenhouse gas emissions almost 13 percent higher than 1990 by 2000. During this period, the automobile industry strongly resisted legislative proposals to set gasoline consumption standards for the huge voracious sports utility vehicles that were becoming ubiquitous in the United States during this period.

By 1995, it was becoming quite clear that the weak nonbinding approaches to global warming contained in the UNFCCC were failing to make much progress on the growing global warming problem. At the first Conference of Parties (COP-1) to the UNFCCC in Berlin in 1995, the parties agreed to begin negotiations on a binding protocol on emissions limitations.

In 1995, the IPCC released its *Second Assessment Report*. For the first time in this report, the IPCC scientists concluded that "the balance of the evidence shows a discernable human influence on climate."[67] In other words, the IPCC scientists, a group created with the strong support of the United States to examine the science of global warming, concluded not only that human-induced climate change was a real issue with likely adverse climate change impacts, a conclusion they had reached in 1990, but also that by 1995 it was possible to observe actual human-caused changes to the world's climate that could be distinguished from natural climate variability. This conclusion was of great significance because the vast natural variability of the climate system made it difficult to separate human- from natural-caused climate changes. Yet the empirical evidence of increased global and regional temperature, rising oceans, increased droughts and floods, and changes in participation patterns and storms, coupled with higher levels of confidence in computer models that[68] were successfully predicting these events, led the IPCC to conclude that "the balance of the evidence" supports the conclusion that human activities were already changing the climate. In other words, scientific evidence available in 1995 supported the conclusion that humans were already changing the climate and therefore, by then, that it was already too late to prevent at least some human-induced global warming. Moreover, because of long lag times in the climate system caused by the time it took for the oceans to heat up, the actual climate change that had already been caused by human activities would take decades to see even if the world were able to stabilize greenhouse gases at 1995 levels—a virtual impossibility. In 1996, the United States reversed its previous position on its unwillingness to accept enforceable targets by announcing its support for negotiations of binding national emissions limitations that would be achieved by a certain date.

The second Conference of Parties (COP-2) to the UNFCCC convened on July 8–19, 1996, in Geneva, Switzerland. On July 18, 1996, the ministers and other heads of delegations present in Geneva released the Geneva Declaration, which was based on a U.S. policy statement delivered July 17 at COP-2. This declaration (1) recognized and endorsed the *Second Assessment Report* of the IPCC as currently the most comprehensive and authoritative assessment of the science of climate change; (2) called for parties to set "legally binding, medium-term targets" for limitations and significant overall reductions of their emissions of greenhouse gases; and (3) accepted the U.S. position that nations should be allowed flexibility in applying policies and measures to achieve emissions limitations and reductions.[69] The chairman of COP-2 called for the parties to consider a "future decision [containing these elements] which would be legally binding on all parties under the UNFCCC." This decision was to be negotiated in Kyoto at the third Conference of Parties (COP-3) to the UNFCCC in 1997. The Clinton administration agreed to this approach and therefore agreed to bind the United States to quantitative emissions limitations.[70]

During this time, there was great nervousness about the Clinton administration's approach to these pending negotiations brewing in Congress, which was being lobbied heavily by fossil fuel interests.[71] Some members of Congress voiced strong concerns, particularly about the principles of "common but differentiated commitments and responsibilities." Under the UNFCCC, this principle would require the developed nations, such as the United States, to commit to begin reducing greenhouse gas emissions while allowing the developing nations to increase their share of global warming–causing emissions.[72] Specifically, questions were raised about whether continued adherence to this principle, along with emission reduction targets, could disadvantage the United States economically and competitively in world markets.[73] Because of the perceived adverse economic impacts to the United States being articulated largely by lobbyists in Washington, Congress continued to resist emerging approaches to reducing the growing threat of global warming that were widely acceptable to other nations. And so the U.S. legislative branch of government during the Clinton administration, similar to the role played by the executive branch in the Reagan and Bush administrations, became the center of resistance to emerging international consensus on greenhouse gas reduction strategies. It apparently made no difference to Congress that the United States had already ratified the UNFCCC in 1992 and in that treaty the United States had already agreed that the developed world needed to reduce greenhouse gas emissions before the developing nations and not use scientific uncertainty as an excuse for not taking action. Also during the 1990s, Congress categorically opposed any programs to reduce greenhouse gas emissions that were not voluntary.

An official U.S. response to the Geneva Declaration was issued on July 19, 1996, to clarify how the United States wanted legally binding targets to be structured. Flexibility in how nations could attain any emission reduction target became an important element in the Clinton administration's approach to reducing U.S. emissions.[74] That is, the U.S. executive branch under the Clinton administration intended to rely on a menu of controversial policy options that would make potential solutions affordable to the United States. These options would include several global emissions trading schemes (see the discussion on trading in chapter 10), options to pick which greenhouse gases any nation could choose to meet national targets, and the liberal use of greenhouse gas sinks, that is, carbon absorption methods, as a way of meeting emission limitation targets. The United States would also require the participation of *all* developed and developing countries, contrary to the express provisions in the UNFCCC that the United States had agreed to.[75] For this reason, the Clinton administration, although more engaged in thinking about solutions to global warming than the Reagan or Bush administration, would introduce into the international negotiations issues that were also very troublesome for most nations and would greatly slow down and complicate negotiations in the years ahead.

Yet members of Congress expressed strong concerns about the announced Clinton administration positions because of Congress's assessment of potential adverse impacts of climate change commitments on the U.S. economy.[76] Congress also expressed great concern about the potential effect on the United States if it agreed to different commitments for developed and developing countries.[77]

At the "Earth Summit Plus Five" Special Session of the UN General Assembly held in June 1997 to assess progress since the 1992 Rio Earth Summit, the United States faced strong criticism for failing to take leadership in setting specific targets and timetables for limiting greenhouse gas emissions. President Clinton addressed this meeting but declined to declare U.S. support for a specific numerical emissions reduction target for greenhouse gas emissions. Yet in this speech, President Clinton acknowledged that the United States had a special responsibility to act on climate change while admitting that there was not strong political support for strong action in the United States. To overcome political apathy in the United States and get domestic support for administration positions, President Clinton announced his intention to hold a White House conference on climate change, scheduled for October 6, 1997, to bring together various contending interests, including industry, scientists, economists, and environmental groups.[78] For the next few months, the Clinton administration acknowledged in a number of speeches that it understood that the United States had certain equitable responsibilities as the largest emitter of greenhouse gases to reduce its emissions.[79] Yet the Clinton administration refused to take equity into account in negotiating specific emissions reductions, and Congress has never recognized the equitable responsibilities of the United States.

During the lead-up to the Kyoto negotiations, industry lobbyists applied increasing pressure to prevent the United States from making commitments that would too quickly limit use of fossil fuel energy, which they argued would create problems for them and for the economy.[80] At the same time, U.S. environmental groups pressed the United States to take leadership at Kyoto to make specific commitments to limit greenhouse gases.[81]

As the then-upcoming November 1997 Kyoto negotiations approached, members of Congress warned U.S. negotiators that they should not agree to any new climate protocol that did not bind all parties, including developing countries.[82] A Senate resolution introduced by Senators Hagel and Byrd along with sixty-four cosponsors passed the Senate by a vote of 95 to 0 on July 25, 1997.[83] This resolution expressed the sense of the Senate that the United States should not be a signatory to any agreement in Kyoto "unless the protocol or other agreement also mandated new specific scheduled commitments to limit or reduce greenhouse gas emissions for developing country parties within the same compliance period" or if it would "result in serious harm to the economy of the United States."[84] In the Hagel–Byrd Resolution, the Senate implicitly repudiated those principles of the UNFCCC already ratified by the United States that called for the developed nations, including the United States, to take the lead in reducing greenhouse gas emissions.

On October 22, 1997, President Clinton announced the long-awaited U.S. positions to be taken at Kyoto in a speech at the National Geographic Society in Washington, D.C. The United States would propose that legally binding greenhouse gas targets for six major greenhouse gases at 1990 emissions levels be met by 2008–12.[85] Therefore, going into Kyoto, the Clinton administration was not willing to commit to anything more than achieving

1990 emissions levels, a level of emissions that the United States had already agreed to try to reach by 2000 in the UNFCCC. Strong protests were quickly made to this proposal by the European Union and the Alliance of Small Island States (AOSIS), who were particularly vocal about the weakness of this U.S. proposal. In response, the United States argued that lowering U.S. emissions to 1990 levels by 2012 would be a reduction of 23 to 30 percent below what emissions would otherwise be. In other words, the United States defended its initial Kyoto position on the basis of the large amount of reductions that would be required from the spiraling greenhouse emissions of the United States.

Additional major elements of the U.S. proposal going into Kyoto were a call for the creation of international emissions trading systems that would reduce U.S. costs and a call for developing countries to make specific commitments on global warming. Therefore, the Clinton administration took the position on developing-nation commitments that were in conflict with the already ratified UNFCCC.

In releasing its initial Kyoto proposal, the Clinton administration further contended that domestic implementation could be achieved through tax incentives, trading, and other measures that would avoid the need for regulations. In this way, the Clinton administration was arguing to Congress that there were relatively painless ways that the United States could make significant reductions in its greenhouse gas emissions.

In addition to the U.S. position, several other proposals were floated by nations before the Kyoto negotiations. The European Union made an early proposal during the summer of 1997 that provided that developed countries commit to reduce emissions for three greenhouse gases by 15 percent below 1990 levels by 2010, with an interim target of 7.5 percent by 2005.[86] The Europeans strongly lobbied the United States to adopt this position at the June 1997 Earth Summit Plus Five meeting that took place in New York five months before Kyoto.[87]

Before Kyoto, AOSIS, the group representing the islands most vulnerable to rising oceans, proposed that nations agree to reduce emissions 20 percent below 1990 levels by 2005.[88] These island nations were very aggressive in climate negotiations because they felt that their very existence was at stake.

The developing nations and China usually negotiated as a bloc known as G-77 and China, where G-77 stood for the seventy-seven nations that originally constituted this group. The G-77 and China initially proposed that developed nations should agree to reduce carbon emissions to 1990 levels by 2000, 7.5 percent below 1990 by 2005, 15 percent below 1990 by 2010, and 35 percent below 1990 by 2020.[89] The developing nations also vociferously rejected specific and legally binding targets for them that were being called for by the United States.

As the United States prepared for Kyoto, an industry coalition of oil companies, electric utilities, automobile manufacturers, and farm groups launched a multi-million-dollar advertising campaign to generate public opposition to a Kyoto treaty.[90] This campaign asserted that devastating impacts on the U.S. economy would follow from a Kyoto treaty that would limit U.S. emissions without obtaining any developing world commitments. One of the television advertisements paid for by this campaign and frequently seen on American television showed a scissors cutting those countries out of a world map that would not have enforceable emissions targets. This advertisement asserted that a Kyoto treaty would unfairly exempt these nations. Yet the advertisement made no mention of the fact that the United States had already agreed that the developed nations should take the first steps to reducing emissions in adopting the UNFCCC.

The Mobil Corporation also placed op-ed articles against binding U.S. commitments in the *New York Times* that continued to stress issues of scientific uncertainty about global warming and crippling U.S. economic impacts.[91] The Mobil articles also urged that any treaty must include commitments from the developing countries.[92]

The Kyoto conference was held on December 1–11, 1997. Attending the conference were 6,000 delegates from more than 160 nations.[93] In addition to the delegates, 3,600 members of environmental groups and 3,500 reporters followed the negotiations.[94] Among the most powerful industry representatives at Kyoto was the Climate Change Coalition, which then included as members, among others, Exxon, Mobil, and Shell Oil, along with the big three U.S. automobile manufacturers, mining and transport companies, steelmakers, and chemical producers.[95] The British environment minister described the presence at Kyoto of the U.S.-based industry lobbyists as follows:

I saw some of the nastiest big business arm-twisting one could imagine. A corps of sixty lobbyists from United States coal, oil, and car industries, masquerading under the label of Global Climate Coalition, stalked the corridors and meeting rooms cajoling and threatening United States' delegates and developing countries alike.[96]

Also attending the conference was a large congressional delegation headed by Republican senator Chuck Hagel, who had introduced the Senate resolution opposing any treaty that would create great costs for the U.S. economy and that did not include developing-world commitments. Many in this congressional delegation appeared to be in Kyoto to prevent the U.S. government delegates from getting out in front of the very restrictive congressional position announced in the Hagel–Byrd Resolution.

Just as in the 1992 Earth Summit negotiations, the United States entered the Kyoto negotiations holding, along with Australia, the least environmentally protective position among major players despite the fact that the Clinton administration had taken a more engaged approach to U.S. global warming responsibilities. In formulating the U.S. position, President Clinton had been convinced by his economic advisers to go slow because of potential adverse economic impacts on the U.S. economy if the proposals of other nations were adopted at Kyoto.[97]

Just as in Rio, the stakes were extraordinarily high in terms of the ability to create losers and winners among and within countries. Energy-intensive industries and fossil fuel and automobile companies in the United States apparently believed that they had a lot to lose. Although these lobbyists fought many battles, during negotiations they focused much of their energy on pushing the United States to hold its position on insisting that the developing nations make specific commitments to reduce greenhouse emissions while fighting various specific proposed emission reduction targets.

As negotiations began, many developing nations lectured the richer countries, and in particular the United States, about the failure to make progress in reducing greenhouse gases since the 1992 Earth Summit. In the first week of negotiations, little progress was made as charges and countercharges were made. In fact, on the fourth day, the *New York Times* declared that only a "near-miracle" could salvage the negotiations.[98] It appeared to many as if the negotiations would fail, in large part because the United States, virtually standing alone again, would not agree to the magnitude of reduction targets being pushed by most developed and developing nations. Not much happened until Vice President Gore arrived in Kyoto on December 8 and told the American delegation to show "increased negotiating flexibility."[99] Gore's arrival broke up the negotiating logjam, although significant disagreements still remained among the parties until the very last moment on the last day of the negotiations. Because so much was at stake, during the last few days intense negotiations took place not only between the negotiators in Kyoto but also between heads of state in their capitals.

At the last moment, a final deal was struck when the United States agreed to commit to a 7 percent reduction below 1990 emission levels in turn for acceptance of much of its position on "flexibility mechanisms," particularly those relating to trading.[100] These flexibility mechanisms would allow the United States to achieve the majority of its greenhouse reduction target not through actual emission reductions in the United States but through paying for greenhouse reduction projects in other countries or by obtaining credit for carbon being stored by American forests.

Despite strong opposition to many aspects of the U.S. trading proposals, at the last moment the developing countries agreed to these trading mechanisms, in part because many of the details of how the trading mechanism would actually work would have to be worked out in future negotiations. In this way, the developing nations believed that they could postpone battles over the specifics of the trading mechanisms to another day.

Many of the core concepts relating to trading and other "flexibility" elements of the Kyoto Protocol that had been pushed by the United States were not resolved in Kyoto because broad, general concepts were agreed to only at the very last moment in Kyoto. These unresolved issues would continue to plague future negotiations.

In the Kyoto Protocol, the United States agreed to achieve a 7 percent reduction of its emissions below 1990 levels between 2008 and 2012, while the European Union agreed to an 8 percent reduction, Japan agreed to a 6 percent reduction, and twenty other countries agreed to be bound to emissions reductions that would in total reduce emissions from the developed nations by 5.2 percent.

In agreeing to its 7 percent reduction target, the United States was successful in getting other nations to agree to several elements of the U.S. strategy that it had been pushing, including the following:[101]

- *Flexibility in which gases could be counted in national targets.* National target reductions could be achieved through reductions in six greenhouse gases (carbon dioxide, methane, nitrous oxide, and three synthetic substitutes for ozone-depleting chlorinated fluorocarbons, i.e., hydrofluorocarbons [HFCs], perfluorocarbons [PFCs], and sulfur hexafluoride [SF_6]) rather than the three proposed by European Union.[102] Because the United States pushed for six gases rather than just a few, nations have flexibility to reduce those greenhouse gases that they find easiest to reduce while allowing others to remain at higher levels. Under this approach, instead of achieving its 7 percent reduction target by lowering fossil fuel use alone, the United States could reduce its emissions of methane or sulfur hexaflouride.
- *Flexibility where a nation must achieve its reduction.* The United States was successful in getting the protocol to include three trading mechanisms that could be pursued by the developed nations, such as the United States, to find least-cost projects to achieve national targets. These mechanisms allowed the developed nations to find inexpensive projects in other parts of the world and to get credit for these projects against national targets. These mechanisms included (1) an international trading mechanism that would allow nations or companies to purchase less expensive emissions permits from countries that have more permits than they need, (2) a joint implementation program that allows developed nations with emissions targets to

obtain credit toward the target by doing emission reduction projects in other nations that have targets, and (3) a clean development mechanism that would allow nations with targets to obtain credit by paying for projects in developing nations.[103]

- *Flexibility in how targets may be achieved.* The United States successfully pushed for flexibility in achieving targets by enhancing carbon-absorbing activities, that is, greenhouse gas sinks, rather than reducing emissions.
- *Flexibility in when targets need to be achieved.*[104] The United States successfully achieved flexibility in when national reduction targets need be achieved in two significant ways. First, the United States successfully fought off earlier dates by which targets have to be achieved, including the European Union proposal that targets be achieved by 2010. Second, under pressure from the United States, the emissions target must not be achieved in a specific year but rather in terms of an average over a five-year period (2008–12).[105]

In achieving its goal in inserting these flexibility elements into the Kyoto Protocol at virtually the last minute, the United States introduced concepts that would be helpful to it in minimizing costs of compliance but made future negotiations much more complex than they would have been without these mechanisms. In fact, many of the flexibility mechanisms successfully pushed by the United States would continue to plague negotiations after Kyoto because many of the details of these flexibility mechanisms continued to be hotly contested and, as we will see in chapter 10, raise equity issues of great concern to the poorest nations.

One of the major objectives of the United States going into Kyoto was not achieved to the satisfaction of the United States. That is, the United States was not successful in achieving its stated goal of securing meaningful participation of developing nations.[106] However, despite the fact that the United States got other nations to compromise their positions in the Kyoto Protocol in return for the U.S. promise to reduce greenhouse gas emissions by 7 percent, the Clinton administration announced after Kyoto that it would not submit the Kyoto Protocol to the Senate for ratification until it secured agreements from developing nations to participate in Kyoto. In this way, the United States was repudiating not only the deal that it had made in Kyoto to support the new Protocol but also the provision in Article 3 of the UNFCCC that stated that the developed world would take the first steps in reducing emissions.

In June 1997, the United States announced to great fanfare that it would pledge $1 billion over five years to help developing nations promote energy efficiency and develop alternative energy sources.[107] However only $250 million of this money was new; the rest was repackaged or redirected money already in the budget of the U.S. Agency for International Development. Yet this commitment was a concrete recognition on the part of the Clinton administration that the United States had some responsibility to help the developing world reduce its greenhouse gas emissions. Despite this acknowledgment, the United States continued to insist that the developing nations make binding commitments to reduce their emissions.

AFTERMATH OF KYOTO

The reaction to the Kyoto Protocol by its U.S. opponents was fierce and swift. Opponents cried that the U.S. agreement to a 7 percent reduction below 1990 in an agreement that did not include developing-world commitments would create economic havoc in the United States. Some fossil fuel interests and others embarked on a massive advertising and public relations blitz, trying to convince the public and the government to shun the Protocol. Senator Chuck Hagel echoed the anger of other U.S. legislators with the Clinton administration's position when he said, "Any way you measure this, this is a bad deal for America."[108] Senator Hagel predicted that the Kyoto agreement would be dead on arrival if it appeared for ratification in the Senate.

In a number of executive branch appropriations acts, Congress also prohibited executive branch agencies, including the U.S. Environmental Protection Agencies (EPA), from working on climate issues that could be construed as "backdoor" ratification of the Kyoto Protocol.[109] This would prove to greatly hinder the EPA from working with states and local governments who desired to take voluntary steps to reduce greenhouse emissions. A House 1999 appropriations bill for the EPA included a ban on spending for any effort to implement the Kyoto agreement, including meetings and educating the public about climate issues.[110] In one case, Pennsylvania invited EPA representatives to a meeting to discuss potential climate change impacts in Pennsylvania, and EPA administrator Carol Browner was hauled in front of Congress to explain why the EPA went to such a meeting in violation of EPA appropriations acts. The Pennsylvania request had nothing to do with ratification of Kyoto, yet such discussions on the part of the EPA were called backdoor ratification of Kyoto. And so at the very time the United States should have been unleashing state and local governments to take voluntary steps to reduce greenhouse gas emissions, Congress was preventing the EPA from discussing climate change issues with state and local governments on the grounds that such discussions were backdoor Kyoto ratification efforts. For this and other reasons, not much was done during the Clinton administration to reduce U.S. emissions of greenhouse gases. Congress was not only hostile to the Kyoto Protocol but was also adamantly opposed to taking serious steps to reduce U.S. emissions. During this time, U.S. greenhouse emissions continued to soar.

In November 1998, the fourth Conference of Parties (COP-4) to the UN-FCCC took place in Buenos Aires. The purpose of the Buenos Aires meeting was to fill in many of the unresolved details needed to implement the Kyoto Protocol.[111] It had been hoped that many of the issues raised but not resolved in Kyoto would be worked out in Buenos Aires, but it quickly became clear that the parties were too far apart to make rapid progress. As a result, not much progress on the major issues was made at COP-4. In lieu of substantive resolution of major issues, COP-4 came out with a two-year plan of action for resolving these issues. The issues included the following:

- Rules and guidelines for the flexible market measurements that had been pushed by the United States. These "market mechanisms" included Emissions Trading, Joint Implementation, and the Clean Development mechanism pushed by the United States (these concepts are explained in chapter 10).
- Issues concerning development and transfer of cleaner technology to developing nations.
- Issues about how to calculate carbon sinks that could be used as credits against national reduction targets.[112]

At COP-4, the European Union had been interested in limiting the amount to which any nation could use emission trading as a method for achieving national targets. The United States strongly resisted this attempt to limit the use of the Kyoto trading mechanisms.

For a year before COP-4, the United States had been pursuing developing-world nations to get some of them to make a break with the majority of the developing nations and show a willingness to make commitments on greenhouse gas reductions. At the beginning of the Buenos Aires meeting, Argentina announced that it would make a commitment to reduce greenhouse gases. The next day, the United States announced that it would sign the Kyoto Protocol but that it would not submit it to the Senate for ratification until it secured more commitments from the developing nations to reduce greenhouse gases.

For the most part, the United States has not been successful in getting many other developing nations to make commitments on reducing greenhouse gases. As a result, the Clinton administration was not in a position to ask the Senate to ratify the treaty.[113] Most of the developing world resisted the pressure from the United States to make commitments to reduce greenhouse gases. One observer on the role played by the developing nations at Buenos Aires said,

The reality is that the views of the developing world have not shifted since the Kyoto Conference. . . . [T]he vast majority [of developing nations] have adopted a wait and see attitude with respect to their obligations—or perhaps we should phrase it a "wait and see if the developed countries begin taking steps to meet the obligations they agreed to in Kyoto." This position dominated discussions on particular commitments from the developing world. Emissions trading and carbon sequestration, of course, still remain suspect, and it will take substantial discussion and negotiation to reach agreement on how to operationalize the Kyoto language.[114]

Many of the nations in the developing world continued to bridle at the U.S. position that they should make commitments while the developing nations' total and per capita emissions are so low compared to the developed world.[115] These developing nations also argued that it is not fair for the United States "with the highest levels of both GDP and emissions to insist on developing country positions when the United States itself seems unwilling to make substantial emissions reductions."[116]

The fifth Conference of Parties (COP-5) to the UNFCCC was held in Bonn, Germany, in October 1999. Few of the issues identified in the two-year plan of action adopted in COP-4 were resolved at COP-5. Again, not much major progress was made at COP-5 on resolving the flexibility mechanisms largely pushed by the United States. The U.S.-pushed flexibility mechanisms continued to be at the very center of controversy in climate negotiations.

The sixth Conference of Parties (COP-6) to the UNFCCC was held in November 2000 in The Hague, Netherlands. The United States continued to press for maximum use of the trading mechanisms and for the right to use its existing forests' ability to remove carbon from the atmosphere as a credit against the 7 percent reduction target that the United States had agreed to in Kyoto. The European Union and many other countries opposed the desire of the United States to have unrestricted use of the Kyoto flexibility mechanisms. The Hague climate conference dramatically failed to make progress on implementing the Kyoto agreements, while most nations blamed the unreasonable position of the United States on forests for the conference failure.

At the beginning of 2001, the IPCC released summaries from its third scientific assessment. This third IPCC report concluded that the earth's average surface temperature could rise by 2.5 to 10.4°F from 1990 to 2100—much higher than the IPCC's estimate of five years earlier, when it predicted a rise of 1.8 to 6.3°F.[117] Should the higher estimates prove accurate, they would spell potential catastrophe for our planet. The third IPCC report also strengthened its prior conclusions that human-caused global warming was already happening.

Just about the same time as the IPCC's summary of its third report was being announced, the U.S. Energy Information Administration released a projection of

U.S. expected energy use and carbon emissions levels in 2020.[118] This official U.S. government projection concluded that in 2020, U.S. energy demand would be up 32 percent from 2000 levels in 2020 while carbon emissions would increase 35 percent. Because the United States was already more than 11 percent above 1990 levels in 2000, this projection forecast that the United States would, under business as usual, be over 45 percent above 1990 levels by 2020. And so, although many governments as early as 1988 had pressed for the developed world to make legally binding commitments to reduce greenhouse gases by as much as 20 percent by 2000, the United States was by 2000 at least 30 percent higher in carbon emissions than might have been possible had it taken climate change seriously in the late 1980s. It is clear by now that the voluntary approaches to global warming pushed by many in the United States have thus far been a colossal failure. The United States also failed to meet its nonenforceable promise to stabilize its greenhouse gas emissions at 1990 levels by 2000.

THE GEORGE W. BUSH ADMINISTRATION

The George W. Bush administration took office in January 2001, apparently either unaware of the enormous international controversy that had arisen around global warming or indifferent to it. On March 13, 2001, President Bush announced that he would abandon his campaign promise to regulate carbon dioxide emissions from electrical generation facilities.[119] In making this announcement, President Bush pointed to the same three reasons that had become an American refrain of excuses for refusing to take action on global warming, namely, scientific uncertainty, cost to the U.S. economy, and the failure of the developing world to make commitments.[120] A week later, the Bush administration announced that it was backing away from Kyoto. The Bush administration's decision to reject the international treaty to combat global warming, so painfully agreed to in Kyoto, provoked a stunned and angry reaction among America's allies in Europe and Japan.[121] Many of them loudly urged the United States to reconsider its decision.

On April 30, 2001, Vice President Dick Cheney gave a preview of the Bush energy strategy. He stressed that the policy will not include austerity measures like the ones the nation adopted in 1974 in the wake of the Arab oil embargo.[122] In this speech, Cheney said, "The aim here is efficiency, not austerity." Cheney also said in this speech that saving energy may be "a sign of personal virtue" but is not sufficient for a national energy policy.[123] Cheney further said that the United States needed to build as many as 1,900 new power plants over the next twenty years to keep abreast of new demand. Cheney argued that coal needed to be the primary source for electric power generation for years to come.

On May 16, 2001, President Bush released a new U.S. energy policy.[124] This policy concluded that over the next twenty years, U.S. oil consumption will increase by 33 percent, and demand for energy will increase 45 percent.[125] Although the Bush policy recognized the need for greater use of renewable energy, the cornerstone of this policy was increased use of fossil fuels to meet rising demand, with coal "playing a significant role" in meeting increased demand along with petroleum, natural gas, and nuclear.[126]

International reaction to the Bush energy plan was harsh for its failure to rein in galloping U.S. energy demand or deal with global warming.[127] Some environmentalists charged that the plan was a "disaster" and a "crime" for failing to take global warming seriously.[128]

On June 7, 2001, the U.S. Academy of Sciences issued a report that had earlier been requested by the Bush administration that confirmed that global warming was a real problem and getting much worse.[129] The Academy of Sciences report was seen to be a huge embarrassment and a rebuke to the Bush administration, which was still relying on scientific uncertainty as a basis for rejecting both the Kyoto Protocol and the regulation of carbon dioxide.

On June 11, 2001, President Bush gave a policy address on global warming in the Rose Garden at the White House.[130] Although this speech acknowledged that the National Academy of Sciences had concluded that recent heating of the earth had been caused in part by human activities and announced new global warming research programs, it also emphasized scientific uncertainty about the consequences of global warming. President Bush also attacked the Kyoto Protocol for excluding developing-world participation, for not basing the Kyoto reduction targets on sound science, and for having a negative economic impact on the U.S. economy were it to be implemented.[131]

CONCLUSION

As the nation that is the greatest emitter of greenhouse gases, with the most financial means to address global warming and the most power to influence international cooperation, the U.S. role in climate change negotiations has been largely that of an obstructionist, preventing agreements that would have been acceptable to most nations. For this reason, the U.S. role in the international global warming negotiations has been extremely disappointing to many around the world who believe that global warming is an immense, growing threat to human health and the environment worldwide.

Throughout negotiations on climate change, the U.S. executive branch (in the case of negotiations leading up to the UNFCC concluded in 1992), Congress and sometimes the executive branch (in the case of negotiations relating to the Kyoto Protocol in 1997), and recently the executive branch in the George W. Bush administration have resisted meaningful greenhouse reduction programs proposed by others nations on several recurring grounds. These grounds for U.S. opposition to global warming programs will be examined in later parts of this book. The recurring arguments against meaningful greenhouse gas reduction programs include the following:

- There is too much scientific uncertainty about the human causes of global warming to justify anything other than voluntary programs to reduce emissions.
- Cost-benefit analyses of carbon reduction strategies in the United States do not justify programs to reduce emissions.
- The United States should not agree to reduce its emissions of greenhouse gases until the developing world makes commitments.
- The United States should not agree to an international program to reduce greenhouse gas emissions unless the rest of the world agrees to create trading regimes that will allow the United States to find least-cost solutions to reducing its emissions.
- The United States should not agree to an international program to reduce greenhouse gas emissions in which national limitations are based on equitable considerations, such as historical emission levels or proportionate share of world emissions.

These arguments are examined through an ethical lens in later chapters of this book. Other chapters identify other significant ethical issues that the United States needs to face if the world is going to agree on a much-needed global solution to the global warming crisis.

NOTES

1. Gene-Baptiste-Joseph Fourier, "Remarques Generales sur la Temperatures du Globe Terrestre et des Espaces Planetaires," *Annales De Chimie et de Physique* 27 (1824): 136–67.

2. Gale E. Christianson, *Greenhouse: The 200-Year Story of Global Warming* (New York: Walker, 1999), 6–11.

3. Svante Arrhenius, "On the Influence of Carbonic Acid in the Air upon Temperature of the Ground," *The London, Edinburg, and Dublin Philosophical Magazine and Journal of Science,* 5th series (April 1896): 237–76.

4. Christianson, *Greenhouse,* 115.

5. G. S. Callendar, "An Attempt to Frame a Working Hypothesis on the Cause of the Glacial Periods on an Atmospheric Basis," *Journal of Geology* 64 (February 1938): 223–40.

6. Environmental Defense Fund, *Global Warming: The History of an International Scientific Consensus* (available at <www.edf.org/pubs/FactSheets/d_GWFact.html>, December 20, 2000).

7. Christianson, *Greenhouse,* 151.

8. David Bodansky, "Prologue to the Climate Change Convention," in I. M. Mitzner and J. A. Leonard, eds., *Negotiating Climate Change: The Inside Story of the Rio Convention* (Cambridge: Cambridge University Press and Stockholm Environment Institute, 1994), 46.

9. Bodansky, "Prologue to the Climate Change Convention," 46.

10. Environmental Defense Fund, *Global Warming.*

11. Wayne Morrissey, *Global Climate Change: A Concise History of Negotiations and Chronology of Major Activities Preceding the 1992 U.N. Framework Convention.* Report for Congress, Congressional Research Service, Washington, D.C., 1998 (available at <www.cnie.org/nle/clim-6.html>, March 9, 2001).

12. Morrissey, *Global Climate Change.*

13. United States Council on Environmental Quality, *Global Energy Futures and the Carbon Dioxide Problem* (Washington, D.C.: U.S. Government Press Printing Office, 1981).

14. Utility Commission of Ohio, *Chronology of Climate Change* (available at <www.puc.state.oh.us/consumer/gcc/chron.html>, June 6, 2000).

15. Morrissey, *Global Climate Change.*

16. Utility Commission of Ohio, *Chronology of Climate Change.*

17. Utility Commission of Ohio, *Chronology of Climate Change.*

18. A campaign speech of George Bush quoted in Shardula Agrarwala and Stiener Anderson, "Indispensability and Indefensibility?: The United States in Climate Treaty Negotiations," *Global Governance* 5, no. 4 (December 1999): 459.

19. Morrissey, *Global Climate Change.*

20. Morrissey, *Global Climate Change.*

21. Utility Commission of Ohio, *Chronology of Climate Change.*

22. Utility Commission of Ohio, *Chronology of Climate Change.*

23. Bodansky, "Prologue to the Climate Change Convention," 52.

24. Bodansky, "Prologue to the Climate Change Convention," 52.

25. Utility Commission of Ohio, *Chronology of Climate Change.*

26. Utility Commission of Ohio, *Chronology of Climate Change.*

27. Morrissey, *Global Climate Change.*

28. The first IPCC report was published as Sir John Houghton, G. Jenkins, and J. Ephraums, eds., *Scientific Assessment of Climate Change* (Boston: Cambridge University Press, 1990).

29. For discussion of the first IPCC report, see Bodansky, "Prologue to the Climate Change Convention," 59.

30. Morrissey, *Global Climate Change.*

31. Morrissey, *Global Climate Change.*

32. Delphne Barione and Jean Ripert, "Exercising Common but Differentiated Responsibility," in Mitzner and Leonard, eds., *Negotiating Climate Change,* 82.

33. Barione and Ripert, *Exercising Common but Differentiated Responsibility,* 82.

34. Chandrashekner Dasgupta, "The Climate Negotiations," in Mitzner and Leonard, eds., *Negotiating Climate Change,* 133.

35. Dasgupta, "The Climate Negotiations," 133.

36. Dasgupta, "The Climate Negotiations," 133.

37. Dasgupta, "The Climate Negotiations," 133.

38. Paul Harris, "Understanding America's Climate Change Policy: Realpolitik, Pluralism, and Ethical Norms" (Research Paper No. 15, Oxford Center for the Environment Ethics and Society), June 1998.

39. Dasgupta, "The Climate Negotiations," 130.

40. Dasgupta, "The Climate Negotiations," 131.

41. Dasgupta, "The Climate Negotiations," 131.

42. Dasgupta, "The Climate Negotiations," 131.

43. Dasgupta, "The Climate Negotiations," 131.

44. Jose Goldemberg, "The Road To Rio," in Mitzner and Leonard, eds., *Negotiating Climate Change,* 181.

45. Bodansky, "Prologue to the Climate Change Convention," 61.

46. Bodansky, "Prologue to the Climate Change Convention," 61.

47. Tariq Osman Hydar, "Looking Back to See Forward," in Mitzner and Leonard, eds., *Negotiating Climate Change,* 209.

48. United Nations Framework Convention on Climate Change (UNFCCC), May 29, 1992, UN Document A:AC.237/18.

49. William A. Nitze, "A Failure of United States Leadership," in Mitzner and Leonard, eds., *Negotiating Climate Change,* 187–200.

50. UNFCCC, Article 2.

51. UNFCCC, Article 4 (a).

52. UNFCCC, Article 4(b).

53. UNFCC, Article 3.

54. UNFCC, Article 3.

55. Nitze, "A Failure of United States Leadership," 187–200.

56. Nitze, "A Failure of United States Leadership," 188.

57. Nitze, "A Failure of United States Leadership," 189.

58. Nitze, "A Failure of United States Leadership," 189.

59. Nitze, "A Failure of United States Leadership," 190.

60. Nitze, "A Failure of United States Leadership," 195–96.

61. United States Environmental Protection Agency, *Inventory of U.S. Greenhouse Gas Emissions and Sinks: 1990–1997.* EPA 236-R-99-003. Washington, D.C.: U.S. Environmental Protection Agency (available at <www.epa.gov/globalwarming/publications/emissions/us1999/index.html>, March 13, 2001).

62. Nitze, "A Failure of United States Leadership," 196.

63. Senator Albert Gore, *Earth in the Balance* (New York: Houghton Mifflin, 1992).

64. Agrarwala and Anderson, "Indispensability and Indefensibility?," 461.

65. United States Department of Energy, *The Climate Change Action Plan of the United States* (Washington, D.C.: U.S. Government Printing Office), 1993.

66. United States Department of Energy, *The Climate Change Action Plan.*

67. Intergovernmental Panel on Climate Change, *The Science of Climate Change Contribution of Working Group I to the Second Assessment of the Intergovernmental Panel on Climate Change, Summary for Policy Makers* (available at <www.ipcc.ch/about/about.htm>, March 9, 2001).

68. Wayne Morrissey and John Justice, *IB89005: Global Climate Change,* Issue Brief for Congress (Washington, D.C.: National Counsel for Science and Environment, Congressional Research Service, March 13, 2000) (<available at <www.cnie.org/nle/clim-2.html>, March 12, 2001).

69. Morrissey and Justice, *IB89005.*

70. Morrissey and Justice *IB89005.*

71. Wayne Morrissey, *Global Climate Change: Adequacy of Commitments under the Framework Convention and the Berlin Mandate* (Washington, D.C.: Committee for the National Institute for the Environment) (available at <www.cnie.org/nle/clim-14.html>, October 25, 2000).

72. Morrissey, *Global Climate Change.*

73. Morrissey, *Global Climate Change.*

74. Morrissey, *Global Climate Change.*

75. Morrissey, *Global Climate Change.*

76. Morrissey, *Global Climate Change.*

77. William Stevens, "5 Years after Environmental Summit, Little Progress," *New York Times,* June 17, 1997, A1.

78. Paul Harris, "Climate Change: Is the United States Sharing the Burden?," in Paul Harris, ed., *Climate Change and American Foreign Policy* (New York: St. Martin's Press, 2000), 30–49.

79. Morrissey, *Global Climate Change.*

80. Morrissey, *Global Climate Change.*

81. Morrissey, *Global Climate Change.*

82. S.R. 98, 105th Cong., 1st sess. (July 22, 1997), *Congressional Record,* 143, S8117, daily ed. (July 25, 1997).

83. S.R. 98.

84. Morrissey, *Global Climate Change.*

85. William Stevens, "In Kyoto, the Subject Is Climate; the Forest Is for Storms," *New York Times,* December 1, 1997, E1, 3.

86. The author of this book attended this meeting as a representative of the U.S. Environmental Protection Agency.

87. The author of this book attended this meeting as a representative of the U.S. Environmental Protection Agency.

88. The author of this book attended this meeting as a representative of the U.S. Environmental Protection Agency.

89. Joy Warick and Peter Baker, "Clinton Details Global Warming Plan Market Incentives, Modest Targets Draw Critics from Left and Right," *Washington Post,* October 23, 1997, A6.

90. Mobil Corporation, "Climate Change: Where We Come Out," *New York Times,* November 15, 1997, op-ed.

91. Mobil Corporation, "Climate Change."

92. Christianson, *Greenhouse,* 253.

93. Christianson, *Greenhouse,* 253.

94. Christianson, *Greenhouse,* 253.

95. John Gummer, quoted in "Business Nonsense," *Down to Earth* 7, no. 12 (November 15, 1998) (available at <www.oneworld.org/cse/html/dte/dte981115/dte_srep2.htm>, July 18, 2000).

96. William Stevens, *The Change in the Weather: People, Weather, and the Science of Climate* (New York: Delacorte Press, 1999), 298.

97. Christianson, *Greenhouse,* 264.

98. Stevens, *The Change in the Weather,* 306.

99. Kyoto Protocol to the United Nations Framework Convention on Climate Change, UN FCC/CP/1997/L.7Add.1, December 10, 1997; see also Gerald Hapka, "Climate Change: The Policy and the Political Process." This paper was released in 1998 by Hapka, who was an observer in Kyoto for the Pew Climate Change Program, Arlington, Virginia.

100. For a discussion of the flexibility objectives that the United States achieved, see The United States of America, "The Kyoto Protocol and the President's Policies to Address Climate Change" (Administration Economic Analysis, WGB-98 0042), July 1998.

101. The United States of America, "The Kyoto Protocol and the President's Policies to Address Climate Change," 22 (available at <www.epa.gov/globalwarming/publications/actions/wh_kyoto/index.html>, March 12, 2001).

102. The United States of America, "The Kyoto Protocol and the President's Policies to Address Climate Change," 23.

103. The United States of America, "The Kyoto Protocol and the President's Policies to Address Climate Change," 23.

104. The United States of America, "The Kyoto Protocol and the President's Policies to Address Climate Change," 23.

105. The United States of America, "The Kyoto Protocol and the President's Policies to Address Climate Change," 23.

106. The United States of America, "The Kyoto Protocol and the President's Policies to Address Climate Change," 23.

107. Curt Tarnoff, "Global Climate Change: The Role of United States Foreign Assistance," Committee for the National Institute for the Environment, Congressional Research Service, November 21, 1997 (available at <www.cnie.org/nle.clim-12.html>, June 2, 2000).

108. William Stevens, "Meeting Reaches Accord to Reduce Greenhouse Gases," *New York Times,* December 11, 1997, A10, International section.

109. See, e.g., Departments of Veterans Affairs and Housing and Urban Development and Independent Agencies Appropriations Act, 1999, Public Law 105-276, 112 Stat. 2496.

110. For a discussion of what is generally referred to as the Knollenburg amendments, for Representative Joe Knollenburg (R-Mich.), see Gary Bryner, "Congress and the Politics of Climate Change," in Harris, ed., *Climate Change and American Foreign Policy,* 116.

111. Morrissey and Justice, *IB89005,* 9.

112. Morrissey and Justice, *IB89005,* 9.

113. Morrissey and Justice, *IB89005,* 10.

114. *Summary of the Fifth Conference of Parties to the Framework Convention on Climate Change* (Toronto: International Institute for Sustainable Development), November 8, 1999.

115. Hapka, "Climate Change," 4.

116. Hapka, "Climate Change," 5.

117. Hapka, "Climate Change," 5.

118. Intergovernmental Panel on Climate Change, *Summary for Policymakers, Wording Group I (Science), Third Assessment Report,* February 2001 (available at <www.ipcc.ch/pub/spm22-01.pdf>, February 21, 2001).

119. Douglas Jehl with Andrew C. Revkin, "Bush in Reversal Won't Seek Cut in Emissions of Carbon Dioxide," *New York Times,* March 14, 2001, A1.

120. Jehl and Revkin.

121. William Drozdiak and Eric Pianin, "U.S. Angers Allies over Climate Pact: Europeans Will Ask Bush to Reconsider," *Washington Post,* March 29, 2001, A01.

122. NBC News, *Cheney Lays Out Energy Strategy,* April 30, 2001. (available at <www.stacks/msnbc.com/news/566483.asp>, June 2, 2001).

123. NBC News, *Cheney Lays Out Energy Strategy.*

124. United States, *National Energy Policy: Report of the National Energy Policy Development Group,* May 16, 2001.

125. United States, *National Energy Policy,* x.

126. United States, *National Energy Policy,* 5–14.

127. Reuters, "Environmentalists Blast Bush Energy Plan," May 18, 2001 (available at <www/nytimes.com/pages/reuters/world/index.html>, June 1, 2001).

128. Reuters, "Environmentalists Blast Bush Energy Plan."

129. Katharine Q. Seelye and Andrew C. Revkin, "Panel Tells Bush Global Warming Is Getting Worse," *New York Times,* June 7, 2001, A1.

130. White House News Service, *Remarks of the President on Global Climate Change,* June 11, 2001 (available at <www.whitehouse.gov/news/releases/2001/06/20010611-2.html>, June 11, 2001).

131. White House News Service, *Remarks of the President on Global Climate Change.*

Chapter Three

Environmental Ethics and Global Warming Policy

This chapter introduces ethical concepts and issues that will be encountered in other parts of this book. It begins by examining the difference between scientific and ethical issues that arise in later chapters. Chapters 7 to 10 examine the ethical dimensions of specific arguments made in opposition to U.S. global warming programs, and chapters 11 and 12 examine other specific ethical issues that the United States needs to face in order to protect human health and the environment from global warming. These later chapters will often use ethical terms and concepts that are introduced here. Those who already have a basic understanding of environmental ethical issues and terms may desire to proceed directly to chapter 4.

ETHICAL STATEMENTS DISTINGUISHED FROM SCIENTIFIC AND ECONOMIC STATEMENTS

As mentioned in chapter 1, global warming can be understood as a problem that raises scientific questions about whether humans are causing climate change and the effects of human-induced climate change on human health and the environment. The use of the term "ethics" in this book is meant to connote the domain of inquiry that attempts to answer the question "What is good?" Ethical statements are propositions of the form that such and such is good or bad, right or wrong, obligatory or nonobligatory. Science, as used in this book, is the discipline that attempts to make "descriptive" statements about the nature of reality through analysis of causes and effects of global warming. Ethical inquiry about global warming is concerned with "prescriptive" statements about what should be done in light of certain understandings about how humans could change the climate.

49

Various positions taken by those who argue for or against specific policy approaches to global warming invariably contain prescriptions such as the United States should not take action on global warming because of scientific uncertainty about the consequences to the climate system from human releases of greenhouse gases. This book critically examines frequent prescriptive statements made in climate change debates in the United States, statements that philosophers classify as ethical statements because they purport to tell what policymakers should do.

A great challenge for all concerned about the ethical dimensions of environmental policy arises from the fact that in day-to-day environmental decision making, many of the ethical positions taken by policymakers are hidden in the details of the scientific, economic, and legal languages in which the environmental issues are discussed. Therefore, to examine the ethical dimensions of proposed environmental decisions, one must be unable to untangle the ethical issues from the scientific, economic, and legal languages that often pretend to be "value free" but that, on further examination, as we will see in later chapters of this book, are heavily value laden.[1]

Climate change science aims at value-free descriptions of the human–climate interactions. However, as will be pointed out in various parts of this book, scientific statements often contain hidden ethical positions throughout analysis of the global warming problem because of, among other reasons, the unavoidable need to (1) deal with scientific uncertainty, (2) assign the burden of proof in scientific reasoning, (3) decide what resources will be spent on problem analysis, (4) choose which disciplines will be used in the analysis of problems and how to synthesize various disciplines in that analysis, and (5) make metaphysical assumptions about the nature of reality.

It is generally accepted that science cannot deduce prescriptive statements from facts.[2] That is, one cannot deduce "ought" from "is" without supplying a new minor premise. One cannot introduce an evaluative term, such as "optimal solution to the global warming problem," into the conclusion of an argument if the prior premises of that argument are entirely nonevaluative (e.g., greenhouse gas warming potentials). Although a description of certain facts may suggest an ethical position, one cannot, through a description of the facts alone, deduce an ethical conclusion. An ethical system, such as utilitarianism, may provide the minor premise needed for ethical reasoning. For instance, if one concludes that global warming policy A will create the greatest happiness, by applying the utilitarian maxim that one should choose the policy option that creates the greatest happiness, one can conclude that option A is the ethically preferable solution and the solution that should be adopted. From a proposition that such and such a human activity creates a particular risk of climate change, one cannot, however, deduce whether that risk is acceptable without first deciding on criteria for acceptability. Therefore, on this largely traditional view of the logic of ethics, science cannot answer ethical questions by itself. Anyone who asserts that we "should' take a particular approach to global warming is making a prescriptive and therefore an ethical assertion leading to a conclusion that science alone cannot compel.

This is not to say, however, that science is irrelevant to ethics. Ethics is concerned with what should be done about particular risks of climate change. Science is extremely important in any global warming ethical judgment because science can help determine which activities cause global warming and pinpoint the various means of protecting against the damages that may be caused by human releases of greenhouse gases. Science can also analyze which climate goals are feasible and can help determine what human health and environmental impacts might be expected from the human release of greenhouse gases. However, science cannot fully determine what to do about human release of greenhouse gases, precisely because no amount of descriptive analysis can logically certify a prescriptive course of action. Thus, science plays an important role in many of the ethical controversies entailed by climate change.

If we agree that the question of whether society should continue to release greenhouse gases is essentially an ethical question while admitting that science could be extremely important in analyzing the ethically relevant facts and thereby giving content to the ethical analysis, it must be admitted that there is no generally accepted consensus in the philosophical community about which ethical system to apply to the problems of global warming. Several major philosophical systems attempt to define good, including utilitarianism, Kantian ethics, natural rights, and Rawlsian contract theory, to name a few. Additionally, it is sometimes difficult to determine which facts should be considered and what weight should be given to these facts in any ethical calculus. Some have argued that the selection of which facts should be considered is itself a question of value. For instance, our concerns about global warming could focus on adverse impacts on cuddly animals, such as polar bears or pandas, or, on the other hand, it could consider impacts on pests, such as mice or bugs. Facts applied to problem solving are not value neutral because choices about which facts to consider usually entail value judgments.

As we will see in chapter 9, economic statements about global warming also frequently contain hidden ethical positions. Economics, like science, often is assumed to contain "value-free" descriptions of economic "facts," such as the "facts" of economic costs and benefits of global warming programs. Yet, as we will see, economic statements often hide numerous controversial yet hidden ethical positions because of the unavoidable need to do the following:

• Measure economic "facts"
• Decide what economic "facts" are relevant to the economic calculations

- Deal with pandemic uncertainty about what costs and benefits will be
- Use mainstream economic methods, such as discounting benefits, that raise a host of ethical questions including but not limited to questions of distributive justice and questions of the value of entities that might be harmed by global warming

Because most of the dominant Western philosophical systems make human interests the measure of value, human interests, some critics argue, are the only interests considered in Western ethical systems that are the foundation of most scientific and economic analyses of global warming problems. The result is that such concerns as the rights of animals are not appropriately included in the traditional global warming debate. In the past twenty years, as concern about environmental problems has increased, environmental philosophers have attempted to create new ethical approaches to emerging environmental problems. In fact, the global environmental crisis has forced a revolutionary reconsideration of ethical theory that dominated public policy debates in the nineteenth and twentieth centuries. This revolution has been responsible for the emergence in the past several decades of biocentric ethics, or an ethics that makes all life the center of value; an ecocentric ethics, or an ethics that makes the natural world itself the focus of ethical concern; and deep ecology, or an ethical approach that strongly rejects many of the basic assumptions of anthropocentric ethics by putting nature at the very center of ethical concern. Ethicists concerned with environmental problems now include anthropocentrists, biocentrists, ecocentrists, deep ecologists, and ecofeminists, among others.[3]

Yet despite the lack of consensus on ethical approaches to environmental problems, this book describes why arguments made against U.S. programs to reduce greenhouse gas emissions are ethically problematic even from the standpoint of mainstream ethical approaches. That is, despite the disagreement among environmental ethicists about many environmental matters, this book argues that strong and noncontroversial ethical judgments can be made about many of the climate change positions taken by the United States. Therefore, no new consensus on an overall environmental ethic is necessary to find many of the U.S. positions on global warming ethically reprehensible. While environmental ethicists will disagree on such questions as whether plants and animals have intrinsic value, most will conclude that many of the arguments made against global warming programs in the United States are ethically unsupportable.

ETHICAL THEORIES AND THEIR LIMITATIONS WHEN APPLIED TO GLOBAL WARMING POLICY

This section describes some of the more common ethical approaches to environmental problems and then identifies some limitations of these approaches when applied to environmental controversies such as global warming. Later chapters examine more comprehensively the ethical issues that might be encountered in discourse about specific global warming policy issues. This section focuses mainly on some of the more conventional Western ethical theories because most debate about global warming policy is already embedded in traditional discourses of science, economics, and law that are usually justified by these Western ethical theories. Therefore, despite growing criticism of traditional ethical approaches to such environmental problems as global warming, as we will see, most arguments for or against various global warming policies take the form of traditional Western ethical arguments. Conventional Western ethical theories are also focused on, for the most part, throughout this book because it will be shown in later chapters that many of the arguments made against programs in the United States to reduce greenhouse gas emissions are abhorrent even to these more conventional ethical theories. Since the more environmentally concerned ethical approaches that arose in the past twenty years would require stronger environmental protection strategies than the conventional Western ethical theories, it is not necessary to spend much time on these recent theories if the U.S. response to global warming is unsupportable even by these less environmentally protective conventional Western theories.

UTILITARIANISM

Arguments for and against global warming programs often are grounded in utilitarian ethical arguments. Utilitarian arguments have been particularly influential in economic analysis of environmental policy. Utilitarian theory is the ethical underpinning of free-market theory and welfare economics and therefore most economic arguments made about global warming policies. For this reason, understanding the ethical strengths and weaknesses of utilitarianism is particularly important to provide a basis for judging many global warming policy arguments.

Jeremy Bentham and John Stuart Mill developed classical utilitarian theory in the nineteenth century. Utilitarian ethical positions assert that those actions are right or good that bring about the greatest happiness. Because utilitarianism makes an action good depending on the results or ends it achieves, utilitarianism is usually classified among "consequentialist" ethical theories. According to utilitarian theory, no act is good or bad in itself; rather, its wrongness depends on the consequences of the action, that is, on the act's ability to increase or lessen happiness. There are two major forms of utilitarian ethics: act utilitarianism and rule utilitarianism.

Advocates of act utilitarianism assert that an act is good if it brings about the greatest good over bad results. That is, actions are good if they produce the greatest good for the greatest number. Accordingly, each individual must assess the good and bad consequences of his or her actions and choose that action that maximizes good. Advocates of act utilitarianism often disdain rules for human action, such as absolute rules on killing and lying, because they believe that each situation is different and that it is the consequences of any action that make an action ethical, not conformance with a rule. To determine whether an act is right or wrong, each actor must determine the consequences of each particular act. The right act is that which brings the greatest utility compared to any other alternative, where utility is often defined as happiness, pleasure, or preference satisfaction.

Because economists often argue that environmental policy should be justified on the basis of cost versus benefit, environmental policy legitimations often implicitly rely on act utilitarian ethical theories, although many actual justifications are often only crudely consistent with sophisticated utilitarian theories. A common criticism of act utilitarianism is that it is difficult for any person to determine what is good for another person and particularly difficult to determine with certainty the consequences of certain actions. This criticism is particularly important for environmental policy, where decisions must often be made in the face of pervasive scientific uncertainty about the consequences of action and where the number of potential consequences are immense. Another criticism of act utilitarianism is that it is a waste of time or impractical to reassess each action's consequences from the beginning before taking any action.

In response to these criticisms, rule utilitarianism was developed. Rule utilitarianism holds that actors should always follow those rules that bring about the greatest good for all concerned. An act's rightness or wrongness, according to rule utilitarianism theory, therefore depends on whether the actor conforms his or her actions to a rule that, if followed by all members of society, would bring about the greatest happiness of the group. Rule utilitarianism overcomes an important problem with act utilitarianism in that an actor does not have to calculate the consequences of every action anew before deciding what to do. In environmental policy, rule utilitarianism is often the ethical basis for regulations that establish general rules for action as compared with a process that would make the environmental consequences of each proposed action determine whether any act is permissible. For instance, some have proposed rules that would require that all industrial plants achieve the best available technology to reduce greenhouse gases even though there are significant differences in costs for different industries to meet the best available technology. Such a rule might be justified on rule utilitarian grounds while being problematic for the act utilitarian.

Both act and rule utilitarianism theories, when applied to environmental controversies like global warming, are subject to the following criticisms:

1. The environmental crisis that first received international attention in the late 1960s has forced ethicists to reassess long-accepted ethical theory. Along with other traditional Western ethical positions, utilitarian justifications for environmental policy are challenged for making human interests the measure of value. Because utilitarianism is usually focused on maximizing human happiness, it often ignores and undermines the value of nonhuman entities, such as plants and animals. Although some philosophers argue that utilitarian calculations could be adjusted to consider the happiness or suffering of any sentient beings, most utilitarian justifications for environmental policy fail to do so. As a result, most utilitarian arguments employed in support of environmental policy are crude utilitarian calculations that many supporters of utilitarianism would reject as incomplete.[4]

2. Utilitarian calculations raise ethical issues that cannot be easily answered from within a utilitarian system.[5] A utilitarian must decide, for instance, which alternatives will be considered in the utilitarian calculus, which consequences of a given action will be considered, whose assessments of harms and benefits will be allowed, and what time scale will be used in assessing the consequences. The utilitarian analysis therefore often rests on imprecise judgments of, and prior to, the utility calculus itself. In other words, utilitarian arguments often are based on hidden nonutilitarian assumptions.

3. Utilitarian methodology cannot easily accommodate the rights that individuals may have to be protected from greenhouse gas damage. Most contemporary philosophers therefore hold that utilitarian approaches must be supplemented by other ethical approaches. These include the deontological approach discussed in the next section and ethical systems that stress such concepts as rights, justice, and due process as fundamental.

4. Utilitarian justifications of environmental policy often assume that questions of value can be reduced to a quantifiable amount. That amount is often money measured in market transactions. Quantification of environmental health and benefits, however, is often difficult and sometimes impossible. What, for instance, is the value of a human life or of an endangered eagle? These difficult issues are often unsatisfactorily dealt with in utilitarian calculations by determining value by measuring individuals' willingness to pay in market transactions.

5. Utilitarian theory cannot determine how benefits or costs of subgroups should be distributed among potential winners and losers. That is, utilitarian theory is indifferent in respect to distribution of utility as long as total utility is maximized. Along this line, environmental program decisions that are based on cost-benefit analysis often fail to identify which subgroups in the

population will suffer the burden of any decision even though those who suffer from environmental problems are a different group than those who cause the problem. As a result, most commentators agree that utilitarianism should be supplemented by concepts of distributive justice.

6. Utilitarianism has difficulty in dealing with valuing the impact of environmental problems on future generations. This difficulty is especially problematic when considering potential environmental impacts that may persist as problems for long periods of time, such as global warming. How should future generations' interests be considered in the calculations, and what present value of these interests should be identified in the utilitarian calculus? To deal with future benefits that are created by current programs, economists recommend that benefits that appear in the future be discounted with a rate of interest that would allow comparison of present costs with future benefits (an issue that is considered at length in later chapters). Yet because benefits of global warming policies may appear a hundred years from the present, any discount rate will make far-off benefits appear as very small compared to present costs. Because the benefits that will be experienced by future generations usually have been discounted, the interests of future generations are given less importance than those of present generations.

Although utilitarian calculations could be adjusted to take into consideration some of these criticisms, utilitarian justifications supporting environmental policy positions rarely deal with these criticisms or, in dealing with them, raise additional ethical questions that cannot be decided on utilitarian grounds. For instance, as we will see in detail in chapter 9, cost-benefit analyses sometimes deal with future generations interests but discount future value in a way that raises questions about the rights of future generations.

It will be shown in later chapters that the use of cost-benefit analysis by the United States to oppose action on reducing greenhouse gas emissions relies on a narrow type of utilitarianism, often referred to as "preference utilitarianism."[6] Those who advocate on behalf of preference utilitarianism do not bother attempting to choose policy options that maximize happiness or pleasure but argue that we should choose policy options that maximize human preferences, often measured by individuals' "willingness to pay" in market transactions. Yet as philosopher Mark Sagoff points out,

Many preferences—for example . . . the urge for a cigarette—are despised by the very people who have them. Why should we regard the satisfaction of preferences that are addictive, boorish, criminal, deceived, external to the individual, foolish, grotesque, harmful, ignorant, jealous . . . or zany to be a good thing in itself.[7]

As we will see when we more closely look at preference utilitarianism in chapter 9, the use of preference utilitarianism to justify nonaction on reducing the U.S. emissions of greenhouse gases raises a host of ethical concerns.

RIGHTS AND DUTIES THEORIES

The second most commonly encountered ethical justifications for environmental or sustainable development policy are justifications that ground action or inaction on the notion that certain actions are intrinsically right or wrong.[8] Because such justifications assume that rightness or wrongness turns on some higher standard than the consequences of the action, these justifications often are classified among ethical theories known as nonconsequentialist theories. Nonconsequentialist theories usually speak of rights of individuals to take certain actions or of duties to refrain from action. Theories that ground ethical behavior on duties usually are classified as "deontological" theories because the word "deontological" is derived from the Greek word for "duty." Deontological ethical theories often are encountered in environmental policy discourse in reaction to the limitations of utilitarian theory. For instance, because of the difficulty in knowing with certainty the consequences of certain human actions on the environment and therefore determining the rightness of consequences, persons who support environmental policies often talk of duties to other humans or future generations to refrain from action in the face of uncertainty.

The best-known Western deontological theory is that of the eighteenth-century German philosopher Immanuel Kant. Kant believed that humans could derive absolute rules of morality on the basis of reasoning alone. Kant held that to determine whether an action was right or wrong, one should look to the rule authorizing the action and ask whether logically it could be universalized. If it could not, it would be unreasonable for individuals to give permission to themselves to do things that they could not advocate should be a generally applicable rule for others in society. Thus, Kant held that humans are capable of being ethical beings because they are rational beings who can freely choose to follow rules that they should be bound by. If one chooses to follow a rule that everyone should follow, one is acting morally. The fundamental ethical duty, called by Kant the "categorical imperative," is to act only in those ways that could be universalized to all rational beings.

An important corollary of the categorical imperative is the notion that because other humans are rational beings, they should always be treated as ends and never as means. Many constitutional protections, especially those that deal with concepts of due process, are often grounded in this Kantian notion that humans are to be respected as autonomous individuals and not to be treated as a means for other humans' interests. Such ideas often become manifest in environmental policy when persons assert that individuals or future generations should not have to suffer the pollution caused by another without consent. Many global warming policy issues, including some discussed in later chapters, undoubtedly will have to deal with questions about the scope of individual procedural rights to consent to global warming decisions of foreign nations that may affect them. For this reason, Kantian notions that people should not be treated as ends are relevant to a number of global warming issues.

The obvious strength of the Kantian approach to global warming policy is that it is an accepted ethical basis for asserting that some actions are wrong without fully knowing the magnitude and timing of global warming. Most Kantians would assert, for instance, that government has a duty to modify behavior that creates a large risk to human health and environment even if it turns out that the most serious damage that many are worried about does not come to be. Similarly, Kantians will argue that humans have a right to a healthy environment undiminished by the actions of another without consent.

Some of the limitations of the Kantian approach to global warming problems are as follows:

1. Many assert that Kantian ethics is difficult if not impossible to apply to most environmental controversies because Kantian ethics is always difficult to apply where a decision involves conflicts of duty between two competing goods. That is, because environmental controversies often involve conflicts between goals that are not objectionable in themselves, such as the use of property for food and shelter versus greenhouse gas sequestration, the categorical imperative is not always useful in giving advice about issues where there are real conflicts between competing "goods."

2. According to Kantian ethics, only humans or other rational beings are intrinsically valuable. This is particularly problematic for environmental controversies because the Kantian ethical system does not contain any basis for giving value to any being that is not rational and therefore provides no basis for asserting intrinsic value for plants and animals. Although some Kantians have attempted to extend rights to nonhumans, most philosophers see rational human beings as the only compelling locus of Kantian morality.

THEORIES OF JUSTICE, FAIRNESS, AND EQUITY

In addition to grounding environmental policy on utility, rights, or duty, proponents of various policy positions often support their positions on grounds of justice, fairness, or equity. Theories of justice are particularly important to environmental policy because the other two common theories used as justification for policy, both utilitarian and deontological theories, give no obvious guidance on how burdens and benefits of environmental policy should be distributed throughout society. In addition, because much environmental policy is grounded on utilitarian justifications by economists, an approach that often ignores questions of distributive fairness, a common criticism of many environmental and sustainable decisions is the failure to satisfy concepts of distributive justice.

There are actually two main types of justice claims that are frequently encountered in environmental policy debates. The first are theories of distributive justice that prescribe ways of distributing the benefits and burdens of society that will flow from an environmental decision. A second type of justice concern that frequently arises in environmental controversies are issues of procedural justice. Procedural justice issues usually arise over whether those affected by decisions should have any say in the decision or whether persons who have been affected by a decision under law have a right to equal treatment under the law.[9]

Theories of distributive justice are not only relevant but also central to many global warming controversies, including how global carbon targets should be allocated among nations, how costs of preventing global warming should be distributed among people of the planet, and who should bear the costs for unavoidable damage from global warming. An understanding of theories of distributive justice is particularly important in environmental controversies because environmental decision making often fails to consider distributional effects of proposed actions. For instance, as we will see in chapter 9, a common argument against global warming programs is some form of cost-benefit analysis. The cost-benefit analyses that have been injected into the global warming debate in the United States have mostly failed to identify which subgroups in society will obtain the benefits or who will suffer the burdens of any decision influenced by the cost-benefit analysis. That is, cost-benefit decisions usually consider only aggregate costs and benefits, not the fairness of how benefits and burdens should be distributed.

Principles of distributive justice assert that benefits and burdens should be distributed according to concepts of equality or merit or some combination of these two.[10] Principles of distributive justice attempt to resolve tensions between treating people equally and making distributions on the basis of merit or deservedness. The problem of global warming raises a number of distributive justice issues, and some of the most important of these questions are examined in chapters 11 and 13 and will continue to grow in importance. This is so because global warming is a problem that has been caused largely by the rich nations but will mostly harm the poor nations, yet the rich nations have not seriously considered their duties to the poorer nations. Moreover, in solving the global warming problem, the world community can no longer assume unlimited ability to consume fossil fuel to expand the economic pie. Because the international community will not be able to ignore the poverty of the developing world in the face of limits on the use of fossil fuels entailed by global warming, issues of fairness of distribution of harms and benefits, that is, matters of distributive justice, will likely become key to achieving international consensus on a global solution.

One theory of justice that has been very influential to philosophers and has great potential relevance to global warming is that worked out by John Rawls in his 1971 work *A Theory of Justice*.[11] According to Rawls, the principles of justice that should be followed are those that would be worked out by rational self-interested people working under a "veil of ignorance" about the class to which they belong. If one follows Rawls on many global warming issues, they will likely side with many of the positions taken by the poorest nations discussed throughout this book. This is so because Rawls generally concludes that public policy should choose options that create the maximum benefits to the least advantaged. In any case, Rawls's theory of justice is particularly relevant to the many rich-versus-poor-country issues that need to be faced in the years ahead to develop solutions to global warming.

BIOCENTRIC, ECOCENTRIC, DEEP ECOLOGY, AND OTHER CHALLENGES TO ANTHROPOCENTRIC ETHICAL PERSPECTIVES ON ENVIRONMENTAL CONTROVERSIES

As a serious academic discipline, environmental ethics began in the early 1970s in reaction to the ever more frequent environmental problems that were getting worldwide attention in the 1960s. Although writers such as Henry David Thoreau, John Muir, Aldo Leopold, and Albert Schweitzer were writing about ethical problems caused by industrial society's disregard of nature in the nineteenth and early twentieth centuries, not until the international media began to give attention to the growing environmental crisis in the past forty years did environmental ethics emerge as a matter for serious study. In the 1960s, the world witnessed environmental disasters, including Japan's Miamata mercury pollution, California's Santa Barbara oil spill, Ohio's Cuyahoga River catching fire because of pollution, Germany's air pollution caused by forest damage, and the world's contamination of food and groundwater by pesticides documented in Rachel Carson's *Silent Spring*. As a result, various challenges to the ethical systems that had dominated Western thought started to arise in debates about the causes of the increasing environmental threats.

The emerging environmental crisis created a powerful challenge to Western ethical systems because ethicists were forced for the first time to deeply consider and articulate the value of nonhuman species of plants and animals. Because utilitarian and deontological ethics as well as more prominent Western theories of justice did not make environmental entities the focus of ethical concern, the emerging environmental crisis became a strong challenge to

Western ethical systems. In fact, some concerned with environmental problems charged that Western ethical systems were at least partly responsible for the environmental crisis. Western ethical theories were often blamed for ecological problems because they failed to value anything other than human happiness or interests with the consequential devaluing of animals, plants, and ecosystems.

Initially, much of the environmental ethics literature in the late 1970s and early 1980s dealt with reforming mainstream consequentialist and deontological ethical systems so that nonhuman species would be considered along with humans.[12] The mainstream approaches were categorized as "anthropocentric" for they assumed that only human interests should be the focus of ethical concern. From the beginning of the emergence of environmental ethics as an academic discipline, environmental ethicists began talking about "biocentric" ethics, that is, ethical systems that put all human life, including nonhumans, at the center of value.[13] Since the 1970s, there have been several approaches to valuing nature that have become common themes in the environmental ethics literature and that may be loosely classified as biocentric in orientation. These new nonanthropocentric ethical theories include (1) biocentric ethics, which attempt to extend ethical concern to all sentient beings; (2) ecocentric theories, which make entire ecosystems or environmental communities the center of value; and (3) deep ecology, which holds that humans, nonhumans, and biotic communities are so intrinsically related to one another that it is a mistake to consider them separately.[14] These ethical approaches are often classified as "nonanthropocentric" ethical theories because human interests alone are not at the center of ethical concern. Other strong challenges to Western ethical approaches have come from Buddhism and ecofeminism.[15]

Much, if not most, of the literature in environmental ethics continues to be concerned with how humans should value nature. Should humans regard nature as inherently valuable or only of instrumental value? Should we regard nature as spiritually empowered or as a wild force to be subdued? These questions are bound to continue to be areas of great concern in environmental policy controversies in the years ahead. These questions are also particularly important in determining how much global warming should be tolerated given that different amounts of warming will affect different species of plants and animals. However, because the solution to the problem of global warming requires a sharing of burdens and benefits among rich and poor people and nations, issues of distributive justice are likely to be the source of greatest conflict in future debates about global warming policy. In addition, as we will see in the following chapters, the world does not need to reach a new consensus on questions of the value of nature to conclude that recent U.S. policy on global warming is ethically reprehensible. Although some issues that must be faced in global warming will directly raise questions that a biocentric, eco-centric, deep-ecology, and ecofeminist ecological ethical perspective are concerned with, this book will demonstrate that many of the most important arguments that have been made against U.S. programs to reduce its greenhouse gas emissions are ethically obnoxious no matter what the ethical perspective. Therefore, although this book most often focuses more on the problems with the U.S. positions on global warming from the standpoint of more traditional anthropocentric ethical theories, one should not conclude that this book intends to ignore the extraordinarily important views of those who hold biocentric, ecocentric, deep-ecology, and ecofeminist ethical perspectives. To the contrary, a few issues entailed by the U.S. positions on climate change, such as the question of the level of protection from global warming that the world should agree on in setting an atmospheric target for greenhouse gases (discussed in chapter 12), directly raise questions of most concern to these nonanthropocentric ethical theories. However, as this book describes in later chapters, many of the most ethically troublesome positions taken by the United States on global warming fail to satisfy even well-accepted principles of distributive justice and other, more mainstream ethical approaches. Because the U.S. positions on global warming can be shown to be troublesome even from the perspective of the less environmentally protective anthropocentric theories, they will be even more problematic from the standpoint of the more environmentally concerned nonanthropocentric ethical theories.

RELIGIOUS GROUNDING OF ENVIRONMENTAL ETHICS

Almost at the same time as the philosophical community awoke to environmental issues in the 1970s, various religious leaders around the world showed a heightened interest in environmental problems. In fact, an article by Lynn White, published in *Science* magazine in 1969, criticized Christianity's treatment of environmental problems and is widely viewed to be a seminal document that led to a reevaluation of the relationship between ethics and the environment.[16]

A growing religious interest in environmental problems has taken two main forms. First, some religious leaders engaged in environmental issues, including Thomas Berry,[17] have been interested in exploring and advocating new connections between religion, science, and environmental issues. Second, other religious leaders have been interested in developing a greater understanding of the religious basis for an environmental ethic that can already be found in major religious traditions. Along this line, the Forum for Religion and Ecology at the Harvard Center for the Study of the World's Religions has been particularly interested in important roles that existing religious traditions play in constructing moral frameworks regarding human interactions with the environment. For this reason, the Forum for Religion and Ecology has conducted research on the environmental ethical concerns of Hinduism, Jainism, Buddhism, Confucianism, Taoism, Shinto, indigenous religions, Judaism, Christianity, and Islam.[18] Mary Evelyn Tucker and John Grim, working with the Harvard Center for the Study of the World's Religions, have brought together religious leaders and scholars from around the world who have been interested in ecological concerns and have helped identify the basis for an environmental ethic that exists in all the world's major religions.[19] Although some religions, including Jainism and Buddhism, appear to more clearly put environmental issues at the center of religious concern, all the world's major religious traditions support an environmental ethic, according to the Forum for Religion and Ecology.

For the most part, recent interest in religious circles about environmental problems has been concerned with whether there is a religious basis for the claim that humans have a duty to protect the environment. For this reason, recent religious concern about the environment is similar in its focus to that of the biocentric and ecocentric environmental ethicists who have argued in support of an ethical duty to protect nature. That is, both the nonanthropocentric environmental ethicists and the ecologically concerned theologians have been interested in arguing for an ethic that values nature for itself, not simply because of nature's value as a resource to humans. Yet, as this book will show, because the U.S. policy on global warming will very likely lead to the death and suffering of humans, one does not need to find a strong ethical duty to animals, plants, or ecosystems derived from either ethics or religion to find much of the U.S. response to global warming reprehensible. For this reason, because most of the world's religions would follow the golden rule to treat your neighbor as yourself, the U.S. response to global warming will be shown to be in conflict with what is often at the very center of concern for the world's religions, namely, the duty to treat your neighbor with dignity and respect.

This book will demonstrate that no matter whether the ethical basis for one's environmental concern is philosophical or religious, the U.S. response to global warming is ethically intolerable.

NOTES

1. For a discussion of how scientific, economic, and legal languages often distort the ethical dimensions of environmental policy, see Donald Brown, "Ethics, Science, and Environmental Regulation," *Environmental Ethics* 9 (1987): 331–49.

2. The relationship between facts and ethical positions is of considerable controversy within the philosophical community. See, for example, J. Baird Callicott, "Hume's Is-Ought Dichotomy and the Relation of Ecology to Leopold's Land Ethic," *Environmental Ethics* 4, (1982): 46–74. Although certain linguistic philosophers have held that moral reasoning made by individuals does not rely on deductive models in which ethical conclusions follow from ethical principles, I believe that it is particularly important in developing public policy that those who make ethical assertions be required to expose ethical premises that support ethical conclusions. See also Don E. Marrietta Jr., "Knowledge and Obligation in Environmental Ethics: A Phenomenological Approach," *Environmental Ethics* 4 (1982): 15–62.

3. For a discussion of the developments in environmental ethics that lead from anthropocentrism to ethical approaches that lead to more concern about environmental issues, see "Environmental Ethics: A Brief History of Environmental Ethics for the Novice" (available at <www.cep.unt.edu/novice.html>, March 14, 2001).

4. For a discussion of the ability to extend utilitarianism to nonhuman entities, see Virginia Sharpe, "Ethical Theory and the Demands of Sustainability" (paper presented at the American Chemical Society Meeting on Ethics and Society, Washington, D.C., October 1995).

5. Alasdair MacIntyre, "Utilitarianism and Cost/Benefit Analysis: An Essay on the Relevance of Moral Philosophy to Bureaucratic Theory," in K. M. Sayre, ed., *Values in the Electric Power Industry* (South Bend, Ind.: University of Notre Dame Press, 1983) 217–93.

6. For a good discussion of the limits of preference utilitarianism, see Peter Wentz, *Environmental Ethics Today* (New York: Oxford University Press, 2001), 100–2.

7. Mark Sagoff, *The Economy of the Earth* (New York: Cambridge University Press, 1988), 102.

8. For a discussion of Kantian theories as they relate to other ethical theories, see David VanDeVeer and Charles Pierce, "An Introduction to Ethical Theory," in *The Environmental Ethics and Policy Book* (Belmont, Calif.: Wadsworth, 1997), 1–42.

9. T. Banuri, K. Goran-Malher, M. Grubb, H. K. Jacobson, and F. Yamin, "Equity and Social Considerations," in J. Bruce, H. Lee, and E. Haites, eds., *Economic and Social Dimensions of Climate Change: Contribution of Working Group III to the Second Assessment Report of the Intergovernmental Panel on Climate Change* (Cambridge: Cambridge University Press, 1995), 85, 79–124.

10. Stanley Benn, "Justice," in Paul Edwards, ed., *The Encyclopedia Of Philosophy* (New York: Macmillan, 1967), 298–301.

11. John Rawls, *A Theory of Justice* (Cambridge, Mass.: The Belknap Press of Harvard University Press, 1971).

12. For a history of environmental ethics, see "Environmental Ethics."

13. For a presentation of a biocentric approach to environmental ethics, see Paul Taylor, "The Ethics of Respect for Nature," *Environmental Ethics* 3 (1981): 261–67.

14. There are several versions of an ecocentric approach to environmental ethics. See J. Baird Callicott, "The Conceptual Foundation of a Land Ethic," in *Companion to a Sand County Almanac* (Madison: University of Wisconsin Press, 1987), 186–217,

and Laura Westra, *An Environmental Proposal for Ethics,* (Lanham, Md.: Rowman & Littlefield, 1974). For deep-ecology approaches to environmental ethics, see Arne Naess, "The Shallow and the Deep: Long-Range Ecological Movement," *Inquiry* 16 (spring 1973).

15. For a good discussion of ecofeminism, see Karren Warren, "The Power and Promise of Ecofeminism," in VanDeVeer and Pierce, eds., *The Environmental Ethics and Policy Book,* 257–70.

16. "Environmental Ethics," 1.

17. Father Thomas Berry has been particularly interested in connecting science's new understanding of evolutionary cosmology and religion's sense of sacred creation. See, for example, Thomas Berry, *The Dream of the Earth* (San Francisco: Sierra Club Books, 1988).

18. Forum for Religion and Ecology (<www.environment.harvard.edu/religion/research/home.html>, May 5, 2001).

19. Tucker and Grim led ten conferences on the world's religions and environmental concerns that were held at Harvard University followed by conferences at the United Nations and the American Museum of Natural History in 1998. They are also responsible for a ten-volume series on religion and ecology published by the Harvard Center for the Study of the World's Religions. For information on this work, see <www.environment.harvard.edu/religion/statements/home.htm#early>, May 5, 2001).

Chapter Four

Global Warming, Ethics, and Foreign Policy

Chapter 2 described how the United States has not only failed to address global warming but has often been an obstructionist blocking approaches to global warming proposed by other nations. Chapter 2 also described how a small group of economic interests in the United States have influenced the U.S. positions on global warming. Yet even if the influence exerted by some members of the fossil fuel industry and other heavy users of fossil fuel could be neutralized, several additional barriers to an ethically based American foreign policy on global warming will remain. This chapter identifies these barriers. This chapter also argues that, despite these difficulties, ethically based solutions to climate change are indispensable to achieving a global consensus.

DIFFICULTIES AHEAD

Solving the problem of global warming problem will not be easy. Among other reasons, global warming creates extraordinarily difficult challenges for foreign policy establishments around the world. This is so for the following reasons:

- The most vulnerable poorer nations are likely to take increasingly tougher positions in climate negotiations.
- The global solution to the climate change problem will need to be crafted at a time when there is growing bitterness between rich and poor nations.
- Hard-to-imagine degrees of international cooperation around difficult issues will be necessary to control global warming.
- Foreign policy establishments are in the business of protecting national interest and avoiding questions of global equity, yet only global warming solutions

that are viewed to be equitable have a chance of getting the global consensus
needed to support a global solution.

- Strong national programs will need to be created to control carbon at a time
  when forces of economic globalization are weakening the role of sovereign
  nations

Each of these issues is addressed in the following sections.

Rising International Criticism of the United States from Poorer Nations

Global warming is a particularly difficult problem for those nations that will
need to most change their behavior to reach an equitable international settle-
ment. Because the United States has 5 percent of the world's population but
emits over 22 percent of the greenhouse gases, global warming promises to
be a particularly tough international relations challenge for the United States.
In fact, global warming not only is likely the most serious environmental
problem facing the world but also may be the worst foreign policy problem
for the United States in the twenty-first century.[1]

Global warming is a historically unprecedented foreign policy problem for the
United States because there is growing international pressure on the United
States to reduce fossil fuel use at rates that are likely to outstrip its willingness
and, perhaps, ability to respond. The growing evidence of climate-induced damage to some of the poorest nations from disease-carrying mosquitoes, storms,
drought and floods, and destruction of habitat and species will likely continue to
increase even if the United States starts to take global warming seriously. More
and more, U.S. action on global warming is seen as irresponsible, and as a result, the trust that is needed to support a global solution is diminishing.

For most of the past decade, the United States has been under great pressure from many nations on climate change. The developing small island states
and other nations that are greatly threatened by rising sea levels are loudly
raising their voices in numerous international fora to complain about the failure of the United States to make meaningful reductions in greenhouse gas
emissions.

An incident that has become a typical example of international reaction to
the U.S. position on climate change took place at the five-year UN review of
the Rio Earth Summit in June 1997. At this meeting, the U.S. ambassador to
the United Nations, Bill Richardson, made opening statements about the U.S.
positions on issues that were under negotiation during this review of progress
made since Rio. This speech was made just five months before the then
much-anticipated Kyoto meeting under the UN Framework Convention on

Climate Change (UNFCCC) to negotiate enforceable emission targets. The normal background noise usually fades in UN conference rooms whenever the United States speaks because delegates are very mindful of the fact that nothing will likely happen unless the world's only true superpower agrees. As a result, when the United States speaks in UN meetings, delegates turn to listen. Yet, as Ambassador Richardson began his speech, the delegates were even more quiet than usual because they were intensely focused on what the speech would reveal about the U.S. position on the upcoming Kyoto negotiations on global warming.[2] About halfway into the speech, Richardson announced that the United States wanted meaningful and enforceable targets and timetables for greenhouse gases to be an outcome of the Kyoto negotiations. As soon as Richardson announced U.S. support for targets and timetables but before the speech was concluded, the British environment minister, John Gummer, a diplomat with a reputation for fiery dramatic oratory, roared so that all could hear, "That will be the day when the United States takes climate change seriously." The feisty British diplomat's display was an extraordinary and unusual breach of diplomatic etiquette in the United Nations and behavior rarely seen in large multilateral international negotiations, which usually are conducted in a culture that expects extreme politeness. Yet, because the United States was being consistently and openly attacked on its global warming policy for many months leading up to this meeting, this incident was merely brushed off by members of the U.S. delegation as another example of growing international derision about U.S. positions on climate change. The open hostility to the U.S. position on global warming had become so common that unusually rude behavior, something that would be greeted with indignation on other issues, had become expected as a typical response to U.S. positions on global warming.

In international negotiations, the U.S. approach to climate change has been under strongest attack from the Association of Small Island Developing States (AOSIS) and some of the poorest nations. As we will see in the next chapter, the poorest nations have the most to lose if global warming is not curbed, while AOSIS is greatly concerned about rising ocean levels. In fact, many AOSIS nations are seriously threatened by rising oceans, and some may lose as much as 80 percent of their territory by the end of the twenty-first century. For this reason, AOSIS and some of the poorest nations are likely to continue to turn up the volume in their complaints about the inequitable share of the U.S. global warming pollution load unless the United States begins to make rapid progress on greenhouse gas reductions. This is so because the more that time passes without the United States making significant reductions in greenhouse gas emissions, the more the United States will be seen to be acting in arrogant disregard to the adverse impacts on the poorest nations.

The United States is also resented for failing to do what it has agreed to do on climate change. As we have seen, under the UNFCCC, the United States and other developed nations agreed to

> protect the climate system for the benefit of present and future generations of humankind, on the basis of *equity* and in accordance with their *common but differentiated responsibilities* and respective capabilities. Accordingly, the developed country Parties should take the lead in combating climate change and the adverse effects thereof.[3] (italics added)

Yet despite this promise it made in ratifying the UNFCCC to take the lead in reducing greenhouse gas emissions on the basis of its equitable share, the United States, under the Clinton administration, announced that it would not submit the Kyoto Protocol to the U.S. Senate for ratification until the developing nations made commitments to curb emissions despite the fact that the United States has dramatically increased its domestic emissions since it ratified the climate treaty in 1992. In 1990, the U.S. share emitted 1,645 million metric tons of greenhouse gases.[4] By 1999, the United States was emitting 1,832.6 million metric tons, or 11 percent greater than 1990.[5]

Figure 4.1 Unbalanced power

Reprinted with the permission of the Centre for Science and the Environment, New Delhi, India, Rustam Vania/CSE.

From the developing world's perspective, the United States often appears as if it is willing to use its political, economic, and military power to avoid its obligations as the world's greatest source of greenhouse emissions. As a result, a large obstacle that the United States will need to face in future climate change negotiations is the lack of trust in U.S. positions.

Need for Trust in a Time of International Suspicion

Another serious barrier to crafting an acceptable global solution to climate change is that an agreement will need to be crafted at a time when there is also growing bitterness and lack of trust between rich and poor nations about a host of sustainable development issues that are related to climate change. Conflicts between rich and poor countries over the role of the richer nations in assisting the poorer nations with problems of poverty have become the most frequent roadblocks to progress in international negotiations dealing with environment and sustainable development. In the past several decades, this conflict between rich and poor nations has continued to deepen as the wealth gap between the richest and poorest nations has widened. Since 1950, as the developed nations tripled their per capita wealth, those at the periphery experienced virtually no change.[6] Because many developing nations feel that they are not sharing in the recent global economic boom, they are likely to continue to see climate change negotiations as an important battle in a larger struggle to redress perceived international economic inequities. They will continue to regard with greatest suspicion global warming proposals that will retard in any way their ability to get out of grinding poverty. Unless the developed nations demonstrate that they are willing to do whatever is necessary to reduce their greenhouse emissions to an equitable share, the developing nations will continue to look askance on developed-world proposals that include developing-world commitments.

Progress since the Earth Summit on a variety of broader sustainable development issues has been blocked primarily because of conflict between rich and poor nations.[7] These issues include the responsibility of the rich nations to help the poorer nations finance sustainable development, the willingness of the rich nations to transfer environmentally protective technology to the developing world, and the failure of the rich nations to reduce unsustainable levels of consumption.[8] Commitments on these issues were made by the developed nations at the 1992 Rio Earth Summit in the UN Program on Environment and Development, Agenda 21.[9] Since Rio, nations have met yearly to review progress in implementing Agenda 21 at meetings of the UN Commission on Sustainable Development (UNCSD). For the most part, these meetings have been marked by increasing conflicts between rich and poor nations amid charges that the developed world, and the United States in particular, has failed to live up to what it agreed to do in Rio.[10]

From the perspective of the poorer nations, the source of this conflict is the belief that the developed world has invented a set of rules and institutions that control the global marketplace. These rules, according to the poorer nations, work to the benefit of the rich nations while enslaving the poor ones. Because developing-world commitments to reduce fossil fuel use could further limit the ability of the developing nations to fight grinding poverty, the poorer nations are likely to bitterly resist making global warming commitments.

From the developed world's perspective, the poorest nations remain poor because of their failure to do what is necessary to take advantage of the potential opportunities that exist in the global economy. The developed nations argue that the best hope for the poorest nations is to take advantage of opportunities for private-sector-led economic growth. To achieve this growth, poorer nations should reform government and economic institutions to give investors confidence in the security of their investments. In making this argument, the United States has often lost sight of the fact that these prescriptions concerning making the economies of poorer nations more attractive to private-sector investment often require cutting back on government programs, including those needed to implement programs to reduce greenhouse gas emissions.

This long-standing conflict between rich and poor nations takes on an added hostility in environmental controversies such as global warming when the greatest amount of the existing pollution problem has been caused by the developed world while the developing world is seen to be asked by the developed world to make a sacrifice for the greater good. As a result, many in the developing world view the global warming problem with tremendous concern and suspicion because of a fear that the developed world will make those who are least responsible shoulder an unfair burden by limiting activities that could help fight grinding poverty.

Thorny Issues to Resolve

To prevent serious harm to human health and the environment from global warming, it will be necessary for the world's nations to reach agreement on a number of thorny issues. Among the most difficult and important issues for which a global agreement is needed is the level at which the international community will attempt to stabilize greenhouse gases in the atmosphere (an issue that is addressed in chapter 12). Should, for instance, the international community seek to stabilize greenhouse gases in the atmosphere from human actions at 450, 560, or 700 parts per million (ppm)? The issue of the level at which to stabilize greenhouse gases will force nations to consider which plants, animals, and ecosystems, not to mention vulnerable people, should be put at risk. The higher the ultimate target stabilization level of greenhouse gases in the atmosphere is, the more human health and some environmental entities will be put at risk.

Because different nations have much more to lose than others, depending on what levels of greenhouse gases are ultimately stabilized in the atmosphere, it is much more in some nations' interest than others to attempt to stabilize greenhouse gases at the lowest possible levels. A nation like the United States, which is a large emitter of pollutants, has less to lose by global warming than those nations that are already threatened by rising sea levels, increased vulnerability to storms, infestations of vector-borne diseases, or drying of agricultural soils. For this reason, it is in some of the poorest nations' interest to stabilize greenhouse gases at the lowest levels possible.

A second difficult issue that must be agreed on to reach the needed global solution arises out of the fact that all nations need to agree on individual national allocations of emissions limitations that in total will achieve stabilization of greenhouse gases in the atmosphere at the agreed-on level (an issue discussed in chapter 11). If, for instance, the world chooses to attempt to stabilize carbon dioxide at 550 ppm in the atmosphere, each nation will need to agree on a target amount of emissions not to be exceeded so that the total from all nations will not cause the atmospheric level to be greater than 550 ppm. It is not in many of the developed nations' national interest to agree on stringent allocations because this will force these rich nations to cut back on certain types of energy while the developing world will be allowed to increase energy use if equity determines national allocation levels. Because large reductions from present levels of emissions could put some of the developed nations' domestic industry at risk, such as the domestic steel industry in the United States (an industry already vulnerable to foreign competition), the United States has continued to resist significant reduction targets and has not shown any interest in reducing emissions to levels dictated by equity. As explained in chapter 2, as a result of its fears about domestic industry impacts, the United States has fiercely resisted proposals that would base national targets on any nation's proportional contributions to the problem.

In addition to the difficult questions about atmospheric stabilization goals and national emission allowances, there are many other issues that need to be faced to reach a global solution and that are equally thorny because of their potential to create winners and losers among and within nations. Included in this list of difficult issues are rules for trading national allowances among individuals and nations, methods for determining baseline levels of emissions, rules relating to how different greenhouse gases will be accounted for in national allowances, credits for carbon sequestration projects, and many more.

Realist Prejudices of Foreign Policy Establishments

This book argues that ethical dimensions of global warming need to be faced to generate a global solution that will receive widespread international support. Yet foreign policy establishments are likely to be barriers to an ethical solution to global warming because traditional approaches to foreign policy are often based on the assumption that national interest, rather than ethics or morality, should be the focus of national foreign policy.[11] This is so because international relations policy has been dominated largely by "realist" theories that encourage nations to protect national interests and ignore moral and ethical considerations. The "realist" is convinced that a focus on ethics in international relations is doomed to ultimately harm the interests of citizens whom the diplomat is representing because the international system of nation-states is one in which only the powerful will prevail. That is, realists argue that the anarchical character of international affairs always works to ensure that power and self-interest will "crowd out international public spirit and moral concern."[12] As one commentator on the role of ethics in international affairs has observed about realist approaches to foreign policy,

> States that follow realpolitik maxims grow and those that irrationally ignore the mandate to egoism decline and lose all influence (except as examples of folly or warnings to not be beguiled by seductive idealism). States may enter into regimes, agreements, and cooperative behavior at times, but only as doing so furthers self-interest.[13]

Because of the dominance of these realist theories, foreign policy institutions around the world, including the U.S. State Department, are often staffed by some personnel who strongly believe in a "balance of power" approach to maintaining international order. As a result, many of these international bureaucrats see maintaining national power as a justifiable preoccupation of their work and view proposals that threaten national interest with great alarm. Because global warming solutions that are capable of achieving widespread international support may require that the United States take action that is motivated more by global than national interest, some elements of the foreign policy establishment in the United States that subscribe to strong realist views on foreign policy are not likely to be friendly to proposals that establish responsibility based on equitable considerations alone.

However, there are some foreign policy theorists who differ with the views of the realists on the proper role of ethics in international affairs. For instance, those foreign policy experts who are often classified as "neoliberals" focus on ways in which "democratic governance, public opinion, mass education, free trade, liberal capitalism, international law and organization, arms control and disarmament, collective security and multilateral diplomacy, and ethically inspired state craft can improve life over the planet."[14]

Those who see a role for ethics and morality in foreign policy have argued that the United States should use its influence to develop a fairer, more just world order.[15] If the world is to become a better place because nations follow laws based on ethical considerations rather than the exclusive pursuit of national power, it would be in the interest of the United States, so this argument goes, to lead the world by taking positions that are justifiable on ethical rather than narrow national interest grounds. However, many realists view such a preoccupation as naive.

Despite the strength of realist approaches to foreign policy in the United States, the United States has in some cases acted out of what appeared to be ethical rather than narrow national self-interest.[16] Examples include cases where the United States sent food to Soviet Russia during a Cold War famine, agreed to destroy its biological weapons, and relinquished control over the Panama Canal.[17] Therefore, it can be demonstrated that U.S. foreign policy has sometimes adopted positions championed by those who were arguing for global rather than narrow self-interest.

Even realists have acknowledged circumstances in which it might be in a nation's self-interest alone to adopt policies that are based on moral principles. For instance, George Kennan, a strong realist who often argued that there was no moral dimension to national interest, also acknowledged that the democratic example that the United States exhibited has a moral power that can influence other nations.[18] That is, if we want others to adopt principles of equity and fairness in international controversies, it is important for the United States to set a moral example. Because the global warming problem is likely unsolvable unless most nations limit carbon emissions to some equitable share of the total, it is arguably a matter of national interest for the United States to limit its greenhouse emissions to an equitable share so that other nations will be willing to do the same. Yet it is more likely than not that many in the United States will vehemently argue that any atmospheric target for stabilizing greenhouse gases that is based on equitable principles alone should be rejected on the grounds of national interest. William Nitze, who was the U.S. deputy secretary of state in charge of several U.S. global warming delegations leading up to the Earth Summit, has admitted that the U.S. position leading up to the Earth Summit was the result of tension between those in the State Department who are of the realist school and those who are more idealistic.[19]

For this reason, those who believe that the United States should agree to greenhouse targets based on equitable considerations must be prepared to show why it is ultimately in the national interest of the United States to agree to a set of rules that equitably share the use of the global atmosphere. Even if the United States looks at the climate change issue from a selfish national interest perspective, a strong argument can be made that it is in the interest of the United States to agree to an equitable allocation of greenhouse gases. As one observer of the equitable issues surrounding global warming has observed, "Once equity becomes a common part of international discourse, it becomes a norm and discussions turn to the subject of how to operate in that norm. Equity takes on a somewhat independent role that is beyond traditional power relationships and calculations."[20]

Because climate change will hurt people and the environment in the United States and cannot be solved by the United States acting alone, the United States will need the cooperation of other countries and will need to appeal to the concept of equity to get cooperation if it does not want to rely on military force or other types of coercion. It is therefore directly in the interest of the United States to encourage international cooperation around equitable principles.

Need for New Programs in a Time of Diminishing Sovereignty

Another great barrier to any global warming solution is that any resolution will likely require all governments that participate in a global agreement to develop strong national programs to live up to their commitments to reduce carbon emissions. In these programs, nations will need to do the following:

- Develop baselines of existing fossil fuel use
- Develop carbon emission strategies
- Monitor rates of fossil fuel usage more intensively
- Allocate allowances among competing uses of fossil fuels
- Enforce elements of carbon reduction strategy

These new government programs will need to be developed at a time when the role of governments is shrinking around the world in response to forces created by the globalized economy. That is, according to many economists, to increase economic growth in a global economy, nations must reduce the size of government spending, decrease the regulatory burden on the private sector, and reduce the number of government employees.

Thomas Friedman, a reporter for the *New York Times* who has been following globalization, has coined the phrase "golden straitjacket" as a metaphor for the path that all nations must take in a globalized economy.[21] According to Friedman, nations must put on the golden straitjacket or else wallow in poverty. Putting on this straitjacket requires a nation to

make the private sector the primary engine of economic growth, maintain a low rate of inflation, and price stability, shrink the size of state bureaucracy, maintain as close to a balanced budget as possible, if not a surplus, eliminate and lower tariffs on imported goods, remove restrictions on foreign investment, get rid of quotas and domestic monopolies, increase exports, privatize state-owned industries and utilities, deregulate capital markets, make its currency convertible, open its industries, stock, and bond markets to direct foreign ownership and investment, deregulate its economy to promote as much domestic competition as possible, eliminate government corruption, subsidies and kickbacks as much as possible, open its banking and telecommunications systems to private ownership and competition, and allow its citizens to choose from an array of competing pension options and foreign-run pension and mutual funds.[22]

According to Friedman, nations have little choice in following these rules, and, "unfortunately, one size fits all."[23]

In this increasingly globalized economy where all nations are competing with one another to attract private capital, nations must do many things that are antithetical to developing complicated or strong global warming control programs. In particular, those developing nations that are struggling with grinding poverty will be in a very weak position to develop strong carbon reduction programs. Many governments may not be able to afford the new programs necessary to implement strong carbon emission reduction strategies without much stronger financial support from the richer nations, such as the United States.[24] Yet there is little political support in the United States for dramatic increases in foreign aid.

It will also be particularly difficult for those poverty-ridden developing nations struggling to compete in a global economy to require domestic industries to install technologies that may increase energy costs and reduce any competitive advantage that they currently have to produce goods at a lower cost. For all these reasons, it will be difficult to create strong national programs needed to control carbon at a time when the forces of economic globalization are weakening the role of sovereign nations.

INDISPENSABLE ROLE OF ETHICS IN GLOBAL WARMING SOLUTIONS AND THE WAY FORWARD

Despite these many reasons for pessimism about the possibility of reaching a global solution to the climate change problem, it is virtually inconceivable that any global agreement can be reached unless it is viewed by participating nations as equitable. The first reason, therefore, for facing the ethical dimensions of global warming is that only an equitably based solution is capable of receiving the indispensable broad-based international support needed to achieve a global consensus. As we have seen, the developing world is not likely to agree to participate in a comprehensive global warming treaty unless it feels that it is being treated fairly. In addition, it has been demonstrated that in order to achieve multilateral agreement on environmental issues, it is necessary for nations to believe that they have been treated fairly and that their core demands have been addressed.[25] For this reason, equity is an indispensable element to a global solution to climate change. As one observer of the global warming negotiations has noted, "Effective measures to address global environmental change require nearly universal participation. That participation is largely a function of international justice because developing countries are unlikely to join international cooperative efforts to protect the global environment if they view those arrangements as being unjust."[26]

As the Center for Science and the Environment, an institution in New Delhi, India, and a close observer of the climate negotiations has said,

> Equity is a prerequisite for global agreement, and environmental cooperation can only be possible through solutions that are both equitable and ecologically effective. Without equity or a sense of fair play it is quite unlikely that there will be a long-lasting partnership to solve the global problems. Global equity is particularly important in global negotiations which deal with the pollution or degradation of global common property, such as the stratospheric ozone layer, the atmosphere, or oceans.[27]

Therefore, the United States must encourage an equitable approach to global warming as a matter of national self-interest because an approach that is not seen as fair to the developing world will not be agreed to. Yet there are extraordinarily strong economic forces in the United States that will continue to vehemently oppose a solution to global warming in which the United States agrees to reduce its emissions to an equitable share of total global emissions.

THE WAY FORWARD:
KEEP PROMISES ALREADY MADE BY THE UNITED STATES

On an optimistic note, later chapters argue that some, but not all, of the most important ethical issues that need to be faced could be settled rather easily. All it will take is for the United States and other developed nations to live up to several provisions already agreed to in the UNFCCC, a treaty ratified by the United States in 1993, and other "soft-law" principles that were agreed to at the Rio Earth Summit in 1992. The fact that these provisions have already been agreed to by the United States and most of the nations of the world is a strong indication that there is almost universal agreement on the norms that should be followed by the international community to resolve many of the critical issues that need to be faced in reaching a global solution on climate change.

International "soft law" is created when nations negotiate a set of principles in an agreement, such as the International Declaration of Human Rights, in which the negotiating nations agree that the principles are reasonable approaches to solve international problems. Yet soft-law agreements are not binding on the agreeing parties to the same extent a treaty would be. However, soft-law agreements often have become the basis for negotiating binding treaties. Because soft-law agreements contain principles about which countries agreed, they are sometimes recognized by courts as reasonable ethical norms of behavior that should be applied to resolve international disputes. Therefore, soft-law agreements often work their way into binding law either through incorporation into treaties or in judicial decisions where judges are looking for international norms of behavior to resolve specific disputes.

The binding UNFCCC provisions and soft-law principles that have already been agreed to by the United States are discussed in the following sections.

Special Duties of Developed Nations

As we saw in this chapter and in chapter 2, the United States agreed to the following in adopting the UNFCCC: "The *developed country Parties should take the lead* in combating climate change and the adverse effects thereof" (italics added).[28] Similarly, the Rio Declaration, a soft-law document agreed to by the United States, provides in Principle 7 that

states shall cooperate in a spirit of global partnership to conserve, protect and restore the health and integrity of the Earth's ecosystem. In view of the different contributions to global environmental degradation, *States have common but differentiated responsibilities. The developed countries acknowledge the responsibility that they bear in the international pursuit to sustainable development in view of the pressures their societies place on the global environment and of the technologies and financial resources they command.*[29] (italics added)

If these principles were taken seriously in regard to global warming, the United States would recognize its ethical obligation to reduce greenhouse gas emissions before requiring the developing world to do so and to reduce its share of global emissions to an equitable share of total emissions. Yet, as we will see in chapters 8 and 11, thus far the United States has refused to seriously consider its equitable obligations to reduce emissions.

Duty to Eliminate Unsustainable
Patterns of Consumption and Production

Principle 8 of the Rio Declaration states, "To achieve sustainable development and a higher quality of life for all people, States should reduce and eliminate unsustainable patterns of production and consumption and promote appropriate demographic policies."[30] If this principle were taken seriously, the United States would recognize its duty to curb unsustainable levels of production and consumption of activities that create greenhouse gases.

Duty to Use Precaution

As we saw in chapter 2, the United States agreed to the following in adopting the UNFCCC:

The Parties should take precautionary measures to anticipate, prevent or minimize the causes of climate change and mitigate its adverse effects. Where there are threats of serious or irreversible damage, *lack of full scientific certainty should not be used as a reason for postponing such measures,* taking into account that policies and measures to deal with climate change should be cost-effective so as to ensure global benefits at the lowest possible cost.[31] (italics added)

Similarly, Principle 15 of the Rio Declaration provides that "in order to protect the environment, the precautionary approach shall be widely applied by States according to their capabilities. Where there are threats of serious or irreversible damage, lack of full scientific certainty shall not be used as a reason for postponing cost-effective measures to prevent environmental degradation."[32] If these principles were taken seriously, the United States would refrain from using scientific uncertainty about global warming as an excuse for failing to take action to reduce its greenhouse gas emissions.

"Polluter-Pays" Principle

Principle 16 of the Rio Declaration provides that "national authorities should endeavor to promote the internalization of environmental costs and the use of economic instruments, taking into account the approach that the polluter should, in principle, bear the cost of pollution, with due regard to the public interest and without distorting international trade and investment."[33] If this principle were seriously applied to global warming, the United States would acknowledge its responsibility to reduce its greenhouse gas emissions to a proportional share of world emissions.

If the U.S. position on global warming is not consistent with these principles, nations are not likely to feel that they are being treated fairly, and U.S. positions will be doomed to failure. Moreover, because the United States has already bound itself to these principles in the UNFCCC or recognized them as fair and reasonable in the case of the principles contained in the Rio Declaration, the United States will be seen, accurately, as breaking its promises to the rest of the world if it continues to ignore these principles.

IMPORTANCE OF ETHICAL ANALYSIS

Later chapters of this book review some of the most frequent arguments commonly heard in the political arena against the United States taking strong action to reduce greenhouse gas emissions. These include arguments against action on grounds of scientific uncertainty, cost-benefit analysis to the United States, the need to have the developing world begin to reduce greenhouse gas emissions before the United States acts, and the right of the United States to insist on its use of the Kyoto Protocol's flexibility mechanisms as a method of achieving target greenhouse gas reductions. It will be shown that when these arguments are examined through an ethical prism, they do not withstand scrutiny. Thus, it will be shown that a key to defusing the common objections to U.S. action on greenhouse gas reductions is to understand the problematic but hidden ethical dimensions of these arguments.

As is discussed in later chapters of this book, there are many additional ethical issues that need to be faced in formulating a global solution to the climate change problem.[34] Among these ethical issues are two broad types of ethical issues. The first regards questions of distributive justice that include questions of how allocations should be distributed among nations, who should pay for any increased costs of installing new technologies, who should be responsible for damage that cannot be avoided, and whether it is just for one nation to continue dangerous behavior that might seriously hurt others. The second regards questions of value, including what plants, animals, ecosystems, or human welfare matters should be protected from global warming damage. As we saw in chapter 3, some have argued that the growing environmental crises has been caused by a narrow anthropocentric system of value that has arisen in the West and that has debased the view that plants and animals have intrinsic value. As a result, many call for a new biocentric or ecocentric ethic as a solution to global environmental problems. A question of value that will need to be considered during upcoming climate negotiations includes that of appropriate target levels for stabilizing greenhouse gases in the atmosphere, as this issue should consider the value that we place on plants and animals that could be destroyed by global warming.

Later chapters of this book argue that many of the first type of ethical question (i.e., questions of distributive justice) in the case of climate change should be relatively easy to settle if the United States and other developed nations follow positions that they have advocated on other matters or have agreed to in the previously identified principles. The second type of issue, however, relating to the value of nature, is likely to be more internationally contentious. Yet this book argues that much progress in climate change negotiations could be made if nations focus on the first type of question, questions of distributive justice, because these issues are the ones that most consistently block progress in international negotiations.

From the point of view of poor nations, developed-world lectures on the value of nature that are delivered to the developing world without facing the questions of distributive justice are troublesome. Along this line, one writer from India has said the following about the developed world's need to face questions of distributive justice:

The two fundamental ecological problems facing the world are: (1) overconsumption by the industrialized world and by the urban elites in the Third World, and (2) growing materialization, both in the short-term sense (i.e., ongoing regional wars) and in the long-term sense (i.e., the arms race and the threat of nuclear annihilation). Neither of these problems have any tangible connection to the anthropocentric-biocentric distinction [i.e., questions of value]. Indeed the agents of these processes would barely comprehend this philosophical dichotomy. The proximate cause of the ecologically wasteful characteristics of industrial society and of militarization are far more mundane: at the aggregate level, the dialectic of economic and political structures, and at the micro-level, the life-style choices of individuals. Those causes cannot be reduced, whatever level of analysis, to a deeper anthropocentric attitude toward nature; on the contrary, by constituting a grave threat to human survival, the ecological degradation they cause does not even serve the best interests of human beings! If my identification of the major dangers to the integrity of the natural world is correct, invoking the bogy of anthropocentrism is at best irrelevant and at worst dangerous.[35]

Because questions of distributive justice between rich and poor nations are at the heart of many international disputes over climate change, not until the developed world, and the United States in particular, makes progress on reducing greenhouse emissions to an equitable level is the world likely to agree on a global solution to global warming. The failure of the United States to seriously accept its responsibility to reduce its share of greenhouse gas emissions to an equitable level is therefore both an ethical and a practical problem. Yet, as we have seen in this chapter and as we will discuss in more detail in later chapters, many of the normative approaches that need to be followed have already been agreed to by the United States. If the United States continues to ignore these principles, as it has in the past, it will miss opportunities to forge a global solution around norms that have high levels of acceptability in the international community while setting itself up to continuing charges of breach of its promises to abide by prior agreements.

NOTES

1. An official of the U.S. State Department Office of Oceans and Environment made these statements when the writer of this book was program manager for UN organizations at the U.S. Environmental Protection Agency from 1996.

2. The author of this book was present during the speech as a member of the U.S. delegation to the five-year review of Rio held by the United Nations in 1997.

3. United Nations Framework Convention on Climate Change (UNFCCC), New York, May 9, 1992, UN Document A/CONF.151/26, Article 3, Paragraph 1 (available at <http//194,95,93/default1.htf>, March 16, 2001).

4. United States Energy Information Administration, *United States Emissions of Greenhouse Gases,* Report No. EIA/DOE-0573, 1999 (available at <www.eir.doe.gov/oiaf/1605/ggrpt/index.html>, March 15, 2001).

5. United States Energy Information Administration, *United States Emissions of Greenhouse Gases.*

6. Charles Kegley and Eugene Wittkoph, *World Politics: Trend and Transformations* (New York: St. Martin's Press, 1997), 123.

7. For a discussion of what happened at the five-year review of the Earth Summit in regard to the North-versus-South animosity, see Donald A. Brown, "Making the United Nations Commission on Sustainable Development Work," *Earth Negotiations Bulletin,* April 1998, 1–4.

8. Brown, "Making the United Nations Commission on Sustainable Development Work."

9. United Nations, *Agenda 21,* UN Document A/CONF. 151/26, June 16, 1992.

10. Brown, "Making the United Nations Commission On Sustainable Development Work."

11. For a good discussion of the role of ethics in international relations, see David H. Lumsdaine, *Moral Vision in International Politics* (Princeton, N.J.: Princeton University Press, 1993). For a discussion of the role that ethics has played in American foreign policy, see George Wiegel, *American Interests, American Purpose: Moral Reasoning and U.S. Foreign Policy* (Washington, D.C.: Praeger, 1989).

12. Lumsdaine, *Moral Vision in International Politics,* 8.

13. Lumsdaine, *Moral Vision in International Politics,* 13.

14. Lumsdaine, *Moral Vision in International Politics,* 13.

15. Lumsdaine, *Moral Vision in International Politics,* 13.

16. See Robert W. McElroy, *Morality and American Foreign Policy* (Princeton, N.J.: Princeton University Press, 1992).

17. McElroy, *Morality and American Foreign Policy.*

18. McElroy, *Morality and American Foreign Policy,* 27.

19. William A. Nitze, "A Failure of United States Leadership," in I. M. Mitzner and J. A. Leonard, eds., *Negotiating Climate Change: The Inside Story of the Rio Convention* (Cambridge: Cambridge University Press and Stockholm Environment Institute, 1994), 190.

20. Paul Harris, "Environmental Security and International Equity: Burdens of American and Other Great Powers," *Pacifica Review* 11, no. 1 (1999): 25–42.

21. Thomas L. Friedman, *The Lexus and the Olive Tree: Understanding Globalization* (New York: Farrar, Strauss & Giroux, 1999), 87.

22. Friedman, *The Lexus and the Olive Tree,* 88.

23. Friedman, *The Lexus and the Olive Tree,* 88

24. The United States has supported the Global Environment Facility in the World Bank, which has made several billion dollars available for global warming programs in the developing world. However, most observers agree that this money is only a drop in the bucket compared to the magnitude of support needed to pay for programs needed to seriously move the developing world to noncarbon energy.

25. For a good summary of the role that equity has played in International Environmental Treaties, see Paul Harris, "Considerations of Equity and International Institutions," *Environmental Politics* 5, no. 2 (1996): 274–301.

26. Paul Harris, "Defining International Distributive Justice: Environmental Considerations," *International Relations* 15, no. 2 (August 2000): 1–10.

27. Anil Agarwal, Sunita Narrain, and Anju Sharma, *Green Politics, Global Environmental Negotiations* (New Delhi: Center for Science and Environment, 1999), 2.

28. UNFCCC, Article 4 (a).

29. United Nations, *Rio Declaration on Environment and Development,* UN Document A/CONF.151/5, June 16, 1992, Principle 7.

30. United Nations, *Rio Declaration,* Principle 8.

31. United Nations, *Rio Declaration,* Principle 8.

32. United Nations, *Rio Declaration,* Principle 15.

33. United Nations, *Rio Declaration,* Principle 8.

34. See chapters 6 to 10.

35. Ramachandra Guha, "Radical American Environmentalism and Wilderness Preservation: A Third World Critique," in J. Baird Callicott and M. P. Nelson, eds., *The Great New Wilderness Debate*(Athens: University of Georgia Press, 1996), 231.

Chapter Five

What Is at Stake?
Global Warming's Threat to
Human Health and the Environment

The ethical significance of any nation's response to a problem like global warming will often depend on the consequences of action or nonaction. For this reason, this chapter examines the likely impacts of human-induced climate change on human health and the environment. This chapter first explores what is at stake in changing any nation's climate and then describes more specific global warming impacts that have been predicted by the Intergovernmental Program on Climate Change (IPCC). Next, the chapter describes likely climate change impacts on the poorest nations and people, followed by a discussion of why actual impacts could be much worse than those most frequently cited in greenhouse debates. Finally, this chapter explains why hard-to-imagine levels of international cooperation will be necessary to stabilize greenhouse gases in the atmosphere at levels that will prevent damage from global warming.

IMPORTANCE OF CLIMATE TO NATIONS

Only very recently has human-induced climate change aroused such widespread public concern in the United States to make it a common front-page story. Given what is at stake in changing any nation's climate, this lack of interest is somewhat surprising. This failure to make global warming a burning front-page issue until recently is astonishing given the enormous importance of climate to the well-being of any nation. In the book *The Wealth and Poverty of Nations—Why Some Are So Rich and So Poor,* Harvard professor David Landes describes the importance of a nation's climate to its culture and standard of living.[1] Landes notes that, for the most part, the rich countries lie in temperate climates and the poor ones in the tropics and semitropics. Although Landes sees climate as only one factor in determining whether a nation will prosper, he describes why temperature and the quantity and quality of rainfall are extraordinarily important determinates of national well-being. The quality of any nation's climate determines the following:

- Much of its physical character
- The nature of its natural resources that can be harvested from its ecosystems
- Its potential for growing food
- The type of plants and animals that are indigenous
- The need to use energy to protect from extremes of heat and cold
- The presence of human health threats from natural pathogens
- Citizen vulnerability to damage from intense storms
- The number of hours that are available to citizens to work or recreate in the outdoors in comfort
- The amount of freshwater that is available for a variety of human uses
- The rate of flow in rivers and streams
- The types and cost of materials that need to be used in human structures
- The nature of any weather limitations on travel
- The damage caused by floods
- The difficulties in travel
- The ability to attract tourists

Without doubt, an action by any nation that harms any other nation's climate gravely affects the latter country's national interest. Therefore, if human activities in one nation cause deterioration to another's climate, the affected nation has a serious grievance against those who are responsible. This is so because a nation's climate is an extraordinarily important ingredient in determining a nation's quality of life and its economic possibilities. Because no theory of international relations justifies the right of any nation to act in such a way that it greatly harms another nation's quality of life, those nations that cause global warming violate the most basic international norms. Wars have been fought over much less and have been viewed to be just.

As we will see in this chapter, a worldwide "business-as-usual" approach to climate change is likely to cause unacceptable climate changes, particularly for some nations. These changes will harm some nations more than others, and some will be gravely affected. As we will see, those nations that are most vulnerable include low-lying nations with vulnerable populations close to the ocean, those whose ability to grow food will be diminished by hotter and dryer climates, and those who experience large increases in vector-borne diseases. For this reason, climate change is not only a threat to a nation's natural resources but also a direct threat to human health. Thus, global warming is a direct assault on many things that nations most cherish.

PREDICTED CLIMATE IMPACTS FROM GLOBAL WARMING

How much will a nation's climate change because of human activities? What are the specific risks of human-induced climate change?

Recognizing the need to reduce scientific uncertainties associated with the problem of potential global climate change, the World Meteorological Organization (WMO) and the United Nations Environment Program (UNEP) established the IPCC in 1988.[2] As explained in chapter 2, the IPCC was created partially in response to U.S. concern that the science of global warming was too soft to justify enforceable international action to reduce greenhouse gas emissions that some European nations were calling for at the end of the 1980s. The United States wanted more study, and the IPCC was created to make recommendations to the community of nations on scientific issues entailed by global warming.

The specific task that was given to the IPCC was to assess for the international community the scientific, technical, and socioeconomic information relevant for understanding the risk of human-induced climate change.[3] Although the IPCC has been under constant attack by the political right in the United States, internationally its predictions have become influential in generating a consensus among most nations on what damages to human health and the environment are likely to follow from continued release of greenhouse gases. (The next chapter examines the criticisms of the IPCC's predictions that have been most strongly voiced in the United States.) The IPCC's predictions are influential because many of the participating scientists are from the most prestigious scientific institutions around the world, the IPCC usually strives to generate consensus positions among participating scientists before it speaks out, and the IPCC supports its scientific conclusions with exhaustive analyses and reports.

The IPCC completed its First Assessment Report in 1990. This report led to a generally accepted international consensus that human-induced global warming was a real threat to human health and the environment. This assessment also played an important role in establishing in 1990 the Intergovernmental Negotiating Committee (INC), the organization created to negotiate the United Nations Framework Convention on Climate Change (UNFCCC). In reaching agreement on the UNFCCC in May 1992, negotiators were influenced by the scientific conclusions reached in the IPCC's reports issued in 1990 and 1992. Since then, the IPCC has continued to provide scientific,

technical, and socioeconomic advice to the world community and, in particular, to the more than 170 parties to the UNFCCC through its periodic assessment reports on the state of knowledge of the causes of climate change,
its potential impacts, and options for response strategies.[4]

The IPCC's Second Assessment Report was issued in 1995 and provided
key input to the negotiations that led to the adoption of the Kyoto Protocol in
1997.[5] In this report, the IPCC, as it had before, exhaustively summarized the
state of the scientific knowledge on human-induced climate change, made specific predictions about the risk of climate change, and discussed mitigation options. One of the many conclusions contained in this report was that a "balance
of the evidence showed a discernable human influence on climate."[6] In other
words, by 1995, not only had the IPCC found that global warming was a substantial and real threat, a conclusion that the IPCC reached in its first report in
1990, but it had concluded that the balance of the evidence allowed the scientific community to separate human-caused changes to climate from the natural variability of the climate system. That is, human-caused changes to the climate were already observable by 1995, and by then it likely was already too
late to prevent human interference with the earth's climate system. In addition,
as of 1995, no matter what the international community would do to respond
to the global warming threat, the planet would continue to heat up for over 100
years because of the human release of greenhouse gases. The planet's temperature would rise even if atmospheric concentrations were stabilized because of
thermal lags in the oceans. Yet catastrophic change could still be prevented if
the international community acted decisively.

In February 2001, a summary for policymakers of the IPCC's third assessment report was released. This report, like the other two, made specific predictions about how human actions would change the global climate and how
climate change would affect human health and the environment. This report
confirmed and expanded on previous IPCC reports and concluded that there
was additional evidence that human-induced climate change had already become noticeable around the world. The following specific predictions have
been made by the IPCC in either its second or its third assessment report:

Temperature. In its third report, the IPCC predicted a global average surface temperature increase of 1.4°C to 5.8°C between 1990 and 2100.[7] This
prediction was considerably greater than the 1995 prediction of between 1°C
and 3.5°C.[8] As we will see, this temperature change is enough to do significant damage to human health and the environment. Not only was the upper
end of the predicted temperature range moved upward from 3.5°C to 5.8°C,
but so was the lower end of the range, from 1°C to 1.4°C, reflecting the fact
that it likely was already too late to prevent some global warming. Even if the
actual warming that takes place is close to the lower end of the likely range,

the earth will be transformed into a planet unlike one humans have ever known (see fig. 5.1).

Sea-level impacts. The IPCC's third report predicted a rise in sea level of between 0.09 and 0.88 meters by 2100.[9] This prediction was slightly lower than that made in the second report, mainly because better models were available five years after the second report.[10] As we will see, this rise in sea level greatly threatens some nations more than others.

Temperature impacts on land and water. Not all parts of the world will warm at the same rate.[11] The IPCC predicted greater surface warming of the land than of the sea in winter, a maximum surface warming in high northern latitudes in winter, and little surface warming over the Arctic in summer. Because there will be an enhanced hydrological cycle (the system that determines the amount of water in the atmosphere), there will generally be more

Figure 5.1   Projected changes in global temperature (global average 1856–1999 and projected estimates to 2100)

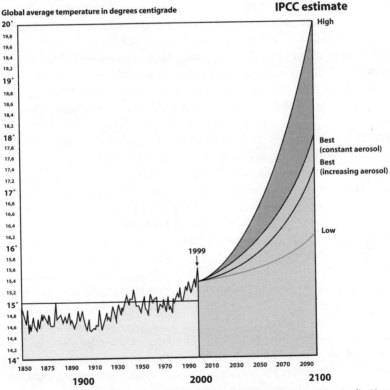

Source: UN Environment Program, Grid Ardenal, Climate Research Unit, University of East Anglia, Norwich, taken from IPCC report 95.

moisture in the atmosphere, and both droughts and floods will increase. There is also a likelihood of more intense storms.[12] This change in precipitation may also affect the geographic distribution of storms such as cyclones so that some nations will be exposed more often to dangerous weather.[13]

Hot and cold days. The IPCC projected that a general warming will lead to an increase in the occurrence of extremely hot days and a decrease in the occurrence of extremely cold days.[14] For this reason, many cities are likely to experience many more days of life-threatening heat waves than they have in the past.

Impacts on ecosystems and biodiversity. The IPCC predicted that the composition and geographic distribution of many ecosystems (e.g., forests, rangelands, deserts, mountain systems, lakes, wetlands, and oceans) will shift as individual species respond to changes in climate; because of these stresses to ecosystems, there likely will be reductions in biological diversity and in the goods and services that ecosystems provide society.[15] For this reason, global warming will put many species of plants and animals at risk while reducing natural resources, such as freshwater, which many people rely on to sustain daily life. Because ecosystems will shift, the character of many places will change. For instance, in Pennsylvania, a place not likely to experience the harshest impacts of global warming, many hardwood species of trees will disappear, and Pennsylvania's brilliant fall foliage might disappear. In addition, Pennsylvania might lose its cold-water trout and much of its winter sports. Thus, even places that are moderately affected by global warming may never be the same.

Modifications of forest. The IPCC stated that a substantial fraction (a global average of one-third, varying by region from one-seventh to two-thirds) of the existing forested area of the world will undergo major changes in broad vegetation types, with the greatest changes occurring in high latitudes and the least in the tropics.[16] Climate change is expected to occur at a rapid rate relative to the speed at which forest species grow, reproduce, and reestablish themselves. Therefore, the species composition of forests is likely to change; entire forest types may disappear, while new assemblages of species and hence new ecosystems may be established.[17] There is also great concern that the forests may not be able to adapt quickly enough to a rapidly changing climate, with the result that there could be massive forest die-off toward the end of the twenty-first century.

Increased temperatures in deserts. The IPCC concluded that deserts are likely to become more extreme in that, with few exceptions, they are projected to become hotter but not significantly wetter. Temperature increases in deserts could be a threat to organisms that exist near their heat tolerance limits. Desertification—land degradation in arid, semiarid, and dry subhumid areas—is more likely to become irreversible if the environment becomes drier and the soil becomes further degraded through erosion and compaction.[18]

Aquatic and coastal ecosystems. The IPCC concluded that in lakes and streams, warming would have the greatest biological effects at high latitudes, where biological productivity would increase, and at the low-latitude boundaries of cold- and cool-water species ranges, where extinctions would be greatest.[19] The geographic distribution of wetlands is likely to shift with changes in temperature and precipitation.[20] Some coastal ecosystems are particularly at risk, including saltwater marshes, mangrove ecosystems, coastal wetlands, sandy beaches, coral reefs, coral atolls, and river deltas.[21]

Melting of glaciers and permafrost. The IPCC stated that models project that between one-third and one-half of existing mountain glacier mass could disappear over the next 100 years.[22] The reduced extent of glaciers and depth of snow cover also would affect the seasonal distribution of river flow and water supply for hydroelectric generation and agriculture. Anticipated hydrological changes and reductions in the aerial extent and depth of permafrost could lead to large-scale damage to infrastructure and additional releases of carbon dioxide and methane into the atmosphere.[23]

Regional water impacts. The IPCC noted that changes in the total amount of precipitation and in its frequency and intensity directly affect the magnitude and timing of runoff and the intensity of floods and droughts; however, at present, specific regional effects are uncertain.[24] Relatively small changes in temperature and precipitation, together with the nonlinear effects on evapotranspiration and soil moisture, could result in relatively large changes in runoff, especially in arid and semiarid regions.[25] The quantity and quality of water supplies already are serious problems today in many regions, including some low-lying coastal areas, deltas, and small islands, making countries in these regions particularly vulnerable to any additional reduction in indigenous water supplies.[26]

Food impacts. The IPCC concluded that crop yields and changes in productivity due to climate change will vary considerably across regions and among localities, thus changing the patterns of production. Productivity is projected to increase in some areas and to decrease in others, especially in the tropics and subtropics.[27]

Human health. The IPCC predicted that climate change is likely to have wide-ranging and mostly adverse impacts on human health, with significant loss of life.[28] Direct health effects include increases in (predominantly cardiorespiratory) mortality and illness due to an anticipated increase in the intensity and duration of heat waves. Temperature increases in colder regions should result in fewer cold-related deaths. Indirect effects of climate change, which are expected to predominate, include increases in the potential transmission of vector-borne infectious diseases (e.g., malaria, dengue, yellow fever, and some viral encephalitis) resulting from extensions of the geographic range and season for vector organisms.[29] Although many places may be able to protect themselves from increased ranges of some vectors, such as mosquitoes, by upgrading human health infrastructure, many places around the world currently do not have the financial resources to do so. In some places, global warming will also create limitations on the availability of freshwater supplies and food and aggravate air pollution. These impacts will also have human health consequences.[30]

EFFECTS OF HUMAN-INDUCED CLIMATE ON THE POOR

Not all nations are equally threatened by these global warming impacts. Many of those nations, such as the United States, that have most benefited from the enormous consumption of fossil fuel are least threatened by global warming. Yet climate change is expected to have the harshest impacts on the poorest nations, which are likely to suffer most from climate for the following reasons.

Vulnerability to storms, flooding, and Rises in sea level. Estimates put about 46 million people per year currently at risk of flooding because of storm surges. The most vulnerable people are in the poorest nations. In the absence of adaptation measures and not taking into account anticipated population growth, the 50-centimeter sea-level rise predicted by the IPCC would increase this number to about 92 million; a 1-meter sea-level rise would raise it to about 118 million. Studies using a 1-meter projection show a particular risk for small islands and deltas.[31] Estimated land losses from sea-level rises include 5 percent for Uruguay, 1 percent for Egypt, 6 percent for the Netherlands, 17.5 percent for Bangladesh, and about 80 percent for the major atoll in the Marshall Islands, given the present state of protection systems.[32] Some small island nations and other countries will confront greater vulnerability because their existing sea and coastal defense systems are less well established. Countries with higher population densities would be more vulnerable. Storm surges and flooding could threaten entire cultures in some countries.[33]

Some poor nations are particularly at risk. Bangladesh is a densely populated country of about 120 million people located in the complex delta region of the Ganges, Brahmaputra, and Meghna Rivers. About 7 percent of the country's habitable land (with about six million population) is less than 1 meter above[34] sea level, and about 25 percent (with about thirty million population) is below the 3-meter contour.[35] Bangladesh is already extremely prone to damage from storm surges.[36] For instance, storm surges in November 1970 and April 1991 are believed to have killed over 250,000 and 100,000 people, respectively.[37] In addition to lives that are threatened by climate change because of increased vulnerability to flooding, climate change creates an increased threat to the intensity of tropical storms and the loss of prime farmland in developing nations that will become covered by rising seas.[38]

Human health. Climate change is expected to have large human health impacts on the poorest nations. The poorest nations are most vulnerable to cardiorespiratory problems caused by the increased intensity and duration of heat waves. The poorest nations are also most at risk from vector-borne infectious diseases, such as malaria, dengue, yellow fever, and some viral encephalitis, resulting from extensions of the geographic range and season for vector organisms. Most of the fifty to eighty million expected additional annual malaria cases will be experienced by the poorest nations as well as new cases of other infectious diseases caused by global warming—such as salmonellosis, cholera, and giardiasis. In addition, scarcities of freshwater supplies caused by droughts and drier soils will be more frequent in the developing world.[39]

Food. Many of the poorest nations are in arid and semiarid regions of Africa, Asia, and Central and South America. Relatively small changes in temperature and precipitation in these places, together with the nonlinear effects on evapotranspiration and soil moisture, can result in a great diminishment in food-growing capability. As a result, many of the world's poorest people—particularly those living in subtropical and tropical areas and dependent on isolated agricultural systems in semiarid and arid regions—are most at risk of increased hunger caused by global warming.[40] Many of these people are already vulnerable to malnutrition, a situation that global warming will exacerbate for some.

The ecological systems of many of the poorest nations are most at risk. Human-induced climate change represents an important additional stress to the many ecological systems already affected by pollution, increasing resource demands, and nonsustainable management practices. The vulnerability of ecological systems depends not only on how stressed they are by human activities but also on the economic resources that are available to take protective action. This implies that systems typically are more vulnerable in developing countries that are already stressed by pollution loading and have the least adequate economic defensive responses. Moreover, some of the harshest climate effects are likely to be experienced in poor nations. For this reason, the poorest nations often contain ecological systems that are most vulnerable to climate change.

Financial and institutional ability to adapt to climate change. The poorest nations are the least prepared to spend money on things that might allow them to adapt to hotter-dryer climates, more violent storms, rising sea level, degraded agricultural resources, and increased burdens on human health organizations.

Air conditioners, irrigation systems, large-scale public works projects to prevent flooding or damage from rises in sea level, food imports, or costly health protection strategies are not affordable in many parts of the world.[41] Those at greatest risk from climate change as well as other sources of shocks are precisely the poor and the vulnerable, namely, groups that lack the capacity and flexibility to protect themselves against unanticipated shocks.

CLIMATE SURPRISES

Most of the frequently quoted IPCC predictions of climate change impacts are based on the assumption that carbon dioxide will double from preindustrial levels, reaching a level of 560 ppm compared to a level of 280 ppm that existed at the end of the eighteenth century. As is discussed in more detail in the next chapter, these predictions were made by the IPCC in reliance on a number of climate models. These models assume that the climate system will react in mathematically describable patterns that are for the most part smooth responses to increases in the human releases of carbon. Yet the IPCC acknowledges that there are a number of plausible more rapid nonlinear responses of the climate system that are not contained in the equations on which the models are based. These plausible nonlinear responses of the climate system are generally referred to as "climate surprises."[42] If climate surprises occur, climate change would be much larger and more rapid than described in the IPCC's predictions. Climate surprises of concern to the scientific community include the following:

Abrupt changes in ocean circulation patterns. Scientists have recently discovered in the historical climate record that sudden shifts in the ocean circulation patterns of the North Atlantic have caused very rapid climate changes. If this were to occur again, there could be dramatic changes in the flow of the Gulf Stream, which would quickly cause sudden and major changes in regional climates much greater than the gradual temperature changes predicted by the climate models.[43]

Large increases in methane release from melting permafrost. Large amounts of methane are trapped in the Arctic permafrosts. If temperature increases rapidly enough, large amounts of methane could be released into the atmosphere, causing even larger amounts of global heating than predicted in the IPCC reports because more carbon will wind up in the atmosphere.[44]

Large, sudden increases in sea level caused by the breakup of the polar ice cap. A large part of the western Antarctic ice shelf could break off and instantaneously increase sea levels by as much as 10 meters.[45] Since the IPCC predicts only a 50-centimeter rise in the next century, this rapid rise in sea level would be much greater than the IPCC's predictions.

Nonlinear responses of the earth's carbon cycle. The carbon cycle is the natural process that circulates carbon through the biosphere among the oceans, atmosphere, terrestrial and aquatic vegetation and animals, and soils. Not all the mechanisms of the carbon cycle are fully understood well enough to include accurate mathematical descriptions in the climate models. Warming could have a nonlinear effect on the ability of natural processes to affect levels of carbon dioxide in the atmosphere. For instance, the solubility of carbon dioxide in seawater decreases with temperature of water, and therefore as oceans increase in temperature, they may be less able to remove carbon dioxide from the air.[46] Higher temperatures could also increase plant respiration, thereby increasing carbon dioxide emissions.[47] For this reason, nonlinear responses of the carbon cycle that are not now included in the climate models could have a greater effect on atmospheric levels of greenhouse gases than are described in the IPCC's predictions. These greater atmospheric levels of greenhouse gases would of course lead to higher temperatures than usually predicted.

Impacts based on these climate surprises have not been included in the IPCC's predictions because either the mechanisms that could trigger these responses are not understood well enough to be described in mathematical equations included in the climate models or the probability of these events taking place were judged to be too low to be included in the IPCC's predictions. Yet the IPCC has acknowledged that these climate surprises are plausible. For this reason, in thinking about the damage that could result from a business-as-usual approach to climate change and the ethical implications of policy responses, these climate surprises cannot be dismissed as too implausible to warrant consideration.

If the United States wants to ignore the possibility of the catastrophic impacts because of the potential costs to the United States of responding, it must be understood as the willingness of the United States to gamble that these responses will not hurt other nations or future generations.

IT IS PROBABLY TOO LATE TO AVOID DAMAGE FROM GLOBAL WARMING

In thinking about the potential impacts of global warming, it is easy to ignore or dismiss warnings of damage that could occur in the distant future on the basis that there surely is enough time to take action to avoid the damage. Yet the full seriousness of these descriptions of the harm that could come from a doubling of atmospheric greenhouse gases can be appreciated by understanding that it is probably already too late to avoid some damage and that the eventual doubling of atmospheric concentrations of greenhouse gases is almost inevitable. Moreover, rapid and enormous changes in the way the world uses energy will be required to stabilize greenhouse gases at the doubling level for carbon dioxide of 560 ppm, which is the level assumed by the IPCC as creating many of the human health and environmental damages and impacts described in the IPCC's reports. This is so because the greenhouse gases of greatest concern remain in the atmosphere for a long time (many decades to centuries for carbon dioxide and nitrous oxide); hence, they will cause warming on long timescales, and slowing down greenhouse gas emissions will continue to cause rises in atmospheric levels unless emissions are drastically reduced.

For this reason, stabilizing greenhouse gas concentrations in the atmosphere will require extraordinary changes in human behavior worldwide. This is so not only because greenhouse gases remain in the atmosphere for long periods but also because worldwide fossil fuel use is increasing at about 2 to 3 percent per year, meaning that current emissions of greenhouse gases are expected to grow under a business-as-usual scenario (i.e., an assumption of moderate economic growth, a doubling of current population, and no strong environmental pressure to cut emissions) to four to six times current levels in 2100.[48] Under the IPCC's business-as-usual scenario, carbon dioxide will rise in the atmosphere from its current 370 ppm to almost 700 ppm by 2100.[49] Average carbon dioxide concentration in the atmosphere is now about 370 ppm, and the average temperature of the earth is believed to have risen about 1°F during the past 100 years because of the human-induced increase from 280 ppm. Yet even if it were possible to stabilize greenhouse gases in the atmosphere at current levels, a clear impossibility, temperature would continue to rise because of the long response time of the oceans.

Many scientists and policymakers believe that a doubling of carbon dioxide from preindustrial levels to 560 ppm may be unavoidable in the next century.[50] This is so because the world's political and economic system cannot respond rapidly enough to make faster changes in polluting sources, such as gasoline-powered automobiles or coal-fired power plants. Some environmentalists, however, believe that it is possible to stabilize greenhouse gases at 450 ppm, a level that would limit the temperature increase, in addition to what has already been caused by anthropogenic causes, to 1.5°F to 2°F during the next 100 years.[51] Virtually no one believes that it is possible to stabilize atmospheric concentrations below 450 ppm, even if the most ambitious proposal currently under consideration were adopted.[52] If all nations could stabilize emissions in 2002, a goal that is virtually impossible, the concentrations of greenhouse gases would continue to rise and would approach 500 ppm by 2100.[53] After that, greenhouse gas concentrations in the atmosphere would continue to rise for several hundred years before stabilization would be achieved.[54] Even to stabilize carbon dioxide at 1000 ppm will require reductions of emissions below current levels.[55]

For all of these reasons, it appears as if many of the climate impacts identified by the IPCC are likely to occur no matter what the international policy response. The issue facing the international community, then, is not whether climate damage can be avoided but whether it is possible to avoid catastrophic change. The longer the world waits to take significant action, the harder it will be to stabilize greenhouse gases in the atmosphere at levels that do not create dangerous interference with the climate system. The U.S. positions in global negotiations are already responsible for at least a decade's delay in concerted international action. As we will see in later chapters, some of the issues that the United States has been pushing in the past few years could easily result in another decade's delay before serious responses are taken. The excuses for this delay are examined from an ethical perspective in the following chapters.

NOTES

1. David Landes, *The Wealth and Poverty of Nations—Why Some Are So Rich and Some So Poor* (New York: W. W. Norton, 1998).

2. Intergovernmental Panel on Climate Change (IPCCa), *About IPCC* (available at <www.ipcc.ch/about/about.htm>, February 10, 2001).

3. IPCCa. The IPCC has three working groups. Working Group I assesses the scientific aspects of the climate system and climate change. Working Group II addresses the vulnerability of socioeconomic and natural systems to climate change, negative and positive consequences of climate change, and options for adapting to it. Working Group III assesses options for limiting greenhouse gas emissions and otherwise mitigating climate change.

4. For a list of IPCC reports see, Intergovernmental Panel on Climate Change, *Reports* (available at <www.ipcc.ch/pub/reports.htm>, February 10, 2001).

5. The 1995 IPCC report was produced in three volumes: (1) John T. Houghton, L. G. Meira Filho, B. A. Callender, N. Harris, A. Kattenberg, and K. Maskell, eds. *The Science of Climate Change: Contribution of Working Group I to the Second Assessment of the Intergovernmental Panel on Climate Change* (IPCCb) (Cambridge: Cambridge University Press, 1995); (2) Robert T. Watson, M. C. Zinyowera, and R. H. Moss, eds., *Impacts, Adaptations and Mitigation of Climate Change: Scientific-Technical Analyses—Contribution of Working Group II to the Second Assessment of the Intergovernmental Panel on Climate Change* (IPCCc) (Cambridge: Cambridge University Press, 1995); and (3) J. P. Bruce, H. Lee, and E. F. Haites, eds., *Economic and Social Dimensions of Climate Change Contribution of Working Group III to the Second Assessment of the Intergovernmental Panel on Climate Change* (IPCCd) (Cambridge: Cambridge University Press, 1995).

6. IPCCb, *Summary for Policy Makers* (available at <www.ipcc.ch./pub/sarsum1.htm>, July 23, 1999), 10.

7. Intergovernmental Panel on Climate Change, *Third Assessment Report: Summary for Policy Makers—Contribution of Working Group I* (IPCCe), January 2001 (available at <www.usgcrp.gov/ipcc/wg1spm.pdf>, March 17, 2001).

8. IPCCb, *Synthesis of Technical and Scientific Information* (available at <www.ipcc.ch/pub/sarsyn.htm>, March 17, 2001).

9. IPCCe, 10.

10. IPCCe, 10.

11. IPCCb, *Synthesis of Scientific and Technical Information,* para. 2.10.

12. IPCCb, *Synthesis of Scientific and Technical Information,* para. 2.11.

13. IPCCb, *Synthesis of Scientific and Technical Information,* para. 2.11.

14. IPCCb, *Synthesis of Scientific and Technical Information,* para. 5.

15. IPCCb, *Synthesis of Scientific and Technical Information,* para. 3.6.

16. IPCCb, *Synthesis of Scientific and Technical Information,* para. 3.7.

17. IPCCb, *Synthesis of Scientific and Technical Information,* para. 3.7.

18. IPCCb, *Synthesis of Scientific and Technical Information,* para. 3.8.

19. IPCCb, *Synthesis of Scientific and Technical Information,* para.3.10.

20. IPCCb, *Synthesis of Scientific and Technical Information,* para. 3.10.

21. IPCCb, *Synthesis of Scientific and Technical Information,* para. 3.10.

22. IPCCb, *Synthesis of Scientific and Technical Information,* para. 3.10.

23. IPCCb, *Synthesis of Scientific and Technical Information,* para. 3.11.

24. IPCCb, *Synthesis of Scientific and Technical Information,* para. 3.12.

25. IPCCb, *Synthesis of Scientific and Technical Information,* para. 3.12.

26. IPCCb, *Synthesis of Scientific and Technical Information,* para. 3.12.

27. IPCCb, *Synthesis of Scientific and Technical Information,* para. 3.13.

28. IPCCb, *Synthesis of Scientific and Technical Information,* para. 3.14.

29. IPCCb, *Synthesis of Scientific and Technical Information,* para. 3.14.

30. IPCCb, *Synthesis of Scientific and Technical Information,* para. 3.14.

31. IPCCb, *Synthesis of Scientific and Technical Information,* para. 3.14.

32. IPCCb, *Synthesis of Scientific and Technical Information,* para. 3.14.

33. IPCCb, *Synthesis of Scientific and Technical Information,* para. 3.14.

34. IPCCb, *Synthesis of Scientific and Technical Information,* para. 3.1.

35. John Houghton, *Global Warming: The Complete Briefing,* (Cambridge: Cambridge University Press, 1997), 111.

36. Houghton, *Global Warming,* 111.

37. Houghton, *Global Warming,* 111.

38. Houghton, *Global Warming,* 111.

39. IPCCb, *Synthesis of Scientific and Technical Information,* para. 3.12.

40. IPCCb, *Synthesis of Scientific and Technical Information,* para. 3.13.

41. IPCCb, *Synthesis of Scientific and Technical Information,* para. 3.18.

42. For a discussion of climate surprises, see D. Streets and M. Glantz, "Exploring the Concept of Climate Surprises," *Global Climate Change* 10, no. 2 (July 2000): 97.

43. Thomas F. Stocker, "Past and Future Reorganizations in the Climate System," *Quaternary Science Reviews* (2000): 301–19.

44. Stocker, "Past and Future Reorganizations in the Climate System," 302.
45. Stocker, "Past and Future Reorganizations in the Climate System," 302.
46. Stocker, "Past and Future Reorganizations in the Climate System," 312.
47. Stocker, "Past and Future Reorganizations in the Climate System," 312.
48. Houghton, *Global Warming,* 193.
49. Houghton, *Global Warming,* 194.
50. William Stevens, "Experts Doubt a Greenhouse Gas Can Be Curbed," *New York Times,* November 3, 1997, A1.
51. Stevens, "Experts Doubt a Greenhouse Gas Can Be Curbed," 1.
52. Stevens, "Experts Doubt a Greenhouse Gas Can Be Curbed," 1.
53. Stevens, "Experts Doubt a Greenhouse Gas Can Be Curbed," 18.
54. Stevens, "Experts Doubt a Greenhouse Gas Can Be Curbed," 1.
55. Stevens, "Experts Doubt a Greenhouse Gas Can Be Curbed," 1.

Chapter 6

Uncertainty in the
Science of Climate Change

As we saw in chapter 2, fossil fuel and other vested interests have frequently argued that the United States should not take action on climate change because the science of climate change is too uncertain to justify the economic pain entailed by programs that reduce fossil fuel use. For years, for instance, Mobil Oil Corporation ran adds on the op-ed page of the *New York Times* and in other periodicals that argued that the United States should not adopt strong climate change mitigation strategies because of the uncertainty embedded in climate change science.[1] This is so that, according to the argument often made in these publications, if human-induced climate change turns out to be not a real threat, increased costs that are incurred to move away from fossil fuels will be wasted drag on the U.S. economy.[2]

Some of the fossil fuel producers went so far as to hire public relations firms to make uncertainty in climate change science the focus of campaigns to prevent government action to reduce fossil fuel use. For instance, Ross Gelbspan, in his book *The Heat Is On,* identified a memo prepared by a public relations firm created by a group of utility and coal companies that stated that it was launching a campaign to "reposition global warming as a theory rather than a fact."[3] Gelbspan also documented additional strategies used by some fossil fuel producers designed to convince the public that global warming was an unproven theory. These strategies included funding the research of several climate scientists who were known skeptics, paying the expenses of these skeptics to appear as witnesses in congressional hearings on global warming, and working to ensure that every mass-media report on climate change issues prominently included these skeptics' positions.[4]

Probably as a result of these efforts, many U.S. citizens doubt whether global warming is a real problem worth worrying about at all. They do not know that a lot of climate change science has never been in question, that many of the elements of global warming science are not seriously challenged even by the scientific skeptics, and that the issues of scientific certainty most discussed by the climate skeptics usually deal with the magnitude and timing of climate change, not with whether global warming is a real threat. Thus, many Americans view global warming as entitled to the same type of respect as other highly speculative and low-probability worries that are sometimes mentioned in the media, such as whether extraterrestrials have visited earth. The fossil fuel producers' strategy of making scientific uncertainty the focus of public debate has managed to create the impression among many U.S. citizens that the global warming problem amounts to nothing more than the exaggerated and unfounded worries of the environmental community. As a result of this strategy, many Americans believe that because human-induced climate change has such little basis in science other than speculation, global warming may not be a real problem deserving our immediate attention.

As we saw in chapter 2, the Reagan, George H. W. Bush, and now the George W. Bush administrations made scientific uncertainty about global warming the basis for resistance to positions of the Europeans and others who wanted to move more aggressively on climate change. In addition, for the past twenty years there have been many members of the U.S. Congress who have opposed programs to reduce U.S. greenhouse gas emissions because scientific uncertainties remain about global warming.

Because the degree of certainty about the consequences of human actions may have relevance to the strength of one's ethical duty, this chapter reviews the state of scientific certainty about global warming. Although this chapter argues that a number of climate skeptics consistently have overstated the amount of scientific uncertainty entailed by the climate change problem, the next chapter argues that it is not necessary to agree that the skeptics have exaggerated the amount of scientific uncertainty to see a strong duty for the United States to reduce greenhouse gas emissions. That is, the ethical responsibility of the United States exists even if one assumes considerable scientific uncertainty about the timing and magnitude of global warming.

How certain are the predictions of the Intergovernmental Panel on Climate Change (IPCC) regarding likely global warming impacts described in chapter 5? As this chapter describes in detail, the IPCC's conclusions about the likely impacts on human health and the environment of human releases of greenhouse gases rests on a scaffolding of scientific planks many of which are quite strong because they are constructed of virtually certain scientific conclusions and others whose strength is less reliable. Yet, as is demonstrated in the next chapter, enough of the scientific planks supporting the IPCC's conclusions are strong to support clear U.S. duties to reduce the real threat of global warming.

SCIENCE OF CLIMATE CHANGE: AREAS OF AGREEMENT

An uninformed observer of the climate change debate that has appeared in the mass media might conclude that there is little agreement among scientists about the greenhouse effect. Yet much of the theory about human-induced climate change has never been, or is no longer, in contention. In fact, much of the basics of the science of global warming were understood over thirty years ago. As we will see, by the end of the 1980s many scientists around the world had concluded that more than enough was known about how humans were changing the amount of greenhouse gases in the atmosphere to justify actions to reduce the growing threat of a rapidly warming planet. Since then, the scientific community has further reduced many of the uncertainties. Currently, there is a vast body of virtually certain scientific knowledge about global warming that has been steadily building for over 100 years and reducing uncertainties.

Global Warming Science up to 1990

As we saw in chapter 2, the scientific community began to think about the fact that humans could actually change the climate with the publishing of Svante Arrhenius's paper in 1896. In fact, the natural greenhouse effect was understood almost 180 years ago with the publishing of Gene-Baptiste-Joseph Fourier's paper in 1826 that concluded that the earth's atmosphere was trapping heat. We also saw in chapter 2 that G. S. Callendar warned the world that humans were changing the climate in the 1930s. Yet the scientific community did not really wake up to the enormous risk of human-induced climate change until Revelle and Suess determined that the oceans were not absorbing the amounts of carbon dioxide then generally assumed and an observatory was placed on Mauna Loa, Hawaii, to measure atmospheric carbon dioxide in the late 1950s.

By the late 1980s, an enormous amount of scientific information had confirmed Callendar's concerns.[5] Some of the most important planks in the uncontested scientific aspects of global warming by the end of the 1980s included the following:

Naturally occurring greenhouse gases warm the planet. Although the earth's atmosphere is comprised mostly of nitrogen and oxygen, which have no effect on warming, the atmosphere contains several gases, including water vapor, carbon dioxide, and nitrous oxide, which are transparent to incoming short-wave radiation from the sun but which trap long-wave radiation that would otherwise be radiated back to space. Most of the outgoing radiant energy is in the long-wave or infrared region, in the wavelengths of

4 to 100 micrometers.[6] Greenhouse gases will absorb some radiation in these wavelengths and prevent it from going back to space and thereby warm the planet. The naturally occurring greenhouse gases raise the temperature of the planet to 15°C, about 30°C warmer than it would be without the natural greenhouse gases. This naturally occurring greenhouse effect is called "natural" because all the natural greenhouse gases were in the atmosphere long before humans came on the scene.

The most important human-released greenhouse gas is carbon dioxide a gas that is also one of the natural greenhouse gases. Because the way in which carbon dioxide works naturally to heat the planet is well understood, the way in which human-caused increases in atmospheric carbon dioxide concentrations tend to heat the planet is also well understood. That is, strong inferences about how increases in carbon dioxide in the atmosphere will tend to warm the planet can be made both by looking at the historical record and by deduction from basic physics.

All this was well understood before the 1980s and has never been very controversial. A book on global warming published in 1989 by Falk and Brownlow says, "The basic mechanism of the greenhouse effect is well understood and the explanation of the role it currently plays is uncontroversial."[7]

Carbon dioxide on Venus and Mars confirms the theory that an increase in greenhouse gases will make a planet hotter. Observations of other planets confirm the theory that the more heat-absorbing gases a planet has in its atmosphere, the hotter the planet is. For instance, Venus is completely cloud covered, thereby retaining less sunlight than the earth, but the surface temperature of Venus is very high. The high temperature is caused by high amounts of carbon dioxide in Venus' atmosphere, as 97 percent is comprised of carbon dioxide.[8] Mars is just the opposite: It has little carbon dioxide and a cold surface. Therefore, in addition to the inferences that can be made from the earth's historical record about how greenhouse gases change surface temperatures, scientists can confirm some of these inferences by learning from other planets how greenhouse gases have affected their surface temperatures. This is not to say that the information from other planets will tell us exactly what will happen on earth; rather, we may conclude that knowledge about the concentration of greenhouse gases in the earth's atmosphere allows strong inferences about likely heating tendencies.

An understanding of the role that carbon dioxide was playing in regulating the temperatures of our neighboring planets was also well understood by the late 1980s. By then, human probes of the planets had brought back information about temperatures and atmospheric chemical concentrations that could be investigated together with the uncontested role of the greenhouse gases in heating these planets.[9]

Human activities are adding to the natural greenhouse gases quantities of carbon dioxide, methane, nitrous oxide, and other gases that are known to trap infrared radiation. Human activities are emitting greenhouse gases into the atmosphere—carbon dioxide, mostly through the burning of fossil fuel; methane, mostly through various agricultural practices and landfills; nitrous oxide, through combustion and agriculture; and chlorinated fluorocarbons (CFCs), mostly through refrigeration, air conditioning, and insulation activities. As a result, carbon dioxide has increased about 31 percent since the beginning of the industrial revolution from about 280 parts per million (ppm) to a level of about 360 ppm at the end of the 1980s and above 370 ppm at the present time.[10] Methane has increased almost 151 percent since 1750 to over 1.6 ppm.[11] Concentrations of other anthropogenic greenhouse gases have also increased. The 31 percent increase in atmospheric carbon dioxide observed since preindustrial times cannot be explained by natural causes alone.[12] Carbon dioxide concentrations have varied naturally throughout earth's history. However, these concentrations are now higher than any seen in at least the past 450,000 years and are likely higher than any seen the past twenty million years.[13] The fact that carbon dioxide had risen to almost 360 ppm by the end of the 1980s was well established and without controversy by the end of that decade.[14]

Greenhouse gases emitted by human activities will absorb infrared radiation at known rates. The ability of each greenhouse gas to absorb infrared radiation is known. For instance, the greenhouse effect of a molecule of methane is about 7.5 times that of carbon dioxide.[15] In fact, because of the relative simplicity of determining how much heating will follow from increased concentrations of greenhouse gases in the atmosphere in the absence of feedback mechanisms, the first relatively successful attempt to calculate the likely global temperature increase that would be caused by a doubling of carbon dioxide was performed in 1896.[16] As we have seen, Svante Arrhenius, who would win the Nobel Prize for Chemistry in 1903, knew at the end of the nineteenth century that industrialization was changing the environment in a way that should lead to a warming. He also knew that two gases, water vapor and carbon dioxide, naturally made the planet warmer by absorbing infrared radiation.[17] In 1896, after immersing himself in tedious calculations more than seventy years before computers were available, Arrhenius concluded that a doubling of carbon dioxide from industrial processes would increase the earth's average temperature by 5°C to 6°C. This 100-year-old prediction is only 2°C to 3°C greater than the 2.5°C warming that our most sophisticated computers are now predicting will be caused by a doubling of carbon.[18] As we will see, what makes predicting a future global warming temperature difficult is not the ability to predict how greenhouse gases will absorb radiation but, as will be explained, a number of nonlinear feedback mechanisms in the climate system that will determine how much heating actually occurs. In other words, predicting the amount of global warming that would come from increased levels of greenhouse gases alone would be quite simple as a matter of elementary physics. If the only changes from greenhouse gas absorption were air and surface temperatures, it would be easy to predict a 1°C to 1.5°C warming by 2100 assuming that current emissions trends continue.[19] But this "direct response" figure (which is less than the current "best guess" of future warming) is almost meaningless because it is physically impossible for the climate system to warm up by over 1°C without any changes to the earth, such as reductions in ice or increases in clouds, which would cause further temperature changes. For this reason, computers are needed to model complex temperature, air, surface, and ocean interactions among other complexities in the climate system. Yet the reaction of the climate system to increased levels of greenhouse gases in the atmosphere without these feedback systems is without scientific controversy. For this reason, increasing greenhouse gases in the atmosphere is known to increase the heating of the planet. The only question is, How much heating will be produced given nonlinear feedbacks of the earth's carbon and climate systems? It can be said, however, without fear of contradiction, that increasing the level of greenhouse gases in the atmosphere will mean that warming will occur.

Since the beginning of the industrial revolution, greenhouse gases emitted by human activities are increasing in the atmosphere in proportion to their use by humans. It is relatively easy to calculate how much coal, natural gas, and oil are being burned each year for human needs.[20] Currently, about 6 gigatons of carbon are entering the atmosphere from the combustion of fossil fuels.[21] It is also known that atmospheric carbon has been increasing in rough proportion to the amount of these fuels that are being burned.[22] Currently, carbon levels in the atmosphere increase at a rate of about 1.5 ppm per year.[23] It is also known that since the beginning of the industrial revolution, carbon dioxide has increased in the atmosphere in proportion to the amount of fossil fuels consumed. Although a minority of scientists claim that this undisputed recent rise in carbon in the atmosphere may have been caused by natural events rather than the human release of carbon, they cannot deny that increases in atmospheric carbon are in proportion to human activities. The fact that atmospheric carbon is rising in proportion to the human use of carbon has created a very strong inference that increases in atmospheric carbon are caused by human releases of carbon.

Again, the fact that carbon has been rising in proportion to human use was well understood by the mid-1980s. This had been well established by thirty years of measurements from the Mauna Loa monitoring station, among others, and by worldwide records of the human use of fossil fuels (see fig. 6.1).[24]

Figure 6.1   Global emissions and atmospheric concentrations of CO_2 since 1790

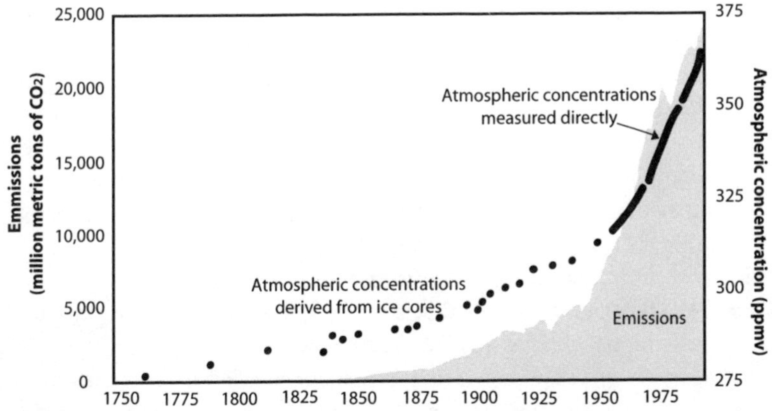

Source: United States Environmental Protection Agency.

There are now many other reasons why increases in atmospheric carbon are believed to be caused by human activities. For one, carbon dioxide emitted from the human combustion of fossil fuel has a different chemical signature than naturally occurring carbon dioxide. In addition, recent chemical analysis of greenhouse gases points to the human causation of the recent atmospheric buildup of carbon dioxide. However, the most compelling reason for this conclusion was stated in 1989 in a book by Falk and Brownlow that concluded, "If industrial activity has been a major factor in creating the recently observed dramatic rise in atmospheric CO_2, then one would expect the rise to have begun with the Industrial Revolution and accelerated as industrialization spread globally . . . this expectation is confirmed by measurements over the last thirty years."[25] Although the increase in carbon in the atmosphere in direct proportion to the release of carbon by human emissions does not establish irrefutably that the carbon in the atmosphere is human caused, it establishes a very strong inference that there is a relationship between human activities and increases in atmospheric greenhouse gases.

Historical records dating back tens of thousands of years show a correlation between temperature and quantities of carbon dioxide in the atmosphere. The last major ice age began about 120,000 years ago and ended about 20,000 years ago.[26] During this period, carbon dioxide and temperature have varied in proportion to each other.[27] For this reason, it is reasonable to conclude that if humans increase the concentrations of greenhouse gases, temperatures eventually will increase. This is supported not only by the physics of the greenhouse gases but also by the historical record of the relationship between greenhouse gases in the atmosphere and global temperatures. This is not to say that all past warming has been caused by increases in greenhouse gases; in fact, as we will see, other natural factors, such as changes in the sun's energy output, are believed to be responsible for natural temperature variability. It is simply to say that there is strong presumptive evidence that when atmospheric concentrations of greenhouse gas increase, it is likely that global temperature will increase.[28] Given that carbon dioxide is now greater in the atmosphere at 370 ppm than it has been for 420,000 years and is likely higher than it has been for the past twenty million years, there is strong evidence that temperatures will rise to levels higher than they have been at least in 420,000 years because temperatures have historically risen in proportion to greenhouse gas concentrations.[29] By the late 1980s, it was already known that carbon dioxide had risen to levels higher than at any time in the past 160,000 years.[30]

For thousands of years before the industrial revolution, quantities of carbon dioxide in the atmosphere were relatively stable at approximately 280 ppm and then rose as the industrial revolution began to use fossil fuel. Although there is great variability in the historical climate record of carbon dioxide and temperature, with ice ages being followed by warm periods, the 8,000 year period before the beginning of the industrial revolution has been unusually stable.[31] For several thousand years before humans started to change the atmosphere, carbon dioxide varied no more than 10 ppm from a mean of 260 ppm.[32] Although there were slow changes in temperature during the past 8,000 years, there were no abrupt changes of the type seen in earlier periods in the historical record.[33] As far as scientists can tell, global temperatures have varied by less than 1°C since the dawn of human civilization.[34] Against the apparently extreme and sometimes rapid climate fluctuations of the preceding 100,000 years, this stands out as a relatively peaceful interglacial period.[35] By the late 1980s, it was well known that carbon dioxide in the interglaciation period varied between 270 and 300 ppm, and therefore the late 1980s buildup to 360 ppm should be of concern.[36]

Since the industrial revolution, the surface temperature of the earth has been slowly heating up in proportion to the use of fossil fuels. Over 7,000 surface temperature–monitoring stations around the world indicate that the average temperature of the earth has been rising steadily during the past 100 years. In addition to these direct measures of temperature, both the temperature and the chemical composition of greenhouse gases have been determined through analysis of ice-core and tree-ring data covering tens of thousands of years. These data show that the earth has heated up an additional 0.6°C from the approximate average temperature of about 15°C since the end of the industrial revolution.[37] By the late 1980s, it was known that 0.5°C of heating had occurred through the analysis of 63 million temperature recordings made from 1861 to 1984 from 15 different regions of the world.[38]

Global Warming Science in the 1990s

Despite the irrefutable scientific inferences that could be drawn about the relationship between human activities and potential planetary heating before 1990, as we saw in chapter 2 the Reagan and George H. W. Bush administrations took the position, in opposition to much of the world, that there was still too much scientific uncertainty to justify taking action to reduce U.S. emissions. Yet a closer inspection of most of those resisting action on the grounds of scientific uncertainty reveals that they were not denying the basic physical facts (described in this chapter) that had been well established by the end of the 1980s. Those who resisted U.S. government actions on the ground of scientific uncertainty usually focused on two issues. The first was the ability to know how much warming would actually take place in the future. The second was what is generally referred to as the signal-to-noise problem, that is, the question of whether it could be proven that humans had already made the planet warmer given the natural variability in the climate system. Therefore, by the beginning of the 1990s, opponents of U.S. government action on global warming had been successful in focusing the public scientific debate not on the issue of whether the burning of fossil fuels was a large risk to many things of profound human importance but rather on the question of whether we could say with a high degree of scientific certainty whether global warming had begun and what precisely the future had in store in terms of climate change. These questions are more difficult scientific questions than establishing whether the United States was involved in irresponsible, risky behavior.

During the 1990s, record heat continued while glaciers and polar ice melted and storm damage set records. In 1990, the IPCC, an institution created with the strong support of the United States as the organization to advise the international community on the science of global warming, issued its first report. After bringing together almost every scientist who had by then made a significant contribution in the field, this first IPCC report concluded with certainty that atmospheric concentrations of greenhouse gases were increasing in a way that should lead to a warming of the earth's surface.[39] The first IPCC report stated that to stabilize atmospheric concentrations of carbon dioxide, 1990 emissions would have to be reduced by 60 to 80 percent.[40] Under a business-as-usual scenario (i.e., no changes in current policies), the 1990 IPCC report forecast a rise of 0.3°C per decade in global mean temperature and a rise of 6 centimeters per decade in the average sea level.[41] The 1990 IPCC report also concluded that climate change impacts on agriculture, forestry, natural ecosystems, water resources, human settlements, oceans, and coastal zones are likely to vary widely from region to region and that rising populations, technological advances, and changes in natural events, such as El Niño, could influence regional impacts.[42] Thus, in 1990, the very institution that the United States had supported to give advice on the science of global warming to the international community concluded that certain troubling global warming impacts were likely and that some of the poorest people around the world were the most vulnerable. Yet the United States would largely ignore the conclusions and recommendations of the very institution that it had said was needed to resolve scientific uncertainties about global warming.

The 1990 IPCC report made it clear that global warming was a serious problem that needed to be addressed, although it conceded that it was not possible to specify precisely what amount of heating would take place and acknowledged that further research would be helpful in reaching higher levels of confidence about impacts. Yet the serious impacts described in the 1990 IPCC report were clearly likely if the world did not take strong steps to reduce emissions of greenhouse gases. The 1990 IPCC report was widely interpreted as saying that the international community was engaging in dangerous behavior that prudence demanded be halted. Yet the United States resisted making binding commitments, apparently because it wanted high levels of certainty about what exactly would happen before imposing burdens on the U.S. economy to reduce greenhouse gas emissions. The United States was willing to gamble that the IPCC's predictions would not happen. It was willing to allow further buildup of greenhouse gases in the atmosphere until scientific uncertainties were resolved.

As we saw in chapter 2, the United States was successful in weakening the climate change treaty in 1992 while relying on the excuse that global warming science could not precisely describe specifically what the continued human releases of greenhouse gases would produce in terms of climate change impacts. And so the treaty agreed to in Rio in 1992 and later ratified by the United States contained no binding obligations to reduce greenhouse gas emissions. It did, however, contain the "precautionary principle" (a provision more fully discussed in the next chapter), a decision-making principle that said that scientific uncertainty should not be used as an excuse for nations not taking cost-effective action to reduce domestic greenhouse gas emissions. Thus, by the beginning of the 1990s, the international community, persuaded by the enormous, well-documented danger entailed by the many undisputed elements of global warming science, agreed no longer to use scientific uncertainty as an excuse for further delay. Yet despite the fact that the George H. W. Bush administration agreed to the reasonableness of the Precautionary Principle in 1992, many U.S. politicians, including George W. Bush, would continue to use scientific uncertainty as an excuse for delaying U.S. action on global warming into the twenty-first century. In the meantime, greenhouse gases continued to accumulate in the atmosphere as record heat was experienced throughout the 1990s.

In 1995, the IPCC issued its Second Assessment Report. In the intervening five years since its first report, the IPCC was able to gain greater confidence in the climate models that in the early 1990s were making rapid advances in sophistication and in the ability to predict what temperatures were later being experienced. These more sophisticated computer models were continuing to support the earlier scientific consensus that humans were conducting a dangerous experiment in continuing to emit ever larger amounts of greenhouse gases.

On the issue of the signal-to-noise problem, the 1995 IPCC report was able to declare for the first time that "the balance of the evidence shows a discernible human influence on climate"[43] In other words, the IPCC's scientists concluded in 1995 not only that human-induced climate change was a serious threat to human health and the environment, a conclusion they had reached in 1990, but also that it was possible in 1995 to observe actual effects of human activities on climate that could be distinguished from natural climate variability. No longer, as Bill McKibben has pointed out, could humans assume that the good and bad weather they experienced was something provided by a nature unaffected by human actions.[44] As far as weather is concerned, nature had ended, if by nature is meant something unaffected by human activities. For the first time in the history of the world, temperatures and storms would be at least partially caused by human activities. There would be no part of the planet that would not be affected. There would be no pure wilderness unaffected by the impacts caused by driving sports utility vehicles. Although the human-caused changes to the weather might have been very small in 1995, one could not rule out the possibility that some portion of extreme weather events could be traced to the burning of fossil fuels even then. One could no longer say that a hurricane that killed 5,000 people was just an act of natural forces.

In the 1990s, the Clinton administration took the position that scientific uncertainty about global warming should no longer be an excuse for not taking action. Yet many members of Congress continued to rigidly resist Clinton administration initiatives on global warming in part on the basis that scientific uncertainties should be eliminated or greatly minimized before the United States adopts major programs to reduce U.S. greenhouse gas emissions.

Recent Global Warming Science

In 2000, the National Resource Council of the National Academy of Sciences claimed that it settled a long-running dispute in climate change science about whether the earth's surface was actually warming. This report concluded that the earth's surface has been warming in proportion to the human use of fossil fuels and that this warming has been very close to what the models had predicted should happen from the human-induced climate change.[45] In line with this warming, ice caps and glaciers are melting, and record temperatures are being experienced around the world. Although as we will see later in this chapter, some scientific skeptics continue to dispute that this warming is human caused, prior skeptics' arguments that the earth's surface was not warming have been put to rest according to the National Resource Council report.[46]

As we saw in chapter 2, at the beginning of 2001 the IPCC released summaries from its third report. Five years after the IPCC's second (1995) report, the third report concluded that the earth's average surface temperature could rise by 2.5°F to 10.4°F by 2100—much higher than the IPCC's estimate five years before, when it predicted a rise of 1.8°F to 6.3°F.[47] The third IPCC report also made stronger conclusions than the 1995 report about the ability to detect human agency in recent warming. In other words, by 2001 there was even stronger evidence than there was in 1995 to support the conclusion that it was already too late to prevent some human-caused global warming. Therefore, some of the heating that was being experienced, particularly in the past two decades of the twentieth century, was human caused (see fig. 6.2).

In summary, contrary to the understanding of many Americans, much of the science supporting concerns about human-induced global warming is not now in question. As a result, few scientists seriously dispute that if humans continue to add greenhouse gases to the atmosphere, the climate will change and human health and the environment may suffer severely. We do know with certainty that the human generation of greenhouse gases is a serious threat to our climate and that greenhouse gases have increased in the atmosphere in proportion to human use. These facts are clear and unassailable. That is not to say, however, as we will see, that science can predict with a high degree of certainty what global warming actually has in store for us in terms of the timing and magnitude of the warming.

The only way that science can know the timing and magnitude of future climate change with high levels of scientific certainty is to develop computer models that accurately describe the entire climate system, including interactions among oceans, soils, vegetation, and the atmosphere; the effects of global ice and snow cover on the reflection or absorption of incoming solar radiation; solar variability; the type and extent of cloud formations; and the natural carbon cycle. As we will see in the next section, the computer models that attempt to describe these complex interactions suffer from some inherent limitations that are not likely to be resolved in the near future.

After constructing models that mathematically describe the physical connections of the climate system, predicting future climate events that result from the human release of greenhouse gases requires running models that make different assumptions about future levels of human population, tech-

Figure 6.2   Important milestones in global warming science

1824 Fourier identifies natural greenhouse effect.
1896 Arrhenius calculates doubling of CO_2 will increase global temperature by 4 to 6°C.
1936 Callendar argues that human induced global warming may be beginning.
1950s Revelle and Suess determine that oceans are not absorbing expected amounts of CO2. Mauna Loa observatory created to monitor CO2.
1960s Mauna Loa observations determine that CO_2 is steadily building in the atmosphere in proportion to human use. Computer models start to be used to predict global warming from increases in atmospheric CO_2.
1970s CEQ admits that United States has responsibility for global warming. U.S. National Academy of Science concludes that "wait and see" policy on global warming may be too late.
1980s Villagio conference concludes some warming is inevitable. Hansen testifies that warming has started. IPCC formed. National Academy of Science warns that future welfare of human society is at risk from warming. UNEP warns that climate change may outstrip ability to adapt.
1990s IPCC first assessment concludes that global warming is real and getting worse. UNFCC is adopted including Precautionary Principle. Second IPCC assessment concludes that the "balance of the evidence" demonstrates a discernible human effect on climate. Clinton administration asserts that science is not an issue.
2000–2001 U.S. National Academy of Science says that Earth is warming. George W. Bush asserts that science is a basis for repudiating Kyoto and campaign promise to regulate CO_2. Third IPCC report: Earth warms faster than expected. U.S. National Academy of Science agrees with IPCC.

nology, and fuel use. Therefore, future predictions of human-caused climate events suffer both from scientific uncertainty about how the global physical system will react to increases in greenhouse gas emissions and from ignorance about what levels of these gases will be emitted by human activities in the years ahead. Therefore, if we make high levels of scientific certainty about what will actually happen in the future a test for the rationality of public policy on global warming, we will probably never meet the test, and if current climate science is roughly correct about global warming, catastrophic impacts may be experienced if significant action is not taken soon.

Therefore, the question we should ask about the timing and magnitude of global warming predicted by the models should be whether the models point in the direction of what is likely to happen if certain scenarios are followed, not whether they accurately describe what will actually happen. Models can make only plausible descriptions of future climates under assumed scenarios, not scientifically proven descriptions of future climates. Yet fossil fuel interests have made us ask the wrong question about the models and the science of global warming. By playing up issues of scientific uncertainty in the models, economic interests and other global warming skeptics have convinced citizens and many politicians in the United States that there are fundamental questions about whether global warming is anything we should worry about at all. The climate skeptics have been successful in making Americans focus on a number of issues of scientific uncertainty in the climate models and have diverted our attention from the many elements of sound science on which global warming concern is based. In making issues of scientific uncertainty about the models the focus of public debate, opponents of serious greenhouse gas reduction programs have rested their case on two dubious but hidden assumptions.

The first assumption is that despite the fact that adding greenhouse gases to the atmosphere is virtually certain to warm the planet, only when we know how much warming will take place is policy justified to prevent the warming even if it will be too late to prevent significant warming by the time the uncertainties are eliminated. In other words, the status quo in emitting greenhouse gases should be allowed to continue until we know what damage will be caused by current greenhouse emission tendencies. The burden of proof should be on those who are concerned about harm to prove what the harm will be. Conversely, those who desire to continue emitting greenhouse gases have no responsibility to show that their behavior is harmless.

The second assumption is that in determining how much warming will take place, only high levels of scientific certainty should be accepted in reaching conclusions about the magnitude of warming. That is, in meeting their burden to prove what the actual harm will be, those concerned about global warming should be able to meet this burden through the use of unassailable scientific evidence. Reasonable projections that rely on unproven assumptions are not usable by those who have the burden of proof in showing what harm will take place.

As we will see, these two assumptions, which are implicit in many of the scientific skeptics' arguments made in opposition to global warming programs in the United States, are ethically dubious.

SCIENCE OF CLIMATE CHANGE:
SOME MAJOR SOURCES OF UNCERTAINTY

To make future projections of climate change, computer models have been used to simulate complex interactions among major components of the climate system since 1969.[48] Since that time, the models have gained in sophistication yet are limited in the ways described in the following sections.

Feedback Uncertainties

A feedback is a change in some variable that tends to change another variable. A positive feedback is a change in one variable that causes a change in another variable in the same direction.[49] A negative feedback, on the other hand, diminishes the initial variable. Among feedbacks in the climate system that are of great importance are the following:[50]

- *Water vapor amount.* Because water vapor is a greenhouse gas, the amount of water vapor in the atmosphere is a positive feedback because increases in water vapor tend to increase temperature. If increased warming creates higher levels of water vapor in the atmosphere, global warming will be stronger.[51]
- *Clouds.* Clouds can either reflect incoming radiation and act as a negative feedback, thus decreasing warming, or insulate the earth like a blanket, thus increasing warming. Whether clouds are positive or negative feedbacks depends on the amount, altitude, and characteristics of the clouds.[52]
- *Aerial extent of ice and snow.* Because ice and snow reflect rather than absorb incoming radiation, decreases in ice and snow act as a positive feedback because such decreases reduce the surface reflectivity, tending to increase warming.[53] Snow and ice reflect sunlight very effectively. If a small warming melts snow earlier in the year, more energy will be absorbed by the ground exposed underneath it, in turn causing more warming. This is the main reason that wintertime northern regions are expected to warm the most.[54]
- *Vegetation.* Changes in vegetation around the world could be a positive or a negative feedback because different types of vegetation reflect radiation differently. Changes in the type and distribution of forests caused by global warming could have feedback effects on global temperatures because such changes would change the amount of the sun's incoming radiation that is reflected back to space.
- *The carbon cycle.* Carbon is naturally cycled among oceans, the atmosphere, and the terrestrial biosphere. The amount of carbon in the atmosphere will depend on the ability of the terrestrial vegetation and the oceans to absorb or release carbon. Changes in the carbon cycle can create both positive and negative feedbacks for many reasons, including the fact that changes to the oceans or biosphere caused by climate changes are likely to alter the sources and sinks in carbon dioxide and methane and thereby work to increase or decrease

warming. The carbon cycle is not fully understood. Only about half the carbon released into the atmosphere by humans winds up in the atmosphere, suggesting that higher atmospheric concentrations have triggered some enhanced or new processes that remove this gas from the air.[55]

Not all these feedbacks are well understood at this time.[56] Until they are, computer calculations of climate consequences may over- or underestimate climate change. In addition, as we saw in chapter 5, the climate is believed to be capable of changing in a rapid, nonlinear manner, that is, in ways that scientists refer to as "climate surprises." For the most part, these climate surprises have not been considered in the equations that make up the global climate models.

Model Limitations

There are a number of inherent limitations with the models able to predict future events. These include the following:

- *Computing limitations.* A climate model that explicitly included all our current understanding of the climate system would be too complex to run on any existing computer.[57] Therefore, for practical purposes, compromises must be made in attempts to model climate. The "art" of modeling includes selecting different complexities of models for different aspects of the climate system. Differences between models include the following:

  1. *The number and size of spatial dimensions of the model.* Because some physical quantities, such as temperature, humidity, and wind speed, must be understood as they vary in space, it is necessary to represent these quantities at different locations in space in the computer model. The most general models for climate change employed by the IPCC are called general circulation models, which describe interactions among the atmosphere, oceans, and terrestrial ecosystems.[58] Many of the more complex climate models array variables in three dimensions with the typical horizontal grids of several hundred kilometers and vertical layers of 1 kilometer. The greater the number of grids, or blocks, the more the complexity of the computing challenge and the greater the cost of running various scenarios. Because of the large number of variables entailed by this scheme, computer models are limited in their ability to model phenomena at smaller scales.[59]

  2. *The need to parameterize some variables.* Computing limitations do not allow models of high enough resolution to resolve important subgrid processes, that is, processes that form at smaller scales than the

size of the grids used in the models. (The average grid size is about the size of the state of Arizona.) Subgrid size phenomena include clouds and vegetative radiation. To account for subgrid phenomena, models average rather than compute subgrid effects, such as cloud formation and cloud interactions with atmospheric radiation. This process of substituting empirical averages for subgrid phenomena is known as "parameterization" of subgrid phenomena.[60]

3. *The number of physical processes represented.* Models make simplifying assumptions about the nature of reality to make the calculations manageable. Not all variables of concern can be included in the models, and choices among variables must be made.

- *Assumptions about future events.* In addition to these inherent limitations of the models, to make predictions about the future impacts of human activities on the climate system, scientists must make assumptions about future population levels, the mix in use of different fuels, the efficiency of future combustion techniques and energy use, and the amount of economic activity that will create increased demand for energy. Assumptions about how much greenhouse gases humans will put into the atmosphere must be made because the amount of climate-changing gases that humans will put into the atmosphere cannot be known in advance. To accommodate this unknown, computer models usually are run for a limited number of scenarios. In 1995, the IPCC reviews adopted six scenarios, including a business-as-usual one. These scenarios made different assumptions about population growth, the cost of energy supplies, deforestation rates, and economic growth rates.[61] For the 2001 IPCC assessment, many new scenarios were run.

- *Ecological impact uncertainties.* Moreover, even if predictions about future temperature increases could be made with acceptable levels of certainty, predicting the consequences of specific temperature increases on ecological systems requires confronting many additional issues that are plagued by scientific uncertainty. That is so because the science of ecology is much too soft to predict ecosystem-wide responses to stress.[62]

For these reasons, attempts to make accurate predictions of the actual future impacts of human activities on the climate system and the how changes in climate will affect people and ecological systems are now and are likely to be frustrated in the future by considerable scientific uncertainties. Particularly difficult to predict are the unexpected, large, and rapid climate system changes (as have occurred in the past) that are referred to as climate surprises.[63] In other words, human intervention in the climate system is a dangerous experiment, and we likely will not find out what will happen for sure until it happens.

SCIENCE OF CLIMATE CHANGE:
CONFIDENCE IN CLIMATE PREDICTIONS

Despite the numerous uncertainties in the climate models, the IPCC reported in 1995 that it was gaining higher levels of confidence in the climate models.[64] In reaching this conclusion, the IPCC noted that "atmospheric models have shown some improvement since 1990, and are markedly superior to the models in use in the 1970's and early 1990's."[65] The IPCC reported increased confidence in the ability of the models to simulate important aspects of human-caused climate change for the following reasons:

• The most successful climate models are able to simulate the important large-scale features of the climate well that actually have been observed, including seasonal, geographic, and vertical variations of climate in space and time.[66]
• Different models are consistently predicting climate change,[67] while all models predict warming caused by human release of greenhouse gases.[68]
• The models have accurately predicted observed regional climate variations, the response of the climate system to the volcanic eruptions such as Mount Pinatubo, and other historical and recent climate events.[69]
• The models can predict natural variability of the climate system over a broad range of time and space scales.[70] For instance, they predict greater warming at the poles and less at the equator. These predictions have been observed in the climate system.
• The recent models have been improved through successful incorporation of additional physical climate processes, including cloud microphysics and the effects of sulfate aerosol pollutants.[71]

In his book *Global Warming: The Complete Briefing,* Sir John Houghton, cochair of the Scientific Assessment Group of the IPCC and cochair of Britain's Royal Commission on Environmental Pollution, elaborates on some of these reasons why the climate models have received new respect from the scientific community that makes up the IPCC:

• Once a comprehensive climate model has been formulated it can be tested in three ways. Firstly, it can be run for a number of years of simulated time and the climate generated by the model compared in detail to current climate. For the model to be seen as a valid one, the average distribution and seasonal variations of appropriate parameters such as surface pressure, temperature and rainfall have to compare well with observation. In the same way, the variability of the model's climate must appear to be similar to the observed variability. Climate models which are currently employed for climate prediction stand up well to such comparison.[72]

- Secondly, climate models can be compared against simulations of past climates when the distribution of key variables was substantially different than at present, for example the period around 9,000 years ago when configurations of the Earth's orbit around the sun was different. . . . These [computer] simulated changes are in qualitative agreement with paleoclimate data. For example, computers accurately describe the period (around 9,000 years ago) of lakes and vegetation in the Southern Sahara about 1,000 km north of the present limits of vegetation.[73]
- Thirdly, climate models can be compared to large perturbations in the climate system such as El Nino and associated climate anomalies and volcanic eruptions. Good progress is being achieved with the prediction of El Nino events and the models successfully simulated the Mount Pinatubo eruption in 1991 at its actual effect upon the climate.[74]

The *New York Times* also reported in 1997 that the climate models were being viewed by much of the scientific community as worthy of higher levels of respect.[75] Andrew Ingersoll, a planetary scientist at the California Institute of Technology, was quoted as saying, "Despite all the uncertainties, you can make useful estimates of climate change with the models. You just have to be aware of the uncertainties, it is just like any other scientific process."[76] Even though actual climate changes could be more or less than levels predicted by the models because of the feedback mechanisms and climate surprise discussed in chapter 5, the models are being viewed more frequently as generating reasonable predictions of climate changes caused by human activities at the global scale.

The IPCC's Third Assessment Report indicated even higher levels of confidence in the climate models.[77] The IPCC's scientists report that they have even greater confidence in the climate models since the Second Assessment Report in 1995 because of (1) a better understanding of climate processes and their incorporation in models, (2) satisfactory simulations of current climate with little need to adjust the models, (3) successful predictions of late twentieth-century climate, and (4) successful predictions of monsoons and other recent, more local scale events.

That is not to say that the models can yet accurately predict climate events at local or regional scales, as global climate models are less accurate the smaller the geographic scale.[78] That is, although the climate models are believed to give a fairly reasonable prediction of likely global average temperature increases, there is much less confidence in the models' ability to predict climate impact at any one place on the planet.

In its 2001 report, the IPCC concluded that it had various "levels of confidence" in its predictions of future climate and its impacts. To explain how much confidence it had in its predictions, the IPCC classified its predictions into predictions that were virtually certain (a prediction that the IPCC's scientists had more than 99 percent confidence in), very likely (90 to 99 percent chance), likely (66 to 90 percent chance), medium likely (33 to 66 percent chance), unlikely (10 to 33 percent chance), very unlikely (1 to 10 percent chance), and exceptionally unlikely (less than 1 percent chance).[79]

For instance, in the third assessment report, the IPCC concluded that the following were changes in climate that were very likely in the twenty-first century:[80]

- Higher maximum temperatures and more hot days over nearly all land areas,
- Higher minimum temperatures and fewer cold days and frost days over nearly all land areas
- Reduced diurnal temperature range over most land areas
- Increased heat index—a measure of a combination of temperature and humidity that indicates human comfort—over all land areas
- More intense precipitation events

Examples of those climate changes in the twenty-first century that were classified as likely are the following:[81]

- Increases in summer continental drying and associated risk of drought
- Increases in tropical cyclone peak wind intensities
- Increases in tropical cyclone mean and peak precipitation intensities

From these classifications of the IPCC's predictions into confidence levels, it is quite clear that the IPCC has very high levels of confidence in concluding that there will be major changes in climate in the next 100 years due to human interference in the climate system despite some uncertainties. According to many observers, those scientists who disagree with the IPCC's conclusions that humans are conducting a very dangerous experiment by continuing to release large quantities of greenhouse gases are a distinct minority.[82] For this reason, the cochair of the IPCC working group on the science of climate change, John Houghton, has stated that "the IPCC reports can be considered as authoritative statements of the contemporary views of the international community."[83]

Some prominent scientists are willing to go much further than the IPCC in declaring their levels of confidence in global warming impacts. For instance, Jerry Mahlman, professor of atmospheric and ocean sciences at Princeton University, has asserted that some of his predictions are "very probable."[84] By "very probable," Mahlman means that these projections have a greater than nine out of ten chance of being true within the predicted range. Mahlman's "very probable" projections include the following:

- A doubling of atmospheric carbon dioxide over preindustrial levels is projected to lead to an equilibrium warming in the range of 1.5°C to 4.5°C. These generous uncertainty brackets reflect remaining limitations in modeling the radiative feedbacks of clouds, details of the changed amounts of water vapor in the upper atmosphere (5 to 10 kilometers), and responses of sea ice. In effect, this means that there is roughly a 10 percent chance that the actual equilibrium caused by doubled atmospheric carbon dioxide could be lower than 1.5°C or higher than 4.5°C. For the answer to lie outside these bounds, we would have to discover a substantial surprise beyond our current understanding.
- Sea-level rise could be substantial. The projections of 50 $\forall$ 25 cm by 2100, caused mainly by the thermal expansion, are below the equilibrium sea-level rise that would ultimately be expected. After 500 years at quadrupled carbon dioxide, the sea-level rise expected due to thermal expansion is roughly 2 $\forall$ 1 meter. Long-term melting of landlocked ice carries the potential for considerably higher values but with less certainty.
- By 2050 or so, the higher latitudes of the Northern Hemisphere are also expected to experience temperature increases well in excess of the global average increase. In addition, substantial reductions in the northern sea ice is expected. Precipitation is expected to increase significantly in higher northern latitudes. This effect occurs mainly because of the higher moisture content of the warmer air, which, as it moves poleward, cools and releases its moisture.

Mahlman asserts that the following projections, among others, are "probable."[85] By "probable," Mahlman means they have a greater than two out of three chance of being true:[86]

- Model studies project eventual marked decreases in soil moisture in response to increases in summer temperatures.
- Recent research suggests that tropical storms, once formed, might tend to be more intense in the warmer ocean, at least in circumstances where weather and geographic (e.g., no landfall) conditions permit.

Many atmospheric scientists from prestigious institutions believe that the science is clear and irrefutable and that the science supports the conclusions that humans have begun to change the climate. For this reason, according to Dr. Mahlman,

None of the known uncertainties [about climate change] can make the problem go away. It is virtually certain that human-caused greenhouse gas warming is going to continue to unfold, slowly but inexorably, for a long time into the future. The severity of the impacts can be modest or large, depending on how some the remaining key uncertainties are resolved through the eventual changes in the real climate system, and our success in reducing long-lived greenhouse gases.[87]

SCIENCE OF CLIMATE CHANGE: VIEW OF THE SCIENTIFIC SKEPTICS

Despite high levels of confidence on the part of most scientists that humans are affecting the climate, there are a number of scientists, often referred to as the "skeptics," who continue to dispute the more mainstream scientific conclusions about global warming that are represented by the IPCC's projections. Although some of the skeptics' research has been paid for by the fossil fuel industry and several Middle Eastern nations that oppose action on global warming, just because this is the case does not make the skeptics' scientific conclusions wrong.[88]

Most of the scientific uncertainties associated with climate science that the climate skeptics point to deal with three issues:

• The timing and magnitude of global warming and its impacts
• Whether human-induced global warming is already discernible
• Whether more harm than good will come from global warming

Uncertainty about the Timing and Magnitude of Global Warming

Some of the most frequent challenges to the work of the IPCC from the climate skeptics are directed at the IPCC's conclusions that global warming is likely to result in serious increases in global temperatures in the twenty-first century under a business-as-usual scenario. Although there have been a host of issues raised by the skeptics, a few of the most frequently heard criticisms of the IPCC's conclusions include the following:

• The models do not accurately describe specific elements of the climate system.
• The models are overly simplistic and rely on false assumptions.

It should be pointed out that most of these criticisms of the IPCC's work do not deny that global warming is a serious threat; rather, they are more in the nature of attacking whether the IPCC's use of models should be accepted as proof of the actual timing and magnitude of warming. That is, the critics are not claiming that they have proven the obverse of the IPCC's prediction, namely, that climate change is nothing to be concerned about. Because they are not making this claim, the skeptics are implicitly making an argument about who should have the burden of proof in making the IPCC's conclusions. For this reason, the skeptics' arguments should be understood as a claim that no one should take global warming seriously until those who are concerned about global warming prove what will happen. But questions about who should have the burden of proof are questions of ethics and values, not science. In this way, the skeptics' attacks contain a hidden ethical assumption about who should have the burden of proof.

There are a number of charges frequently made by the skeptics that concern specific elements of the IPCC's reasoning:

- The models do not accurately describe how water vapor in the atmosphere, the most potent natural greenhouse gas, will respond to a warmer climate.
- The models do not accurately describe how clouds will be formed that will tend to reduce global warming, that is, act as a negative feedback.
- The models are not reliable because satellite temperature measurements of the atmosphere demonstrate that the atmosphere is not heating up as predicted by the models.

The claim that the models do not accurately describe the response of water vapor in the atmosphere is a charge that has been most forcefully made by Richard Lizden, an atmospheric scientist from the Massachusetts Institute of Technology. Lizden has argued that increased heat will move water vapor into the upper atmosphere, where it will be dried out and thus put a limit on the buildup that would have otherwise fueled global warming.[89] The IPCC's scientists disagree with Lizden on the basis that satellite and balloon observations show that with more heating of the atmosphere, water vapor increases.[90] Yet Lizden remains a powerful voice for the skeptics.

The water vapor controversy is typical of many of the controversies in the climate science debate. That is, a few prominent skeptics disagree with the mainstream view about an element of how the climate system will respond to increased human use of fossil fuels.

The claim that the models do not accurately describe the potential negative feedback effect of clouds is a charge that has been made by one of the more prominent skeptics, Fred Singer, among others.[91] It is generally acknowledged by all scientists, including those who are members of the IPCC, that the models need to be improved to get a better handle on the role that clouds will play in future climates. This is so because the models used by the IPCC do not adequately deal with clouds because cloud generation and behavior will take place at scales smaller than the smallest grids that can currently be used in the models. Yet, as mentioned previously, the size of grid that can be used is limited by the number of variables that the computers can deal with. As also explained previously, for phenomena that take place at scales smaller than the grids, the models "paramaterize" these variables; that is, they rely on averages rather than compute the specific phenomenon.

Determining what type and size of clouds will be created by future warming is an issue worth consideration because some clouds will produce a positive feedback and tend to warm the planet, and others will generate a negative feedback that acts as a force for cooling. To get around the inherent limitations created by model grid size, the models make assumptions about how and what types of clouds are likely to form. Because it is recognized that higher-power computers could deal more effectively with smaller grids, it is hoped that future climate models will more satisfactorily describe cloud formation and their effect on climate. This is not to say, however, that the models' current assumptions about clouds lead to the conclusion that the models underestimate the role that clouds will play in dampening global warming. Later research or actual experience may demonstrate that the type of clouds that will be formed in response to human actions may make global warming worse than the levels currently projected by the computer models relied on by the IPCC.

Because there are both theoretical and practical limits to the use of models to predict complex phenomena such as future cloud formation, identifying uncertainties in the models has been and will continue to be quite easy. Yet the unstated assumption entailed by advice from climate skeptics against government action to curb greenhouse gases because of uncertainties in the computer models is that the models should not be used to support government policy until they reach high levels of certainty. However, this is a goal that the computer models may never be able to fully achieve or will achieve too long after serious damage is done.[92]

By harping on various weaknesses in the models, such as their ability to compute cloud changes, the skeptics often give the impression that the entire global warming theory is groundless. Yet as we have seen, much of the climate change science is not now, nor has it ever been, in contention, while many other elements of climate science, such as the fact that greenhouse gases are building up in the atmosphere in proportion to human use, are not grounded on the models. Although ideally we may want to know what type of clouds will be formed to gain levels of confidence in the computer models, we do not need the models to conclude that if humans increase the quantity of greenhouse gases in the atmosphere, the temperature will rise, as this is a deduction that can be made directly from the historical record and basic physical laws.

The skeptics' attack on elements of the models also often fails to acknowledge that there are other reasons to respect the models' predictions as likely projections of future climate, such as the IPCC's reasons for increased confidence in the models described here. That is, even if one recognizes the weaknesses of certain elements of climate science on which the models are built, there may be valid reasons for taking the models seriously notwithstanding uncertainties about some of a models' building blocks. Some of the models' building blocks may prove to be wrong, yet the general conclusions of the models might be sound because some blocks may overestimate human impacts on climate while others underestimate climate response. This is why it is important to know whether the models' predictions are matching observed temperatures, a fact that the IPCC has identified as giving it more confidence in the models.

An argument currently receiving much attention by the climate skeptics to cast doubt on the mainstream science of climate change comes from the fact that satellite measurements from 1979 to the present do not show the same heating in the atmosphere that is being experienced on the ground.[93] Measurements of the earth's surface for the past twenty years shows a warming of 2.25°F to 3.6°F per century, while warming in the atmosphere determined by satellites is between zero and 1.8°F per century.[94]

The 2000 report by the National Resource Council has settled one controversy created by this disparity between apparent atmospheric and surface warming while intensifying another.[95] Up until the time when this report was published in the winter of 2000, some of the climate skeptics were arguing that the failure of the atmosphere to warm like the surface undermined the conclusion that the earth is warming at all. According to the skeptics, the surface–atmosphere warming discrepancy discredited the claim that the planet is warming because surface temperature measurements were susceptible to errors from such phenomena as increases in heat from growing cities that absorb and retain heat and thereby make it appear that the planet is getting warmer while it is actually an effect of the growing city. Yet the National Resource Council's report found that the "surface warming in the last twenty years is undoubtedly real and is substantially greater than the rate of warming during the twentieth century."[96] Therefore, the argument that the planet is not heating up that has been based on the satellite measurements of atmospheric temperatures has been put to rest by the recent National Resource Council report, according to the National Academy of Sciences.

Some skeptics, however, argue that the National Resource Council's report supports an argument that any warming that is occurring has natural causes because the report concluded that the atmosphere is not heating to the same extent that the surface is warming.[97] The skeptics argue that if the surface warming is being caused by increased levels of carbon dioxide in the atmosphere rather than by natural causes, such as an increased output of solar radiation, the lower atmosphere should show the same type of warming experienced at the earth's surface. This is so because increased greenhouse gases should make the atmosphere as well as the surface warm up. Therefore, the skeptics argue, the fact that the National Resource Council's report has determined that the atmosphere is not warming to the same extent as the earth's surface supports arguments that warming is being caused by natural causes.

However, the National Resource Council's report states that the atmosphere may not be heating up like the surface because of other human causes. These include human-caused decreases in the ozone layer as well as emissions of pollutants that block incoming radiation.[98] Therefore, the fact that the atmosphere is not warming like the earth's surface is acknowledged to be an unsettled issue in climate change science. It does not, however, disprove the mainstream scientists' conclusion that the earth is warming because of human causes. Given that it is now virtually indisputable that humans have greatly increased the level of greenhouse gases in the atmosphere and that it is certain that once the greenhouse gases get into the atmosphere, they will absorb and reradiate more heat to earth, the argument made by the skeptics that the heating we are seeing on the surface of the earth is due to natural causes is highly implausible.

There Is No Reliable Evidence That the Climate Is Already Changing in Response to Human Activities

A second argument frequently heard from the climate skeptics is that it cannot be proven that human activities are already changing the climate. This is the signal-to-noise problem identified earlier. The question of whether recent abnormally warm weather has been caused by human agency is also a very difficult scientific question. It is a much harder question than the issue of whether human-caused increases in the concentrations of atmospheric greenhouse gases will eventually cause climate change, an issue about which there is virtually no question, although there is admitted uncertainty about the timing and magnitude of warming. Whether any one climate event has been caused by human actions is an extraordinarily difficult scientific issue because of the natural variation in the climate system. That is, without human intervention, climate is believed to have varied greatly in the earth's history because of the following:

- *Earth–sun relations.* These variables include changes of the angle of the earth's axis to the sun, changes in the earth's orbital eccentricity, and the timing of when the earth reaches the farthest and closest points from the sun.[99]

- *Output of solar radiation.* The sun's output varies both over long and short cycles.[100]
- *Atmospheric modifications.* Natural variations in carbon dioxide, water vapor content, ozone, and oxides of nitrogen can cause natural temperature change.[101]

Despite the natural variability of the climate system, the IPCC's scientists concluded in their 1995 report that "the balance of the evidence demonstrates a discernible human influence on climate."[102] And as we have already seen, the 2001 IPCC report has concluded that the evidence that humans are already changing the climate is now even stronger. That is, notwithstanding the difficulty of separating human from natural causes of changing climate, the IPCC has recently concluded again that scientific evidence supports the conclusion that human-caused climate change is already being experienced. According to the IPCC, this is so because of the following:[103]

- Actual observed temperatures are matching models' predictions about human-caused changes.
- Climate models are better able to simulate the type of natural variability in the climate that would be expected without human intervention.
- Statistical studies show that annual observed averaged temperatures over the past century are not likely to have been caused by natural fluctuations of the climate system alone.
- A number of recent studies of observed patterns of temperature change (i.e., the actual temperature change occurring at different latitudes, longitudes, heights, and time) would be difficult to achieve unless human agency were the cause of the changes.

The climate skeptics disagree that it is now possible to identify the signal of human-caused temperature change and separate it from the noise of natural variability. Relying on the skeptics' arguments, ExxonMobil, in a recent op-ed piece in the *New York Times*, said that "it is impossible for scientists to attribute the recent surface temperature increase to human causes."[104] Yet the IPCC never claimed that it has been absolutely proven that recent warming is being caused by human agency; the IPCC claimed in 1995 only that the "balance of the evidence" supported the conclusion that humans are already changing the climate and in 2001 that there was stronger evidence to support this conclusion. By denying the ability for science to prove human agency in recent warming, ExxonMobil is implicitly arguing that only high levels of proof should be taken seriously. Yet on the very next day after the ExxonMobil op-ed piece appeared in the *New York Times,* the same newspaper reported that scientists had determined that to the extent the planet is being warmed by emissions of greenhouse gases like carbon dioxide, only part of that heating has materialized so far.[105] Because of this, the amount of damage already done to the planet by human agency is probably only half the damage that will be experienced from existing pollution levels.[106] This is so, according to this article, because "about half the greenhouse warming is still in the oceanic pipeline and will inevitably percolate to the air in the decades just ahead."[107] As we have already seen, neither the scientific skeptics nor ExxonMobil claim that they have proven or have any reliable proof that recent undisputed warming is natural; they simply disagree with the IPCC's conclusions that the balance of the evidence shows human agency in recent warming.

The ExxonMobil op-ed piece, as well as arguments made by climate skeptics in opposition to government action on climate change, does not advise the public that if the mainstream scientists are right about human-induced global warming, the damage to the planet, its people, and natural heritage could be very serious if not catastrophic if we wait until high levels of proof about the timing and magnitude of climate change are achieved. The climate skeptics and their corporate patrons also do not acknowledge that a U.S. policy to do nothing or to slowly implement climate change mitigation strategies is a high-stakes wager where the biggest losers, if the gamble is lost, will be future generations and the poorest people on the planet.

Global Warming Will Be Good for Us

Another common argument made by the skeptics is that global warming will turn out to be good for us. That is, global warming will benefit agriculture by lengthening the growing seasons, and higher atmospheric carbon dioxide will increase plant growth.[108] Glossy brochures produced by fossil fuel interests promise a greener future from global warming and enhanced plant growth.

It is undoubtedly true that some parts of the world may benefit from increased warming and that increased carbon dioxide will increase plant production by making more carbon available to be used by plants in photosynthesis. Yet the skeptics who are arguing that the world will be a better place because of global warming conveniently forget to mention how global warming will also cause rising oceans that will destroy some small island developing states and coastal communities in many of the poorest nations, cause large increases in some types of human health problems (particularly from vector-borne diseases), decrease agricultural productivity in those parts of the world that become drier, increases stresses on ecosystems and species that are already threatened by human activities, and cause many other adverse effects to humans and ecological systems. The skeptics who are celebrating the benefits of global warming are ignoring the disaster that global warming is likely to be for hundreds of millions of the world's poorest people even if it proves to be a benefit for some. Because people in some places may be big losers even though others may gain from global warming, the argument that we need not do anything because global warming will be good seriously overlooks issues entailed by distributive justice, as we will see in later chapters. These arguments that global warming will be good for us also conveniently fail to mention that the people who will be harmed have not consented to U.S. policy to resist fifteen years of international efforts to develop an international approach to global warming, nor has the United States agreed to compensate all those who will be harmed by climate change.

CONCLUSION

Despite the fact that the IPCC's reports and the U.S. Academy of Sciences have recently made strong conclusions about the seriousness of the global warming threat, the George W. Bush administration has recently indicated that because of scientific uncertainty, it will further delay strong U.S. action on climate change. Although there is admittedly scientific uncertainty about where in the 1.4°C to 5.8°C range temperatures will be in this century, as predicted by the IPCC, even if the temperature increase turns out to be at the lower end of this range, the earth likely will be a different place than previously known to humans. Those who continue to fight U.S. programs to reduce greenhouse gas emissions confuse people by talking about the scientific uncertainty as if it were uncertainty that goes to the heart of whether global warming should be seen as a dangerous threat to human health and the environment. Yet those who make scientific uncertainty arguments against global warming programs usually focus on the signal-to-noise problem and the scientific uncertainties embedded in the models' predictions of likely temperature changes. Even on these two issues (issues that we will see are irrelevant to the ethical duty of the United States to act), the skeptics hold minority positions in the scientific community. Yet Americans have been confused by the diversionary rhetoric of the skeptics' arguments on scientific certainty.

NOTES

1. See, for example, Mobil Corporation, *New York Times,* December 12, 1997, op-ed.
2. Mobil Corporation.
3. Ross Gelbspan, *The Heat Is On* (Reading, Mass: Perseus Books, 1998), 34.
4. Gelbspan, *The Heat Is On,* 34.

5. For a good discussion of what was known about global warming by the late 1980s, see Jim Falk and Andrew Brownlow, *The Greenhouse Challenge: What's to Be Done?* (New York: Penguin Books, 1989).

6. John Lemons, Rudolph Heridia, Dale Jamieson, and Clive Splash, "Climate Change and Sustainable Development," in John Lemons and Donald Brown, eds., *Sustainable Development: Science, Ethics, and Public Policy* (Dordrecht: Kluwer Academic Publishers, 1995), 110.

7. Falk and Brownlow, *The Greenhouse Challenge*, 19.

8. Falk and Brownlow, *The Greenhouse Challenge*, 22.

9. Falk and Brownlow, *The Greenhouse Challenge*, 22.

10. Intergovernmental Panel on Climate Change (IPCC), *Third Assessment Report: Summary for Policy Makers—Contribution of Working Group I*, January 2001 (available at <www.ipcc.ch>, March 19, 2001), 4.

11. IPCC, *Third Assessment Report*, 4.

12. IPCC, *Third Assessment Report*, 4.

13. IPCC, *Third Assessment Report*, 4

14. Falk and Brownlow, *The Greenhouse Challenge*, 22.

15. Gale E. Christianson, *Greenhouse: The 200-Year History of Global Warming* (New York: Walker, 1999), 110.

16. Christianson, *Greenhouse*, 110.

17. Christianson, *Greenhouse*, 114.

18. Christianson, *Greenhouse*, 114.

19. United Nations Framework Convention on Climate Change (UNFCCC) Secretariat, *Frequently Asked Questions* (available at <www.unfccc.de/resource/iuckit/fact07.html>, March 18, 2001).

20. John Houghton, *Global Warming: The Complete Briefing* (Cambridge: Cambridge University Press, 1997), 24.

21. Houghton, *Global Warming*, 24.

22. Houghton, *Global Warming*, 26.

23. Houghton, *Global Warming*, 25.

24. Falk and Brownlow, *The Greenhouse Challenge*, 36.

25. Falk and Brownlow, *The Greenhouse Challenge*, 37.

26. Houghton, *Global Warming*, 53.

27. Houghton, *Global Warming*, 54.

28. Lemons et al., "Climate Change and Sustainable Development," 113.

29. The recent IPCC report released in January 2001 concluded that carbon dioxide is higher than it has been in 420,000 years and likely is higher than it has been in the past 20 million years. IPCC, *Summary for Policy Makers: Contribution of Working Group I—Third Assessment Report*, January 30, 2001 (available at <www.ipcc.ch>, March 17, 2001).

30. Falk and Brownlow, *The Greenhouse Challenge*, 37.

31. Houghton, *Global Warming*, 24.

32. Houghton, *Global Warming*, 24.

33. Houghton, *Global Warming*, 24.

34. UNFCCC Secretariat, *Frequently Asked Questions*.

35. UNFCCC Secretariat, *Frequently Asked Questions.*

36. Falk and Brownlow, *The Greenhouse Challenge,* 35.

37. Houghton, *Global Warming,* 24.

38. Falk and Brownlow, *The Greenhouse Challenge,* 41.

39. United Nations Environment Program (UNEP), *Intergovernmental Panel on Climate Change* (available at <www.unep.ch/iucc/fs208.htm>, June 28, 2001).

40. UNEP, *Intergovernmental Panel on Climate Change.*

41. UNEP, *Intergovernmental Panel on Climate Change.*

42. UNEP, *Intergovernmental Panel on Climate Change.*

43. IPCC, *The Science of Climate Change: Contribution of Working Group I to the Second Assessment of the Intergovernmental Panel on Climate Change—Summary for Policy Makers* (available at <www.ipcc.ch/about/about.htm>, March 9, 2001).

44. Bill McKibben, *The End of Nature* (New York: Anchor Books, 1989).

45. See the discussion in this chapter on the skeptics' arguments about the difference between surface and satellite measurements of heating. See also National Resource Council, *Reconciling Observations of Global Temperature Change* (Washington, D.C.: National Academy Press, 2000).

46. National Resource Council, *Reconciling Observations of Global Temperature Change.*

47. IPCC, *Summary for Policymakers: Working Group I (Science)—Third Assessment Report,* February 2001 (available at <www.ipcc.ch/pub/spm22-01.pdf>, February 21, 2001).

48. Houghton, *Global Warming,* 31

49. IPCC, *An Introduction to Simple Climate Models Used in the Second Assessment Report,* 1997 (available at <www.ipcc.ch/pub/IPCCTP.II(E).pdf>, March 17, 2001).

50. UNFCCC, *Climate Change Information Kit* (available at <www.unfccc.de/resource/iuckit/fact07.html>, March 18, 2001).

51. UNFCCC, *Climate Change Information Kit.*

52. UNFCCC, *Climate Change Information Kit.*

52. UNFCCC, *Climate Change Information Kit.*

53. UNFCCC, *Climate Change Information Kit.*

54. UNFCCC, *Climate Change Information Kit.*

55. IPCC, *An Introduction to Simple Climate Models Used in the Second Assessment Report.*

56. IPCC, *An Introduction to Simple Climate Models Used in the Second Assessment Report.*

57. IPCC, *An Introduction to Simple Climate Models Used in the Second Assessment Report.*

58. IPCC, *An Introduction to Simple Climate Models Used in the Second Assessment Report.*

59. IPCC, *An Introduction to Simple Climate Models Used in the Second Assessment Report.*

60. IPCC, *Report of Working Group I, Technical Synthesis,* 1995 (available at <www.ipcc.ch/pub/sarsyn.htm>, March 18, 2001).

61. Kristen Shrader-Frechette and Edward D. McCoy, *Methods in Ecology* (Cambridge, Mass.: Cambridge University Press, 1993).

62. See discussion on climate surprises in chapter 5.

63. K. L. Gates, A. Henderson-Sellers, G. J. Boer, C. K. Folland, A. Kitoh, B. J. McAveney, F. Semazzi, N. Smith, A. J. Weaver, and Q. C. Zeng, "Climate Models: Evaluation," in John T. Houghton, L. G. Meira Filo, B. A. Callander, N. Harris, A. Kattenbverg, and K. Maskell, eds., *The Science of Climate Change: Contribution of Working Group II to Working Group II* (Cambridge: Cambridge University Press, 1995), 223–36.

64. Houghton et al., eds., "Climate Models," 252.

65. John Houghton, L. G. Meira-Filo, B. A. Callander, N. Harris, A. Kattenbverg, and K. Maskell, "The Technical Summary," in *The Science of Climate Change* (Cambridge: Cambridge University Press, 1995), 1–9.

66. Houghton et al., "The Technical Summary," 31.

67. Houghton et al., "The Technical Summary," 33.

68. Houghton et al., "The Technical Summary," 33.

69. Houghton et al., "The Technical Summary," 33.

70. Houghton et al., "The Technical Summary," 33.

71. Houghton et al., "The Technical Summary," 34.

72. Houghton, *Global Warming,* 81.

73. Houghton, *Global Warming,* 84.

74. Houghton, *Global Warming,* 84.

75. *New York Times,* November 4, 1997, F6.

76. *New York Times,* November 4, 1997, F6.

77. IPCC, *Third Assessment Report,* 5.

78. Houghton, *Global Warming,* 157.

79. IPCC, *Third Assessment Report,* 1.

80. IPCC, *Third Assessment Report,* 5.

81. IPCC, *Third Assessment Report,* 5.

82. According to Ross Gelbspan in the *Heat Is On* (p. 9), the climate skeptics are a "tiny band."

83. Houghton, *Global Warming,* 159.

84. J. D. Mahlman, "Uncertainties in Projections of Human-Caused Climate Warming," *Science,* November 1997, 51–54.

85. Mahlman, "Uncertainties in Projections of Human-Caused Climate Warming."

86. Mahlman, "Uncertainties in Projections of Human-Caused Climate Warming."

87. Mahlman, "Uncertainties in Projections of Human-Caused Climate Warming."

88. For a good discussion of who has paid for the research of the scientific skeptics, see Gelbspan, *The Heat Is On,* particularly chapter 2.

89. Gelbspan, *The Heat Is On,* 49.

90. Gelbspan, *The Heat Is On,* 49.

91. S. Fred Singer, *The Scientific Case against Global Climate Treaty* (Fairfax, Va.: The Science and Environmental Policy Project, 1997), 25–29.

92. For a discussion of the limits of models, see John Lemons, Kristen Shrader-Frechette, and Carl Cranor, "The Precautionary Principle: Scientific Uncertainty and Type I and Type II Errors," *Foundations of Science* 2 (1997): 207–36.

93. For an excellent summary of the controversy over satellite measurement of atmospheric temperatures, see William Stevens, "Global Warming: The Contrarian View," *New York Times,* February 29, 2000 (available at <www.nytimes.com/library/national/science/0229000sci-environ-climate>, March 18, 2001).

94. National Resource Council, *Reconciling Observations of Global Temperature Change.*

95. National Resource Council, *Reconciling Observations of Global Temperature Change.*

96. National Resource Council, *Reconciling Observations of Global Temperature Change,* 2.

97. Stevens, "Global Warming."

98. National Resource Council, *Reconciling Observations of Global Temperature Change,* 3.

99. John Hidore and John Oliver, *Climatology: An Atmospheric Science* (New York: Macmillan, 1993).

100. Hidore and Oliver, *Climatology.*

101. Hidore and Oliver, *Climatology.*

102. Houghton et al., "The Technical Summary," 36.

103. Houghton et al., "The Technical Summary," 35–37.

104. ExxonMobil, *New York Times,* March 23, 2000, op-ed.

105. William Stevens, "The Oceans Absorb Much of Global Warming, Study Confirms," *New York Times,* March 24, 2000, A16.

106. Stevens, "The Oceans Absorb Much of Global Warming, Study Confirms."

107. Stevens, "The Oceans Absorb Much of Global Warming, Study Confirms."

108. For an argument in support of why climate change will be good for us, see Thomas G. More, *Climate of Fear* (Washington, D.C.: Cato Institute, 1998).

Part II

ETHICAL ANALYSIS OF U.S. EXCUSES FOR LACK OF ACTION ON GLOBAL WARMING

Chapter Seven

Ethical Duty to Reduce Emissions in the Face of Scientific Uncertainty about Global Warming Consequences

In chapters 2 and 6, we saw that certain economic interests in the United States have vigorously fought against government global warming programs by charging that global warming science was too uncertain to justify programs that might turn out to be an unnecessary drag on the U.S. economy. This campaign has been so successful that many in the United States question whether climate change is a problem worth worrying about at all. More recently, President George W. Bush once again identified scientific uncertainty as a reason for backing away from the Kyoto Protocol. Yet in chapter 6 it was shown that, contrary to the understanding of many Americans, much of the science of climate change, including the basics for the conclusion that adding greenhouse gases to the atmosphere will cause some warming, is quite sound and either has never been in controversy or is not now seriously questioned. We also saw in chapter 6 that some scientific skeptics have attacked mainstream science's conclusions in regard to the following:

- The timing and magnitude of global warming and its impacts
- Whether human-induced global warming is already discernible

These attacks on the mainstream science of global warming do not challenge the notion that global warming is a dangerous threat to human health and the environment but rather are based on the unstated assumption that nothing should be done about such a serious threat until the damage that will be caused by the threat has been proven with high levels of scientific certainty.

Chapter 6 not only identified some of the climate skeptics' positions but also gave responses to the skeptics' arguments. In so doing, that chapter sought to describe why many mainstream scientists are dismissive of many of the climate skeptics' scientific arguments. However, this chapter explains why, even if one assumes that there is considerable scientific uncertainty about the timing and magnitude of human-induced climate change, the United States has a strong ethical duty to reduce its greenhouse gas emissions. First, this chapter explores the general relationship between ethics and scientific uncertainty in environmental controversies. Next, it examines the ethical basis for the strong duty of the United States to reduce its greenhouse gases, notwithstanding some uncertainty about the timing and magnitude of global warming. Finally, it examines the responsibility that the United States has to reduce greenhouse gas emissions that stems from its adoption of the "precautionary principle" in the UN Framework Convention on Climate Change.

ETHICS AND SCIENTIFIC UNCERTAINTY IN ENVIRONMENTAL CONTROVERSIES

Climate change scientists around the world have been working to determine the nature of the threat from global warming. From a proposition that a problem like global warming creates a particular threat or risk, one cannot, however, deduce whether that threat is acceptable without first deciding on certain criteria for acceptability. The criteria of acceptability must be understood as an ethical rather than a scientific question. For instance, although science may conclude that a certain increased exposure to solar radiation may increase the risk of skin cancer by one new cancer in every 100 people, science cannot say whether this additional risk is acceptable because science describes facts and cannot generate prescriptive guidance by itself. The scientific understanding of the nature of the threat is not irrelevant to the ethical question of whether the risk is ethically acceptable, but science alone cannot tell society what it should do about various threats. In environmental controversies such as global warming, where there is legitimate concern, important ethical questions arise when scientific uncertainty prevents unambiguous predictions of human health and environmental consequences.[1] This is so because decision makers cannot duck ethical questions such as how conservative scientific assumptions "should" be in the face of uncertainty or who "should" bear the burden of proof about harm. To ignore these questions is to decide to expose human health and the environment to a legitimate risk; that is, a decision to not act on a serious environmental threat has consequences. Science alone cannot tell us what assumptions or concerns should be considered in making a judgment about potentially dangerous behavior.

For this reason, environmental decisions in the face of scientific uncertainty must be understood to raise a mixture of ethical and scientific questions. Yet the scientific skeptics on global warming often speak as if it is irrational to talk about duties to reduce greenhouse gases until science is capable of proving with high levels of certainty what actual damages will be. The skeptics seem to dismiss the conclusions of the Intergovernmental Panel on Climate Change (IPCC) on the basis that they have not adequately proven that the IPCC's identified impacts will happen as described. This condemnation comes despite the fact that the IPCC claims only that their descriptions of global warming impacts are likely or very likely, that is, not proven, consequences of the continuing human release of greenhouse gases. The skeptics often attack the scientific proponents of global warming action on scientific grounds, accusing them of doing "bad" science for relying on unproven assumptions even though the IPCC's conclusions are based on its review of peer-reviewed science of global warming.[2] Yet the skeptics not only offer no proof for their alternative predictions but usually simply attack the assumptions of the mainstream scientists by offering their own unproven and non-peer-reviewed theories about the likely timing and magnitude of global warming.[3] By attacking the mainstream scientists' views of likely impacts, the skeptics are implicitly arguing that only proven "facts" should count in the debate. They do this despite the fact that climate models will probably never be able to prove with a high degree of certainty what future temperatures will actually be. This is the case because the climate models will always need to simplify a complex and chaotic climate system; rely on speculation about future population, technology, and use of fossil fuels; and make reasonable guesses about human health and environmental impacts of temperature change through the use of environmental impact science, an inherently uncertain science. Therefore, the skeptics' attack on mainstream climate science on the grounds of its use of unproven assumptions hides a controversial but unstated ethical position, namely, that governments should not act until absolute scientific proof is in. For this reason, the skeptics appear to be opposed to the use of science to describe potentially dangerous behavior. In the case of global warming, the skeptics want only proven science to count in public policy formulation about potentially catastrophic human activities. In taking this position, the skeptics are implicitly arguing that the burden of proof should be on those who may be victims of global warming to show that damages to them will actually occur. At the same time, the skeptics appear to be denying that those who are engaged in dangerous behavior have any responsibility to refrain from threatening others.

In response to the skeptics' attack on the science on which proposed global warming policy is based, the mainstream scientists often defend their position on scientific rather than ethical grounds, explaining why their view of the "facts" is scientifically respectable rather than arguing that ethics demands that plausible but unproven consequences should be considered in public policy debates. The public, watching this debate between the scientists, is often confused because the real difference between the contending parties, that is, differences about what one should do in the face of uncertainty, is hidden in scientific attack and response. Unless the contending parties' assumptions about how science should proceed in controversies where consequences are uncertain are visible to the public, an interested party cannot make sense of the debate. Environmental decision making about actions that could cause plausible but unproven serious adverse consequences, such as clearly is the case in global warming, must be understood to raise ethical issues along with scientific questions.

By attacking the science of proponents of action on global warming, economically interested parties have invited the public to focus on the wrong question from the one that ethics would have us ask. Ethics would have us ask whether there is a reasonable basis to be concerned that certain activities could damage human health and harm the environment, violate rights, or lead to injustice before the uncertainties are resolved. That is, as a matter of ethics, potentially serious but unproven harm from global warming is a relevant consideration. If one is concerned with "potential" harm, however, one needs to consider possible adverse impacts, not just those that have been proven will occur.

From the standpoint of ethics, those who engage in risky behavior are not exonerated because they did not know that their behavior would actually cause damage. Under law that implements this ethical norm, for instance, to be convicted of reckless driving or reckless endangerment, a prosecutor simply has to prove that the defendant acted in a way that he or she should have known to be risky. Many types of risky behavior are criminal because societies believe that dangerous behavior is irresponsible and should not be condoned. As a matter of ethics, a relevant question in the face of scientific uncertainty about harmful consequences of human behavior is whether there is a reasonable basis for concluding that serious harm to others could result from the behavior. In the case of global warming, as we saw in chapter 2, humans have understood the potential of humans to change the climate for over 100 years. In addition, for the past twenty years, the threat of human-induced climate change to human health and the environment has been widely discussed in the scientific literature. In fact, for more than a decade, the IPCC, a scientific body created with the strong support of the United States, a body whose function is to give advice to governments after evaluating the peer-reviewed science on climate change, has been telling the world that the great harm from global warming is not only possible but also likely. As we saw in chapter 6, by the end of the 1980s there was widespread understanding of the threat posed by rising concentrations of atmospheric greenhouse gases, more than enough to trigger an ethical duty to act. The United States cannot deny that its release of greenhouse gases creates a great risk to human health and the environment around the world, even if one disagrees with the specific predictions of the timing and magnitude of global warming impacts now being made by mainstream science. Therefore, it can be said without fear of contradiction that the United States has been engaged in risky behavior in regard to global warming and that risky behavior has ethical significance even if there is uncertainty about actual consequences.

As we saw in chapter 6, most of the skeptics' arguments have been directed to either the signal-to-noise problem or the ability of the models to predict with certainty what impacts will be caused by global warming. Yet even in the unlikely event that the skeptics turn out to be right on these issues, their arguments have no bearing on whether the United States is engaged in risky behavior. This is so because even if the skeptics are correct in pointing out that the IPCC has not proven that recent warming has been caused by human agency because it is impossible to scientifically distinguish human- from natural-caused climate change, the skeptics have not even tried to prove that recent global warming has been caused by natural variability. Furthermore, if the signal of human-caused climate change has not yet emerged from the noise of natural variability, it might do so in the near future. If the IPCC's predictions about likely global warming impacts rest on models that contain unproven assumptions, as the skeptics argue, the skeptics have not proven that impacts from increasing atmospheric concentrations of greenhouse gases will be different than those identified by the IPCC or even that the IPCC's predictions are unreasonable. In fact, explained in chapters 5 and 6, the IPCC's predictions might actually underestimate global warming impacts, particularly in light of the potential "climate surprises" discussed in chapter 5. For this reason, even if one accepts some of the arguments advanced by the skeptics, the United States is engaged in very risky behavior in failing to reduce its greenhouse gas emissions.

ETHICAL DUTY OF THE UNITED STATES TO REDUCE GREENHOUSE EMISSIONS IN FACE OF SCIENTIFIC UNCERTAINTY ABOUT CONSEQUENCES

The argument that the United States need not reduce its greenhouse gas emissions because of scientific uncertainty about the consequences of timing and magnitude does not withstand minimum ethical scrutiny because of the following:

- The enormous adverse potential impacts on human health and the environment from human-induced climate change (see chapter 5)
- The disproportionate effects on the poorest people of the world (see chapter 5)

- The real potential for potentially catastrophic climate surprises much greater than often-quoted predictions that rely on assumptions of linear responses to climate change (see chapter 5)
- The fact that much of the science of the climate change problem has never been or is not now in dispute even if one acknowledges some uncertainty about timing or magnitude (see chapter 6)
- The fact that global warming damage is probably already being experienced (see chapter 6)
- The strong likelihood that serious and irreversible damage will be experienced before all the uncertainties can be eliminated (see chapter 6)
- The fact that the longer nations wait to take action, the more difficult it will be to stabilize greenhouse gases at levels that do not create serious damage (see chapter 5)

It is inconceivable that any ethical system would condone the status quo in the United States on global warming on the basis of the excuse that we do not know for sure how bad damage will be or when it will be experienced. As we have seen in earlier chapters, concerns about the harm that will be caused by global warming are based in large part on accepted and sound principles of physics, and there are huge adverse potential consequences to others who do not have a say in the decisions of the United States. The potential consequences include increased human death and sickness, and the consequences to other forms of life on earth are potentially profound and catastrophic. It is very likely that humans are already changing the planet to the detriment of those who have no say in U.S. policy. As we have seen, the second and third IPCC reports have found strong evidence to support the conclusion that the current heating of the earth is being caused at least in part by human activities.

It may take decades to resolve some of the remaining major uncertainties in the climate models, and even then it may be too late to avoid additional damage caused by the buildup of greenhouse gases that results from inaction in the meantime. The whole world is waiting for the United States, the largest polluting nation and the nation in the best economic position to take action, to accept its global warming responsibilities. Yet almost a decade after the adoption of the UN Framework Convention on Climate Change (UNFCCC), the overall fuel economy for cars and trucks sold in the United States is at its lowest since 1980.[4] And as we saw in chapter 2, the U.S. Energy Information Administration recently predicted that greenhouse gas emissions in the United States would increase by 34 percent by 2020 rather than stabilize at 1990 levels, the goal that the United States agreed to shoot for when it ratified the UNFCCC in 1992.[5] And so, a decade after the United States agreed to stabilize greenhouse gases at 1990 levels, it has allowed its emissions to spiral upward and is expected to be as much as 45 percent higher than 1990 levels by 2020.[6]

All major ethical systems would strongly condemn behavior that is much less threatening and dangerous than global warming. This is a problem that, if not controlled, may cause the death of tens or hundreds of thousands of helpless victims in intense storms and heat waves, the death or sickness of millions who may suffer dengue fever or malaria, the destruction of some nations' ability to grow food or provide drinking water, the devastation of forests and personal property, and the accelerated elimination of countless species of plants and animals that are already stressed by other human activities. In summary, global warming threatens many of the things that humans hold to be of most value, that is, life, health, family, the ability to make a living, community, and the natural environment. Therefore, the nature of the risk from global warming is enormous, and using scientific uncertainty as an excuse for doing nothing is ethically intolerable.

The ethical norm that one should not engage in behavior that could seriously damage others without their consent is a corollary of the golden rule that one should not treat others in a manner different from the way one would like to be treated. The golden rule is the philosophical underpinning for many widely accepted international documents, such as the Universal Declaration of Human Rights, a document that has broad international support.[7] All nations strongly condemn reckless behavior of outsiders that could seriously harm the health and welfare of their citizens. This condemnation has often been made more specific in international treaties, including those dealing with nuclear waste, hazardous chemicals, and the loss of atmospheric ozone, among many others.

The fact that there is widespread cross-cultural acceptance of the idea that one should not engage in risky behavior that could cause great harm to things to which people attach great value is clear from the acceptance of the precautionary principle in a growing number of international treaties and agreements, including the Rio Declaration, the Treaties on Hazardous Substance and the Ozone Layer, and, as we will see in this chapter, the UN Convention on Climate Change.[8]

The ethical duty to avoid risky behavior is proportional to the magnitude of the potential harm. Because global warming is likely to cause death to many if not millions of people through heat stroke, vector-borne disease, and flooding; annihilate many island nations by rising seas; cause billions of dollars in property damage in intense storms; and destroy the ability of hundreds of millions to feed themselves in hotter, drier climates, the duty to refrain from activities that could cause global warming is extraordinarily strong even in the face of uncertainty about consequences.

The following discussion describes what several conventional ethical theories have to say about this duty to take action on global warming in the face of scientific uncertainty about climate change impacts. This discussion focuses on more conventional ethical theories rather than those recently developed environmentally focused ones, such as the biocentric and ecocentric theories identified in chapter 3. There is no need to examine the newer nonanthropocentric environmentally focused ethical theories because they would find an even stronger ethical duty to refrain from activities that could cause global warming.

UTILITARIANISM

The most common arguments used by vested interests in the United States to resist global warming programs are a species of a crude utilitarianism, namely, cost-benefit arguments that philosophers sometimes call "preference utilitarianism." Although proponents of cost-benefit analysis as a prescriptive tool to make environmental decisions often employ a logic that many utilitarians would reject, proponents of the use of cost-benefit analysis as a decision-making tool, including many economists, ground their ethical position on the idea that governments should select options that maximize utility.

Chapter 9 more thoroughly examines ethical problems entailed by the cost-benefit analysis arguments most often made in the United States against global warming programs. This discussion in chapter 9 will show that these cost-benefit arguments fail to withstand minimum ethical scrutiny because they usually ignore impacts to the rest of the world outside the United States. This section simply discusses how utilitarians would deal with issues of scientific uncertainty.

As pointed out in chapter 3, utilitarians assert that those actions are right or good that bring about the best end results. According to utilitarian theory, no act is good or bad in itself; its wrongness depends on the consequences of the action. Some economists argue for the use of cost-benefit analysis to calculate which alternative course of action will maximize utility. Because scientific uncertainty about the consequences of human actions creates difficulties in calculating the actual benefits that will occur, scientific uncertainty about outcomes creates problems for cost-benefit calculations particularly because it is somewhat speculative to identify the harms that will be avoided by taking action.

Because utilitarians advise that humans choose behaviors that will maximize happiness and because global warming will potentially cause death and misery for tens of millions of people around the world in present and future generations and thereby create unhappiness much greater than the costs to the

United States of moving out of fossil fuels, even in the face of scientific uncertainty about consequences, utilitarians would find the status quo in the United States ethically unacceptable.

Some utilitarians and economists urge that expected utility should be calculated in the face of uncertainty by looking at various options and weighting the potential benefits according to the probability that certain consequences will actually occur.[9] According to some utilitarians, that option that creates the greatest utility determined by a calculation that ascertains total damages by multiplying the damages by the probability that the damages will occur should be the preferred option.[10] For instance, if option A has a 50 percent probability of causing harm that if it occurs will create $1 million of damages while option B is certain to create $550,000 worth of damages, option A is the preferred option because it puts less money at risk. That is so because option A puts only $500,000 at risk (i.e., $1 million times .5), and option B puts $550,000 at risk (i.e., $550,000 times 1). Applying this approach to the global warming problem would entail determining the costs of stabilizing greenhouse gases at various levels, comparing these costs with the value of human health and environmental entities that would have been damaged if greenhouse gases were not stabilized at the identified level, and multiplying the difference by the probability that the damage would occur. This is one way that some utilitarians would deal with scientific uncertainty about global warming impacts.

Because mainstream scientists believe that the probability of harm from global warming is very high and, as we saw in chapter 6, because the damages to human health and the environment are huge, even after discounting the amount of potential damages from global warming by the probability that these damages will occur, utilitarian theory would condemn the status quo on global warming in the United States.

Many ethicists, including some utilitarians, would not condone such an ethical calculus because of its failure to allow those who may be harmed to participate in the process and consent to potential damage. Yet as we have seen, utilitarian ethical analysis is, in theory, capable of making ethical judgments about problems where consequences of human actions are uncertain. What utilitarian theory cannot easily deal with, however, is determining which probability number to assign to potential consequences when scientists disagree about what the probability is that a particular harm will occur. In these cases where there is uncertainty about harm, most ethicists would argue that utilitarian theory must be supplemented by other ethical considerations, such as due process and other procedural requirements entailed by procedural justice, that would recognize the rights of those who might be harmed to participate in and consent to decisions that might affect them.

Of course, other nations and people who might be harmed by the U.S. releases of greenhouse gases not only have not participated in U.S. policymaking on global warming but also, as we saw in chapter 2, some nations, including the small island developing states, have vehemently condemned the failure of the United States to meaningfully respond to global warming.

Yet, as we will see in chapter 9, the most obvious ethical loathsomeness of the cost-benefit analysis arguments made to thwart global warming programs in the United States follows not only from the failure of the cost-benefit analyses to consider the views of those who will be harmed by global warming; it also follows from the failure of U.S. cost-benefit analyses on global warming to consider any harm and damage to those outside the United States. This narrow focus on cost and benefits to the United States alone is shown in chapter 9 to be ethically inexcusable.

RIGHTS AND DUTIES THEORIES

As we saw in chapter 3, mainstream rights and duties theories, often classified as deontological ethical theories, require that humans act only in those ways that treat humans as if they have inherent dignity. According to these theories, people should always be treated as ends with certain rights and never as means. For this reason, rights and duties theories condemn risky behavior that could seriously harm others without their consent. Uncertainty about consequences is irrelevant to these theories because actions of individuals can be wrong without knowing their consequences. Therefore, according to rights and duties theories, the question of the moral acceptability of U.S. greenhouse gas emissions does not turn on the probability that harm will occur but rather on whether one is engaged in behavior that one has a duty to avoid. Because individuals have a duty to refrain from reckless behavior, the United States has recognized rights "to a healthy and productive life in harmony with nature,"[11] and because global warming will likely diminish the human health and productivity of millions, U.S. activities that cause global warming violate deontological ethical principles.

According to rights and duties theories, one must not engage in actions that could harm others without their consent. For this reason, rights and duties ethical theories condemn risky behavior, particularly when that behavior could kill or greatly diminish others' quality of life. Therefore, a defense of the status quo on greenhouse gas emissions in the United States on the basis of uncertainty about actual consequences is ethically unacceptable according to mainstream rights and duties ethical theories. This is particularly true because of the very real potential of global warming to kill hundreds of thousands of human beings and to greatly diminish the quality of life for tens, if not hundreds, of millions of living people and future generations.

In thinking about how to consider the uncertain consequences of problems like global warming, some ethicists, following deontological theories, have argued that humans have a duty to be guided by a "heuristic of fear" in predicting consequences.[12] That is, humans should give preference to the bad over the good predictions. Particularly where there are possible serious irreversible consequences from human actions and where the stakes are high, decision makers should give more weight to prognoses of doom rather than of bliss. The philosophical reason for this duty to give more weight to the prediction of harm is premised on the notion that present generations do not have a right to gamble with the interests of other generations or to act so that life on earth is jeopardized.[13] For this reason, in the face of uncertainty about global warming consequences, the United States should consider potential "worst-case" scenarios of global warming impacts when making policy. Yet throughout global warming policymaking in the United States, whether in the calculation of costs and benefits to the United States considered in chapter 9 or in the description of likely global warming impacts to the world discussed in chapter 5, the United States has not assumed worst-case consequences. In fact, the United States has not even accepted the IPCC's projections that are based on the smooth responses of the climate system assumed by the climate models, not to mention the possibility of climate surprises discussed in chapter 5.

THEORIES OF JUSTICE

As we saw in chapter 3, theories of justice are particularly relevant to the global warming problem because they provide guidance on how benefits and burdens of climate change should be distributed throughout society. Because, as we saw in chapter 5, some of the poorest nations have much more to lose than the United States, the poorer nations shoulder a much greater burden of risk than the United States. At the same time, as we will see in chapter 9, the benefits and costs that have been considered in supporting U.S. global warming policy are those that accrue to the United States alone. For this reason, the U.S. approach to global warming in regard to a fair and equitable sharing of the burdens and benefits has been unjust.

As we also saw in chapter 3, theories of justice are particularly relevant also to the international climate change debate because they call for fair procedural rules that allow for all potentially affected people to participate in decision making that may affect their interests. Because the United States has not invited other nations to participate in domestic decisions relating to the degree of risk about uncertain consequences of global warming that is acceptable before reducing greenhouse gas emissions, the maintenance of the status quo by the United States in the face of potentially serious damage to others around the world must be seen as procedurally unjust. Therefore, if the United States uses scientific uncertainty as a basis for doing nothing while failing to get consent from the rest of the world on its use of the uncertainty excuse, it is ethically problematic as a matter of procedural justice.

PRECAUTIONARY PRINCIPLE

If there is any doubt about the ethical duty for the United States to reduce its emissions of greenhouse gases, notwithstanding some scientific uncertainty about the timing and magnitude of climate change, one need only examine the UNFCCC that has been ratified by the U.S. Congress. The UNFCC contains the precautionary principle that has been adopted in other treaties to deal with dangerous behavior. As we have seen, Article 3 of the UNFCCC states in relevant part,

> The Parties should take precautionary measures to anticipate, prevent or minimize the causes of climate change and mitigate its adverse effects. Where there are threats of serious or irreversible damage, lack of full scientific certainty should not be used as a reason for postponing such measures, taking into account that policies and measures to deal with climate change should be cost-effective so as to ensure global benefits at the lowest possible cost.[14]

Therefore, the United States already has a legal duty under the UNFCC to apply the precautionary principle to climate change problems notwithstanding the position taken by many economic interests in the United States that action should not now be taken because of issues of scientific uncertainty.

The precautionary principle is based on the rather uncontroversial ethical norm discussed previously that persons should not engage in risky acts that could cause serious and irreversible harm to others even if there is some uncertainty about which consequences will actually occur. Many societal decisions follow the precautionary principle without controversy. For instance, we have some scientific doubts about whether the so-called mad cow disease can be transmitted to human beings. Yet great effort is expended to ensure that people do not eat meat that could cause mad cow disease. The precautionary principle simply implements the saying, "Better safe than sorry." Because Congress has ratified the UNFCCC that contains the precautionary principle, those climate skeptics who are urging no serious U.S. action to reduce greenhouse gas emissions until the scientific uncertainties about the timing and magnitude of global warming are resolved are encouraging the United States to act in violation of its international legal commitments that have been based on well-grounded ethical considerations. Because the United States has already consented to be bound by the precautionary principle in relation to global warming science, the failure to apply the precautionary principle to global warming will also violate the ethical norm that a nation should keep its promises. As we saw in chapter 2, the United States, in negotiating the UNFCCC, got a lot of what it wanted because it promised to live up to other things that nations cared about. It is therefore a major breach of trust for the United States to disavow the precautionary principle at this late stage of international negotiations.

CONCLUSION

For these reasons, the continued use of scientific uncertainty by the United States as an excuse for not taking serious action to reduce greenhouse gases does not withstand minimum ethical scrutiny. Continuing to use the excuse of scientific uncertainty, given the fact that it probably is already too late to prevent global warming from taking place and for carbon dioxide to rise to twice the preindustrial levels of 550 parts per million, is ethically inexcusable. Much less risky behavior by a nation would appropriately receive international condemnation.

NOTES

1. For a general discussion of the relationship of science to ethics in environmental decision making, see John Lemons and Donald Brown, "The Role of Science in Sustainable Development and Environmental Decisionmaking," in John Lemons and Donald Brown, eds., *Sustainable Development: Science, Ethics, and Public Policy* (Dordrecht: Kluwer Academic Publishers, 1995), 11–35.

2. Sebastian Oberthur and Herman Ott, *The Kyoto Protocol: International Climate Policy for the 21st Century* (Berlin: Springer Publishing, 1999), 10.

3. Oberthur and Ott, *The Kyoto Protocol*, 10.

4. Keith Bradsher, "Fuel Economy for New Cars Is at Lowest Level since '80," *New York Times*, May 18, 2001, A15.

5. United States Energy Information Administration, *Annual Energy Outlook 2001 with Projections to 2020*. Report No. DOE/EIA-0383(2001), December 22, 2000.

6. See the discussion of this in chapter 2.

7. United Nations, *Universal Declaration of Human Rights*, G.A. Resolution 217A (III), UN Document A/810, at 71, December 10, 1948, adopted by the General Assembly of the United Nations (without dissent).

8. United Nations, *Rio Declaration on Environment and Development*, June 14, 1992, 31 ILM 874; United Nations, *Protocol on Substances That Deplete the Ozone Layer,* September 16, 1987, 26 ILM 1541; Bamako Convention on Hazardous Wastes within Africa, January 30, 1991, 30 ILM 773.

9. For a discussion of utilitarian approaches to scientific uncertainty in environmental decision making, see R. Kerry Turner, David Pierce, and Ian Bateman, *Environmental Economics: An Elementary Introduction* (Baltimore: The Johns Hopkins University Press, 1993). See also Kristen Shrader-Frechette, "Methodological Rules for Four Classes of Scientific Uncertainty," in John Lemons, ed., *Scientific Uncertainty and Environmental Problem Solving* (Cambridge, Mass.: Blackwell Scientific Press, 1996), 12–39.

10. See Turner et al., *Environmental Economics,* and Shrader-Frechette, "Methodological Rules for Four Classes of Scientific Uncertainty," 12–39.

11. United Nations, *The Rio Declaration on Environment and Development,* Sales No. E.73.II.A.14 and corrigendum\chap. I, 1992.

12. For a discussion of why in some circumstances decision makers should consider the worst potential consequences in dealing with serious actions in the face of uncertainty, see Hans Jonas, *The Imperative of Responsibility* (Chicago: University of Chicago Press, 1984).

13. Jonas, *The Imperative of Responsibility.*

14. *United Nations Framework Convention on Climate Change,* UN Document A/CONF.151/26, reprinted at 31 ILM 849, Article 3, 1992.

Chapter Eight

U.S. Obligations to Act Even if the Developing World Does Not

Another common, strongly expressed objection to U.S. action on global warming is the argument that the United States should not take action until the developing world agrees to reduce greenhouse gas emissions. This argument rests on the fact that the United States cannot solve the climate change problem by itself and that the developing world continues to grow as a larger percentage of total world emissions. If the United States acts and the developing world does not, so goes this argument, climate change will still happen, and U.S. industry will put itself in an uncompetitive position versus the rest of the world (see fig. 8.1).

Figure 8.1   2020 projected carbon emissions

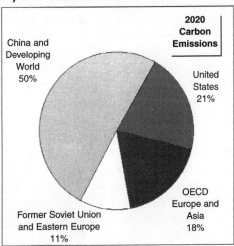

Note: Emissions measured from China and Developing World, United States, OECD countries in Asia and Europe, and countries that were part of former Soviet Union or Eastern Europe.
Source: United States Environmental Protection Agency.

This concern about developing world participation has been a major basis for opposition to climate change commitments by the United States for the past few years. As we saw in chapter 2, because of this alarm about the lack of developing world participation, there has been very strong opposition to the Kyoto Protocol in the United States. As we also saw in chapter 2, U.S. Senators Byrd and Hagel, along with sixty-four cosponsors, introduced a Senate resolution relating to the then-upcoming Kyoto negotiations that passed the Senate by a vote of 95 to 0 on July 25, 1997. This resolution expressed the sense of the Senate that the United States should not be a signatory to any agreement in Kyoto "unless the protocol or other agreement also mandated new specific scheduled commitments to limit or reduce greenhouse gas emissions for developing country parties within the same compliance period."[1]

As the United States prepared for Kyoto, an industry coalition of oil companies, electric utilities, automobile manufacturers, and farm groups launched a multi-million-dollar advertising campaign to generate public opposition to a Kyoto treaty. This campaign asserted that devastating impacts on the U.S. economy would result from a Kyoto treaty that would limit U.S. emissions without obtaining any firm developing-world commitments. One of the television advertisements paid for by the campaign showed someone using scissors to cut developing countries from a world map while the announcer warned that the Kyoto treaty would be economically disastrous because these countries had been exempted from the treaty's obligations. Since 1997, economic interests in the United States have continued to attack the Kyoto agreement on the grounds that it would be disastrous to the U.S. economy to accept a treaty that exempted the developing nations.

Despite strong opposition from economic interests and the U.S. Congress to any agreement that did not require developing nations to cut emissions, in Kyoto the Clinton administration agreed to a 7 percent reduction in greenhouse gas emissions between 2008 and 2012. Yet because of pressure from Congress, the Clinton administration announced that it would not seek Senate ratification of the Kyoto Protocol until it obtained developing-world commitments on global warming. After Kyoto, the Clinton administration attempted to obtain these developing-world commitments while Congress let it be known that it would not fund any U.S. greenhouse gas reduction programs on the basis that such programs would amount to backdoor ratification of Kyoto.

Although the Clinton administration demanded developing-world commitments, it did not articulate what type of developing-world reduction commitments it would seek. The administration also appeared to accept some responsibility of the United States to reduce its emissions to an equitable level.[2] For instance, on October 22, President Clinton, in a major speech on climate change, acknowledged that "the United States has a special responsibility for the problem: The United States has less than 5 percent of the world's population, enjoys 22 percent of the world's wealth, but emits more than 25 percent of the world's greenhouse gases."[3]

In a variety of other settings, the Clinton administration made it clear that the United States, in calling for developing-world commitments to reduce emissions, was not taking the position that the developed and the developing world had an equal responsibility to reduce emissions or that the United States would require the developing world to take action on climate change that would interfere with their ability to continue with economic development.[4] In fact, the Clinton administration sometimes acted as if it would accept almost any commitment from the developing world to limit greenhouse gas emissions before approaching the Senate for ratification of Kyoto. Yet the administration stuck to its position that the developing world would have to agree to reduce emissions while it never proposed limiting U.S. greenhouse gas emissions in a way that was based on an equitable share of safe total global emissions. The administration simply admitted that the developed world had a greater responsibility than the developing world to reduce its emissions while requesting that the developing world make commitments to reduce emissions. Thus, the Clinton administration was vague about the nature of the developed world's greater responsibility for greenhouse gas reductions, seeming to want to keep its negotiating options open.

When the United States negotiated its 7 percent reduction target in Kyoto, the negotiations focused on what was affordable to the United States, not on what the obligations of the United States were in relation to developing-world responsibilities. And so the Clinton administration's view of what was the developing world's responsibility to reduce emissions was mostly a matter of conjecture. All that can be said for sure is that the administration took the position that the developing world must make legally binding commitments to reduce greenhouse gas emissions. If a developing nation would have made a proposal that would allow it to expand rather than reduce its emissions, it is not clear how the Clinton administration would have reacted. Yet, as we will see, as a matter of equity a strong case could be made that some developing nations should be able to increase emissions as the United States and other developed nations reduce theirs.

Despite the fact that the Clinton administration made several gestures in the direction of ultimately accepting some version of an equitably based share in a global greenhouse gas target, the majority in Congress have consistently opposed greenhouse gas targets based on equitable considerations. Because the Senate alone has the power to ratify any climate change treaty protocol by a two-thirds majority, the official U.S. position has been seen as that articulated in the Hagel–Byrd resolution, namely, the United States demands that the developing nations make "new specific scheduled commitments to limit or reduce greenhouse gas emissions."[5] Therefore, it would appear that the majority in Congress desired to make U.S. agreements on global warming contingent on the poorest nations actually committing to reduce emissions. As we will see, the U.S. demand that developing nations limit their greenhouse gas emissions as a precondition to any U.S. commitment is ethically troublesome.

Recently, the George W. Bush administration announced that it would repudiate Kyoto for several reasons, including the failure of the Kyoto agreement to require the developing world to make commitments to reduce greenhouse gas emissions. The Bush administration appears to be willing to stake out a position that demands the developing world to commit to reduce its emissions before the United States will bind itself to reductions in greenhouse gas emissions.

This chapter reviews the ethical problems entailed by the continuing insistence by the United States on developing-world commitments as a precondition for U.S. commitments on reductions in greenhouse gas emissions. Chapter 11 examines what equity demands of the United States in the nature of specific commitments.

ETHICAL PROBLEMS ENTAILED BY THE U.S. INSISTENCE THAT THE DEVELOPING WORLD MAKE COMMITMENTS TO REDUCE GREENHOUSE GAS EMISSIONS

As we saw in chapter 3, distributive justice is concerned with a fair distribution of society's benefits and burdens. Notwithstanding the position of Congress that the United States should not make commitments to reduce its greenhouse gas emissions unless the developing world commits to reduce theirs, justice demands that the United States accept a fair share of the burdens of reducing global carbon emissions to a safe level. Yet the United States emits a disproportionate share of greenhouse gases with 4.6 percent of the world's population and 23 percent of the carbon emissions (see table 8.1).

In the twentieth century, the United States has been by far the largest emitter of greenhouse gases in terms of both total pounds of carbon and per capita carbon emissions. Table 8.2 identifies total carbon emissions and per capita emissions for 1996 for the ten largest and smallest emitters of greenhouse gases. It can be seen that the United States has been by far the largest national emitter of greenhouse gases in respect to total pounds emitted even though it contains less than 5 percent of the global population. The United States also by far exceeds all advanced nations in per capita emissions of greenhouse gases and in many

Table 8.1 **United States' share of population and carbon emissions, 1997**

	1997 population (millions)	Percent of total
United States	268	4.6
World	5,868	95.4

	Carbon (Millions of Metric Tons)	Percent of total
United States	1,480	23
World	6,175	77

Source: U.S. Energy Information Agency.

Table 8.2 **Top and bottom ten emitters of carbon, 1996**

Rank	Country	Thousands of tons of carbon	Per capita tons
1	United States	1,446,777	5.37
2	China (Mainland)	917,997	0.76
3	Russian Federation	431,090	2.91
4	Japan	318,686	2.54
5	India	272,212	0.29
6	Germany	235,050	2.87
7	United Kingdom	152,015	2.59
8	Canada	111,723	3.76
9	Republic of Korea	111,370	2.46
10	Italy (including San Marino)	110,052	1.92
201	British Virgin Islands	16	0.84
202	Comoros	15	0.02
203	Falkland Islands (Malvinas)	12	6.03
204	Montserrat	11	0.99
205	Cook Island	6	0.31
206	Kiribati	6	0.07
207	Antarctic Fisheries	5	5.02
208	Somalia	4	0.00
209	Saint Helena	2	0.28
210	Niue	1	0.42

Source: U.S. Energy Information Agency

cases exceeds per capita emissions of many of the developing-world nations by a factor of 10, 20, and sometimes 30. North American per capita emissions has averaged between 4.5 to 6.0 tons of carbon per person, while per capita emissions in most of East Asia and Latin America has averaged 0.5. to 1.0 tons of carbon.[6] At the bottom end, per capita emissions of the Indo-Pakistan subcontinent and in much of Africa rarely exceed 0.3 tons per person.[7] The U.S. demand for commitments to emissions reductions from these developing nations, given the enormous disparity in per capita emissions between the United States and most of the rest of the world, has been judged harshly around the world.

The United States is also responsible for the largest share of historical and cumulative greenhouse gas emissions (see fig. 8.2). The developed countries, including the United States, have contributed ten times more than the developing nations to the recent buildup of greenhouse gases in the atmosphere.[8] In fact, the developed nations have contributed 84 percent of the greenhouse gas emissions from 1800 to the present.[9] Therefore, the United States is the largest both current and cumulative emitter of greenhouse gases. For this reason, status quo emission levels in the United States must be understood to already represent an inequitable use of the global commons. That is, it already can be said that the U.S. share of current emissions is inequitable because it is known that total emissions must be reduced and the U.S. share of the total is not fair given its historical and current levels of emissions compared to the rest of the world. As we will see in chapter 11, because distributive justice demands that the burdens of reducing a problem either be shared equally or be based on merit or deservedness, there is no conceivable equitably based formula that would allow the United States to continue to emit at existing levels

Figure 8.2 Cumulative carbon emissions, 1950–1996

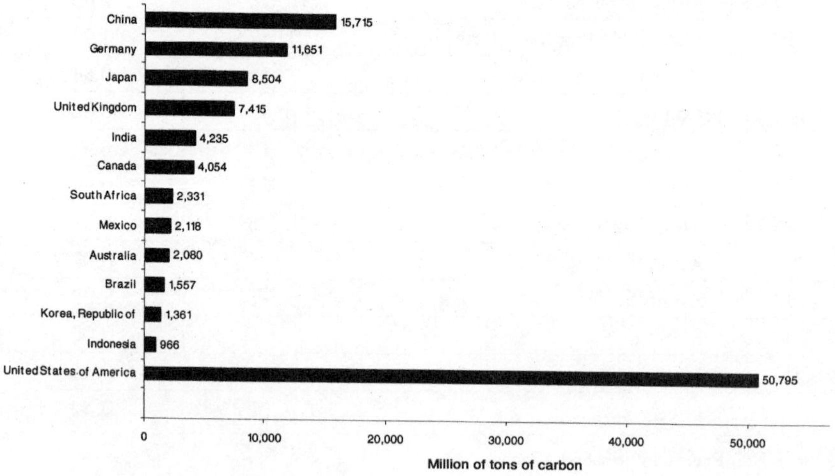

	Million of tons of carbon
China	15,715
Germany	11,651
Japan	8,504
United Kingdom	7,415
India	4,235
Canada	4,054
South Africa	2,331
Mexico	2,118
Australia	2,080
Brazil	1,557
Korea, Republic of	1,361
Indonesia	966
United States of America	50,795

Source: U.S. Energy Information Administration.

once it is understood that reductions are called for. The same cannot be said with as much certainty for almost all developing countries.

Whether the developing world will need to reduce its greenhouse gas emissions from current levels will depend on the amount of worldwide reductions that are necessary and how this total is equitably apportioned among nations. It may be that many developing nations may eventually need to reduce emissions from current levels because of the immense amount of reductions that will be necessary to get global warming under control. As we saw in chapter 5, large reductions from current greenhouse gas emission levels will be necessary because the greenhouse gases of greatest concern remain in the atmosphere for a long time (decades to centuries for most greenhouse gases). Hence, a mere slowing down of greenhouse gas emissions without dramatic reductions will continue to cause increases in atmospheric levels. How much reduction will actually be required to stabilize greenhouse gases in the atmosphere at safe levels will depend on what atmospheric target is chosen for a stabilization level and how much atmospheric levels have risen from the present at the time the atmospheric targets is agreed to. In 1990, for instance, the IPCC said that to stabilize atmospheric greenhouse gases at safe levels, the world would have to reduce 1990 levels by 60 percent.

Nevertheless, what amount developing countries will need to reduce current emissions cannot be determined without prior decisions about acceptable worldwide emissions totals and equitable allocation among nations of the allowable total world emissions. However, because it is known that some reductions from existing levels are necessary and because the United States already has the greatest share of existing and historical emissions, it can be said without fear of contradiction that the United States and other developed nations will need to reduce emissions.

Hypothetically, even if the science turns out to be wrong about the magnitude of reduction necessary to stabilize greenhouse gases at safe levels and the world could maintain current emissions, the developed world will have to reduce its greenhouse gases to ensure that each nation has an equitable share of the total. That is, because some nations more than others have caused the current rise of carbon dioxide to almost 370 parts per million, coupled with the fact, as can be seen in table 8.2, that some nations are currently emitting vastly different amounts of greenhouse gases per capita, a just international allocation of a global target will require some nations, including the United States, to cut back from their current use of the global atmosphere as a carbon sink. This is so because distributive justice requires a fair sharing of burdens based on either equality, merit, or deservedness. Not only would an allocation that reduces the developed nations' share be required by distributive justice principles, but if the poorest nations are not allowed to increase their share of greenhouse gas emissions, they likely will be trapped in grinding poverty for as long as fossil fuels are less expensive than alternatives.

Even if total world greenhouse gas emissions could remain safely at current levels, an assumption strongly disputed by mainstream science, one part of the world must be able to grow and the other part shrink to implement an equitable result. As one observer comments,

> The overall total of greenhouse gases must cease growing while there is a continued growth in one part of the total, the part generated by the poor. Arithmetically, this can be accomplished only if the other part, the part generated by the rich, shrinks. In other words, even if the scientific consensus were wrong and the total overall did not need to shrink, but only needed to be held constant, the contribution to the total by the rich would have to shrink by at least as much as the amount by which emissions by those rising out of poverty increase.[10]

In other words, it can be said with certainty that no matter what one's assumption about the amount of current emission levels that need to be reduced, the developed world will need to reduce its current emission levels. Yet the distribution of developing-world reductions necessary to achieve safe atmospheric levels can be determined only after other decisions are made about a global stabilization target and an equitable allocation of the target.

In summary, because the Untied States is the largest greenhouse gas emitter in terms of both total pounds and per capita and because current worldwide emissions already greatly exceed the ability of the atmosphere to absorb greenhouse gases at safe levels, the current emissions levels of the United States can be seen as an unjust use of the global commons. The same cannot be said for other nations with very low emission levels. For this reason, the calls of the United States for developing-world commitments to reduce greenhouse gas emissions as a precondition for U.S. reductions is obviously problematic as a matter of distributive justice.

Those in the United States who are calling for the developing world to make commitments to reduce greenhouse gas emissions levels appear to be asking poor nations to "settle for levels of emissions per capita far below the current levels of the rich nations."[11] That is, they are calling for the poorer nations to limit certain types of economic activity at levels well below what the United States has relied on to become wealthy. Particularly because many of these nations are fighting grinding poverty, the poor nations see this U.S. demand for them to make commitments to greenhouse gas reductions at levels well below the United States emissions as arrogantly unjust.

As we will see in chapter 11, in response to the U.S. request for developing-world commitments, some in the poorer nations have been calling for the developed world to agree to allocate global greenhouse gas quotas on a per capita basis.[12] This call is based on the notion that every human being has an equal right to use the absorptive capacity of the global commons.[13] The position of

Figure 8.3 The rich nations sharing our planet

Reprinted with the permission of the Centre for Science and the Environment, New Delhi, India, Rustam Vania/CSE.

much of the developing world therefore is not, as commonly understood in the United States, that the developing nations refuse to contribute to a solution to global warming but rather that they want a fair approach to sharing the burdens of reducing the great threats entailed by human-induced climate change. As we will see in chapter 11, the issue of what constitutes an equitable share of each nation's right to use the atmosphere as a sink to absorb greenhouse gases is perhaps the most important ethical question entailed by global warming that the United States needs to face in the future. It is an issue that we will consider in some detail in chapter 11. As a matter of distributive justice, it is particularly disturbing for the United States to argue that it should not have to cut back on its emissions of greenhouse gases until the developing world agrees to cut back.

U.S. LEGAL OBLIGATIONS TO REDUCE GREENHOUSE GAS EMISSIONS BEFORE THE DEVELOPING WORLD

In addition to the ethical duty of the United States to reduce its greenhouse gas emissions immediately, the United States has a binding legal duty under the UNFCCC to take the lead on emissions reductions, which it is ignoring. As we have seen before, under the UNFCCC, the United States expressly agreed that

the Parties should protect the climate system for the benefit of present and future generations of humankind, on the basis of *equity* and in accordance with their *common but differentiated responsibilities* and respective capabilities. Accordingly, the *developed country Parties should take the lead* in combating climate change and the adverse effects thereof.[14] (italics added)

Because the United States has already agreed in the UNFCCC both that it has a duty to reduce its greenhouse gas emissions to an equitable level and that, as one of the developed-country parties, it should take the lead in combating climate change, the U.S. calls for developing-world reduction commitments have been seen by the developing world as a repudiation of the legal obligations of the United States. Along this line, the U.S. congressmen who have called for the United States to condition any U.S. promise to reduce greenhouse gas emissions on commitments by the developing world are acting inconsistently with a treaty that was ratified by a two-thirds majority of the Senate. These congressmen are therefore acting in blatant disregard of existing U.S. law and promises made by the United States to the international community.

The United States has not only agreed in the UNFCCC that it should reduce its global warming emissions on the basis of equity, as we saw in chapter 4; it has also agreed to certain principles that help interpret what equity demands of a nation that emits pollution that harms other nations. For instance, in the 1992 Rio Declaration, the United States agreed that "States have . . . the responsibility to ensure that activities within their own jurisdiction of control do not cause damage to the environment of other States or areas beyond the limits of national jurisdiction."[15] This principle must be understood as establishing the responsibility of the United States to reduce its pollution loading to levels that will not cause harm to other nations.

Also in the Rio Declaration, the United States agreed that whoever causes a pollution problem should be responsible for paying for the problem. This notion is encapsulated in the "polluter-pays" principle. More specifically, this principle states, "National authorities should endeavor to promote the internalization of environmental costs and the use of economic instruments, *taking into account the approach that the polluter should, in principle, bear the cost of pollution,* with due regard to the public interest and without distorting international trade and investment"[16] (italics added).

Thus, the United States has agreed in principle that nations that cause pollution problems for other nations should shoulder the burden of eliminating the pollution and paying for the damages of the pollution. Under the polluter-pays principle, the United States should eliminate that portion of greenhouse gas pollution that comes from the United States.

CONCLUSION

This chapter has demonstrated that the United States has both an equitable and a legal duty to reduce its emissions of greenhouse gases. Because the United States has also agreed in various international agreements to take the lead in reducing its emissions before the developing world must act and to take responsibility for its share of the pollution problem, the U.S. demand that the developing world commit to reduce its emissions is also a violation of its ethical responsibility to keep promises made in international agreements. The U.S. call for the developing world to commit to reduce its emissions when the United States is so clearly exceeding its fair share of use of the global commons is seen by many in the developing world as an extraordinarily arrogant act on the part of the world's only true superpower. As we will see in chapter 11, the unwillingness of the United States to reduce its greenhouse gas emissions to an equitable share of total global emissions is at the heart of many impasses in global climate change negotiations.

NOTES

1. S.R. 98, 105th Cong., 1st sess. (July 22, 1997); 143 *Congressional Record,* S8117, daily ed. (July 25, 1997).
2. For a good discussion of the Clinton administration's position on the type of commitments it has been seeking from the developing world, see Paul Harris, "Sharing the Costs of Climate Change: An Assessment of American Foreign Policy," *Cambridge Review of International Affairs* 12, no. 2 (1999): 289–310.
3. Joy Warick and Peter Baker, "Clinton Details Global Warming Plan," *Washington Post,* October 23, 1997, A6.
4. See Harris, "Sharing the Costs of Climate Change."
5. G. Marland and G. T. Boden, *National Carbon Emissions for 1996,* U.S. Energy Information Agency (available at <www.cdiac.esd.ornl.gov/trends/emis/top96.tot>, March 21, 2001).
6. K. Banuri, K. Goran-Maler, M. Grubb, H. K. Jacobson, and F. Yamin, "Equity and Social Considerations," in James Bruce, Hoesung Lee, and Eric Haites, eds., *Economic and Social Dimensions of Climate Change: Contribution of Working Group III to the Second Assessment Report of the Intergovernmental Panel on Climate Change* (New York: Cambridge University Press, 1996), 94.
7. Banuri et al., eds., "Equity and Social Considerations" 94.
8. Banuri et al., eds., "Equity and Social Considerations," 94.

9. Banuri et al., eds., "Equity and Social Considerations," 94.

10. Henry Shue, "After You: May Action by the Rich Be Contingent upon Action by the Poor?" *Indiana University School of Law–Bloomington Law Journal* 2 (available at <www.law.indiana.edu/glsj/vol11/shue.html>, March 21, 2001).

11. Shue, "After You," 2.

12. "Equity First," *Down to Earth* (available at <www.oneworld.org/cse/html/dte/dte20000815/dte_news.htm>, December 15, 2000).

13. "Equity First."

14. United Nations Framework Convention on Climate Change (UNFCCC), New York, May 9, 1992, UN Document6 A/CONF.151/26, Article 3.

15. United Nations, *Rio Declaration on Environment and Development,* UN Document A/CONF.151/5, June 16, 1992, Principle 2.

16. United Nations, *Rio Declaration on Environment and Development,* Principle 16.

Chapter Nine

Ethical Issues Entailed by the Use of Cost-Benefit Analysis–Based Arguments Made in Opposition to U.S. Greenhouse Gas Reduction Programs

A third common argument made by those opposing government action on climate change in the United States is that the costs of U.S. climate change programs outweigh the benefits of these programs. Cost-benefit analysis (CBA) is a generic term for a variety of techniques designed to allow decision makers to determine in a rigorous way whether the payback from a program will be greater than the costs of implementing it. If the costs of an environmental program are greater than environmental benefits produced by a program, according to mainstream CBA theory, the program should be abandoned. The economic justification for this use of CBA is the notion that society must decide how to spend its scarce resources and should spend its money in the most efficient way possible. If money is spent by society on environmental protection programs that do not produce an environmental payback that is greater in economic value than the cost of the program, it is a bad investment and should not be supported.[1] This is so, according to CBA theory, because public money should be spent on programs that will produce the largest aggregate benefits.

Although CBA may be a very valuable tool for decision makers who are trying to decide whether investment in a particular project will provide an adequate payoff compared to other projects, as we will see, its use in environmental decision making is often ethically dubious, particularly when it is applied to such ethically loaded problems as global warming. Yet economic interests and some economists continue to demand that the United States use CBA to determine whether global warming programs should be implemented. Although some economists recognize the ethical limitations of CBA that will be discussed in this chapter, recent CBA-based arguments made in opposition to U.S. global warming programs ignore the ethical limits of CBA that have been identified by ethicists and acknowledged by some economists. In addition, economic interests that oppose global warming programs in the United States often use the rhetoric of CBA without disclosing its many widely recognized ethical limitations. In this way, they hide the ethical dimensions of analyses that appear on their surface to be only a discussion of economic facts.

As we saw in chapter 2, for the past fifteen years vested interests and certain members of the U.S. Congress have resisted climate change programs on the basis that they would create havoc in the U.S. economy. Sometimes these arguments have been directly couched in cost-benefit language; sometimes arguments are made against global warming programs that have implicitly used CBA-like logic when they assert that the costs to the United States are too high to justify action.

As early as 1988, some nations wanted to take internationally coordinated action to reduce the threat of global warming, but the Reagan and the first Bush administrations resisted because they were worried about the effect such action could have on the U.S. domestic economy.[2] In the late 1980s and early 1990s, the U.S. government acted as if harm to the U.S. domestic economy, if the global warming theory proved to be false, was of much greater concern than damage to the atmosphere that could be avoided by early action if the global warming concerns proved to be scientifically sound. The positions adopted by the Reagan and the first Bush administrations in international negotiations were remarkably similar to the concerns being expressed by the fossil fuel industry that at that time were strongly lobbying the U.S. government about its concerns of costs.

As we saw in chapter 2, during the Clinton administration fossil fuel interests and some members of Congress continued to fight against global warming initiatives on the basis that costs of global warming programs were too high. For instance, opponents of Kyoto asserted that the 7 percent carbon reduction target agreed to by the United States would wreak havoc on the American economy and challenged the Clinton administration on its identification of costs for achieving the Kyoto reduction.

In response to this cost-based opposition to Kyoto, U.S. officials often argued that climate change programs could be implemented at acceptable levels of cost. For instance, to defend itself against charges that climate programs needed to implement the Kyoto Protocol under the UN Framework Convention on Climate Change (UNFCCC) were too costly, the Clinton administration prepared a CBA in July 1998 that showed that costs to the United States of complying with Kyoto would not be great.[3] More specifically, the administration concluded that compliance with Kyoto would cost the United States the following:

- $7 to $12 billion per year or 0.1% of gross domestic product (GDP)
- 4 to 6 cents per gallon of gasoline
- An increase of $14 to $23 in energy costs per household[4]

The Clinton administration's analysis concluded that these costs were justified because damages from a doubling of preindustrial concentrations of greenhouse gases would cost the U.S. economy about 1.1 percent of GDP per year, or $8.9 billion per year.[5] In so doing, the Clinton administration seemed to acknowledge the validity of the vested interests' basic argument that U.S. domestic action should be limited to actions justifiable by CBA. That is, at no time did the Clinton administration assert that the logic of CBA that supported the position of the opponents to Kyoto was ethically problematic; the administration simply asserted that the CBA calculations of those who opposed Kyoto were overly pessimistic.

In making its assessment of the costs of Kyoto, the Clinton administration relied heavily on the broad use of Kyoto's carbon-trading mechanisms that will be discussed in the next chapter. That is, the administration assumed that the United States could achieve most of its Kyoto reductions by financing projects outside the United States and obtaining credit for these projects against the 7 percent reduction target of the United States.[6]

In response to the Clinton CBA, opponents of Kyoto argued that the Clinton administration's analysis understated the costs to the U.S. economy. The fossil fuel industry and others continued to oppose ratification of the Kyoto Protocol on the basis, among others, that the costs of U.S. compliance would exceed benefits. Also, Congress continued to oppose ratification of the Kyoto Protocol, in part, on the argument that costs to the United States would outweigh the benefits of taking action. In making this argument, Congress adopted the fossil fuel industries' view of costs.

As we also saw in chapter 2, soon after coming to office the George W. Bush administration announced that it would not regulate carbon dioxide while repudiating the Kyoto Protocol on the grounds that the costs to the U.S. economy were too high. In fact, President Bush, in defense of his rejection of the Kyoto Protocol, stated that he would take no action on climate change that would harm the U.S. economy.[7]

It can be seen that a common excuse for not taking meaningful steps to reduce greenhouse gas emissions used by most American presidents or members of Congress for the past twenty years is that the costs of reduction programs to the United States are not justified by the benefits of greenhouse gas emissions reductions.

ETHICAL PROBLEMS WITH RECENT U.S. CBAS IN GLOBAL WARMING DECISION MAKING

As we will see in this chapter, there are a number of ethical problems with the use of CBA-based arguments to thwart global warming programs in the United States. In addition to these more general ethical concerns, there is one overriding reason why recent uses of CBA-based arguments in opposition to U.S. global warming programs are ethically bankrupt: They have made the comparison of costs and benefits to the United States alone the criteria for whether the United States should take action. Although CBAs have been prepared that look at worldwide costs and benefits of global warming, the debate in the United States has almost exclusively been about domestic costs and benefits. For this reason, strong opposition to serious carbon mitigation strategies has been centered almost exclusively on the effects of such strategies on the United States.[8] Such a use of CBA arguments ignores the obligations that the United States has to people outside the United States to prevent harm to human health and the environment in their countries.

As we saw previously, when the Clinton administration was attacked with the charge that the Kyoto Protocol's cost in the United State was too expensive compared to the benefits of programs in the United States, it simply developed an alternative analysis that showed lower costs to the United States than those on which the opponents of Kyoto were relying.[9] The Clinton administration's defense of Kyoto ignored the benefits of U.S. global warming programs to others outside the United States. Although the Clinton administration may have simply been attempting to refute arguments against Kyoto, its limited focus on costs and benefits to the United States alone is ethically

Figure 9.1   The United States threatens our planet as the world looks on

CLIMATE CHANGE = 39

Reprinted with the permission of the Centre for Science and Environment, New Delhi, India, Rustam Vania/CSE.

troublesome. Such an insular approach treats foreigners as if their U.S.-caused injury is irrelevant to U.S. decisions. Over and over again, nations around the world that are gravely threatened by rising seas, intense storms, and vector-borne disease hear that the United States is not willing to take global warming seriously because the U.S. costs are viewed to be too expensive for the United States. Their outrage is triggered by their dismay at the unjustifiable selfishness of the United States.

Even if the costs of taking action to the United States are very high, a fact disputed by many in the United States, the United States has a strong ethical responsibility to prevent harm to others who neither consented to the harm nor benefited from U.S. activities that cause harm. Given that the environmental harm from human-induced climate change could be catastrophic for some nations and likely will be grave for many of the poorest nations, the U.S. failure to consider the consequences of its activities on others is ethically inexcusable. This is particularly true because, as we saw in chapter 5, human-induced climate change could be devastating to those nations already vulnerable to heat-caused mortality, tropical disease, floods and droughts, marginal food supplies, and rising sea levels.

As we also saw in chapter 2, there is an international consensus that it is more likely than not that some human-induced climate impacts are already killing people around the world and causing great environmental damage. That is, as early as 1995 the Intergovernmental Panel on Climate Change (IPCC) had already concluded that the "balance of the evidence" supported the conclusion that adverse climate impacts are already being experienced by millions of people vulnerable to climate change. The IPPC report released five years later in January 2001 explained how the evidence is much stronger than it was in 1995 that human activities have already begun to change the climate.

Even if it were true that the U.S. costs of global warming programs were high compared to the benefits that the United States would experience from these programs, the United States would have a responsibility to prevent harm to other nations. No respected ethical system would condone one nation causing great harm to another by using the excuse that the harming nation's costs of reducing its harmful behavior were too high for its economic welfare. Ignoring the harm that could be caused to millions around the world by global warming is inconsistent with the rights-and-duties-based ethical approaches as well as theories of justice discussed in chapter 3. Moreover, even utilitarians require that the consequences of one's actions on all people be considered in analyzing one's ethical duties. For this reason, policies based on CBAs that look only at the costs and harm to the United States alone are ethically problematic according to all the mainstream ethical theories discussed in chapter 3.

By urging U.S. citizens to focus on costs and benefits to the United States alone, economic interests again succeeded in robbing the global warming debate of an ethical focus on U.S. behavior. This is so because CBA-based arguments appear on their surface to be calculations of whether a program is worth the effort but often contain hidden controversial ethical premises that are not acknowledged in public policy debates. In the case of CBAs that look only at the U.S. costs and benefits, the hidden ethical consideration is that the United States appears to be unwilling to consider the interests of others.

ADDITIONAL ETHICAL PROBLEMS WITH THE USE OF CBAS IN GLOBAL WARMING DECISIONS

In addition to the exclusive focus on costs and benefits to the United States alone that have characterized recent CBA disputes in the United States, there are other ethical concerns with any use of CBA as a test of acceptability for global warming programs in the United States. Some of these concerns are outlined in the following sections.

Ethical Limitations of "Preference Utilitarianism"

As we saw in chapter 3, CBA, like other economically based environmental decision-making tools, is usually ethically justified as a species of utilitarian ethical theory sometimes called "preference utilitarianism." Preference utilitarianism holds that governments should choose options that maximize humanity's ability to fulfill its desires where the value of human desires are determined by the market value of human decisions. CBA is classified as preference utilitarianism and is distinguished from mainstream utilitarianism because it is peoples' preferences expressed in market transactions that are maximized according to the logic of this theory. On the other hand, more mainstream utilitarianism is concerned with maximizing happiness, not simply human desires. Preference utilitarianism is a much more ethically controversial theory than mainstream utilitarianism because the latter encourages exploration of what actually makes people happy, not just the preferences people express in market transactions.[10] That is, utilitarians urge decision makers to choose alternatives that will produce the greatest happiness, not simply to assume that happiness is equal to what people are willing to pay for something. For this reason, utilitarians advise careful thinking about which options under consideration will create the most happiness, while preference utilitarianism is interested exclusively in which options will produce the greatest economic value. For instance, a utilitarian may approve of spending money for such economically low-payback activities as schools or parks because a case can be made that these investments produce greater happiness than other investments with higher economic returns. Moreover, utilitarians do not necessarily believe that all human choices made in market transactions lead to happiness. In fact, utilitarians urge that people reflect on their desires and that people sometimes select behavior that is contrary to desires. As Ernest Partridge points out, happiness may require that people not act according to preferences: "A recovering drug addict desires not to have the desires that he does. Which economic transaction is responsive to his wants, and to his interests: with his therapist or with his dealer?"[11]

The very idea of morality requires that people reflect on their preferences and not act in response to them if they are destructive of other peoples' rights or interests. Yet preference utilitarianism assumes that any preference satisfaction is good regardless of whether it is a preference to buy a rapist's knife or a serial killer's gun. For this reason, a preference to buy a gas-guzzling sports utility vehicle is as good as a preference to buy a hybrid fuel cell–powered Honda or Toyota. If the United States were to tighten fuel mileage standards for sports utility vehicles that would increase sticker prices, this would be a cost, according to preference utilitarianism, that would be calculated in CBAs.

Figure 9.2 The earth has been made into a commodity

Reprinted with the permission of the Centre for Science and the Environment, New Delhi, India, Rustam Vania/CSE.

Philosopher Mark Sagoff has argued that preference utilitarianism makes a mistake by confusing a person's action as a consumer with an action as a citizen. "As a citizen, I am concerned with the public interest, rather than my own interest, with the good of the community, rather than simply the well being of my family."[12] Acting as a citizen, according to Sagoff, I may take actions that are inconsistent with actions I might take as a consumer. As a citizen, I may support policies that harm my economic interests. For instance, as a citizen, I might support policies that reduce global warming that might threaten people living on islands through rising sea levels even though I may not be personally threatened by rising seas because I live in Nebraska. I might support these policies even though the policies might drive up the cost of electricity in my home. Yet preference utilitarianism would not acknowledge my vote for global warming as a preference satisfaction while assuming that the increased costs of the global warming program are limiting my individual preference satisfaction and therefore should be categorized as a cost.

Sagoff gives additional examples of conflicts between peoples' roles as consumer and citizen and thereby demonstrates why individuals often have a greater commitment to their role as a citizen over their role as a consumer. One such example given by Sagoff is as follows:

> Last year, I bribed a judge to fix a couple of traffic tickets, and I was glad to so because I saved my license. Yet at election time, I helped vote the corrupt judge out of office. I speed on the highway, yet I want the police to enforce laws against speeding. . . . I love my car: I hate the bus. Yet I vote for candidates who promise to tax gasoline for public transportation. . . . The political causes I support seem to have little or no basis in my interests as a consumer . . . because I take different points of view when I vote and when I shop . . . I have an "Ecology Now" sticker on a car that drips oil everywhere it is parked.[13]

Even though I may prefer to take action as a citizen that might work against my personal economic interest, preference utilitarianism assumes that people only act selfishly.

Preference utilitarianism also does not usually count the beauty of a sunset or poem or the intelligence of public debate. For this reason, preference utilitarianism often fails to measure things that make life worthwhile. For these reasons, preference utilitarianism, the underpinning of most CBAs that have often been relied on in arguments made in opposition to U.S. programs on global warming, is often ethically dubious when applied to environmental issues.

CBA tests to determine the acceptability of environmental programs also raise numerous additional ethical concerns. Although there is a vast economics literature that discusses these limitations of CBAs when applied to environmental problems, many of the CBAs that have been applied to potential U.S. policy on global warming continue to ignore these ethical limitations.[14]

CBA Techniques Make Human Desires the Exclusive Measure of Value

Only human interests are of concern to most utilitarians, and as a result no duties or obligations to nonhumans are usually recognized.[15] CBA assumes not only that human interests exclusively are what matter, in line with most although not all utilitarians, but also that only what people are willing to pay is the exclusive measure of value and worth. Therefore, if people are not willing to pay to keep animals from being harmed by global warming, according to CBA theory, a decision that will make animals suffer is perfectly acceptable. If people are not willing to pay to keep pandas or tigers from going extinct, that is also of no concern to CBA-based prescriptions because only what people are willing to pay for is entitled to respect. Only the quantity of money that people will spend to protect animals or plants is relevant in most CBA calculations. For this reason, no fundamental distinction is made in CBA between rocks and animals that suffer pain or between virgin and planted forests. According to CBA, it is only what people are willing to pay for that should guide environmental decision making. No other ethical considerations are relevant, and for this reason CBA is ethically troublesome because, as was pointed out previously, ethics requires us to consider whether our desires are good and not assume that all desires are good.

CBA-Based Decisions Ignore Rights

CBA methods do not recognize the rights that individuals or nations may have to be protected from greenhouse gas damage. If, for instance, the total costs of implementing global warming programs in the richer nations exceed the benefits of global warming programs to the poorer nations, the poorer nations' pleas about rights to remain unharmed are not relevant to the decision maker who follows the strict logic of CBA. In order to consider human rights, CBA-based decision logic must be supplemented by rights or other ethical theories. Yet if a decision maker follows the logic of CBA theory alone, it is irrelevant that people have rights to be protected from the type of environmental damage that would be avoided if the global warming programs were implemented. Although some ethicists who are otherwise sympathetic with utilitarianism acknowledge that utilitarian ethical theory must be supplemented by considerations of rights and justice, those making arguments that global warming programs in the United States are too expensive to be implemented do not acknowledge that it is ever legitimate to override cost-based decisions because they would infringe on rights or violate duties. Because of the irrelevance of rights and duties to its prescriptive assumptions, CBA-based opposition to global warming programs is also ethically troublesome.

CBA-Based Decisions Ignore the Requirements of Distributive and Procedural Justice

The use of CBA as a test of whether global warming programs should be implemented is also ethically troublesome because CBA has often been applied to global warming policy in a way that is indifferent to how costs and benefits are distributed among those affected by global warming. That is, according to some proponents of CBA, a decision to take action to protect the environment is authorized only when the environmental benefits that would be experienced because of the proposed program exceed the costs of implementing the program.[16] It makes no difference to many advocates of CBA-based decision making that those who might be harmed by the failure to implement a global warming program are different than those who would have to pay the costs of implementing the program. For this reason, if the costs to the United States of implementing global warming protection programs exceed the damages that might be experienced in the rest of the world from global warming, the United States should not implement the global warming programs. In fact, this is the very argument made by many in the United States that oppose U.S. programs to reduce greenhouse gas emissions. It makes no difference, according to the proponents of this use of CBA, that some of the poorest nations might be hurt by global warming if the costs of global warming programs to the United States are high. Yet justice demands that those who cause problems to others should be responsible for that harm.

A few global CBAs that have been prepared show that the harm to the poorest nations will be much greater than the harm to the United States. For instance, a summary of global CBAs prepared for the United Nations found that while damage to the developed nations from the global warming entailed by a doubling of carbon is estimated to be between 1 and 2 percent of GDP, estimates of damages to the developing world range from 2 to 9 percent of GDP.[17] Yet those in the United States who have opposed taking action on global warming because of costs to the U.S. economy usually have not acknowledged the responsibility of the United States to the rest of the world.

CBA procedures also usually violate precepts of procedural justice that require that those who may be harmed by a decision be given a right to participate in that decision. Yet those who perform CBA evaluations of global warming programs feel no need to consult those who may be affected by global warming to determine either (1) the victims' view of how the CBA calculations should put a value on the victims' human health and environment or (2) whether the victims consent to a CBA-based decision to not implement a global warming program. For this reason, the use of CBA-based arguments to thwart global warming programs in the United States violates principles of procedural justice.

In addition to the CBAs that have looked only at costs and benefits to the United States of global warming programs, there have been a number of global-scale CBAs that have been prepared to examine global costs and benefits of climate change programs.[18] These global-scale CBAs usually have come to radically different conclusions about the costs and benefits of proposed global warming programs because they have made different assumptions about such things as what damages are likely from global warming or what and how costs will be considered.[19] Assumptions in CBAs must be understood to value judgments that persons who may be adversely affected by decisions based on the CBA have a right to consent to. Although the U.S. government may have a right to make certain assumptions in CBAs that are used in decisions that affect only Americans, considerations of procedural justice require that the United States allow those who will be affected by its decisions to participate in CBAs that may be used in ways that may adversely affect their interests.

Ethical Problems in the Calculation of Benefits and Costs

The "benefits" of global warming programs are generally understood to include the damages to human health and environment that would otherwise have been caused if the programs were not implemented. So far, we have reviewed some of the ethical problems with the limited kinds of values that CBA recognizes. The following discussion focuses on the ethical problems that are entailed by how the value of entities that are considered in CBA are calculated.

Translation of Benefits into Dollars

Economists advise that benefits of environmental programs be calculated in monetary terms so that they can be compared to costs. That amount of money a benefit is worth is the price that a market establishes according to CBA theory or the willingness of people to pay for protection of threatened environmental benefits. For instance, the worth of trees that are threatened by global warming is the dollar value at which the trees are sold. Yet for many environmental entities that provide important environmental services for the maintenance of life on earth, markets recognize little monetary value. For instance, bugs that live in streambeds are vital to support fish, yet these bugs are worth almost nothing in the market. In addition, quantification of some environmental benefits is often difficult and sometimes impossible. What, for instance, is the value of a human life or of a species that might be exterminated by climate change? How do you value an island nation that ceases to exist after it is submerged beneath the ocean because of a rise in sea level caused by global warming? Is the worth of a threatened island nation civilization equal only to what the real estate is worth plus the value of other submerged property? How should nations value native trout streams or winter sports that might disappear because of global warming? Is the value of the loss simply what markets recognize? What about the climate of nations that become harder to live in because of the discomfort entailed by much hotter weather? If 100 million people per year contract malaria because of the increased range of mosquitoes enabled by global warming, how do we measure the malaria victims' suffering even if they survive?

When values of environmental entities cannot be determined directly from prices, economists often advise that alternate techniques be used to determine value in CBA calculations. In these methods, values are determined by asking individuals about their willingness to pay to have threatened entities protected. In partial recognition of the need to go beyond available market prices to determine the value of environmental entities, economists recommend that these questions attempt to determine values not only for the human use of the threatened environmental entity but also for its "existence" value. That is, people are asked to say what they are willing to pay for its "nonuse" value, that is, the value of the entity's mere existence.

Yet despite the fact that the economists' questions attempt to determine nonuse value, the questions asked of people by these techniques are in all cases what individuals are "willing to pay" to avoid the harm of concern. The ethically dubious nature of such procedures should be obvious when it is applied to human health and the environment if one reflects on the fact that there are many human behaviors that are outlawed without justifying a law's prohibition on people's willingness to pay to prohibit the behavior. For instance, society does not subject laws prohibiting child labor, homicide, or slavery to cost-benefit calculations. Laws outlaw these actions and activities because they are morally offensive, not because the benefits of their prohibition exceed costs. Using "willingness to pay" as a measure of value is to focus on one type of value at the expense of important ethical concerns.

Willingness-to-pay-based procedures are also ethically dubious because such an approach ignores injunctions against any harm entailed by human rights and other ethically based prohibitions. That is, asking willingness-to-pay questions about permitting damage to human health and the environment takes off the table the idea that behavior that kills people or destroys important environmental entities should be avoided as morally offensive. The very process of converting environmental entities' worth into monetary values is to transform something that some believe should be protected from consumption into a commodity available for human use. These willingness-to-pay techniques for determining value in CBA assume that everything's worth is reducible to its price as if everything is for sale and available for consumption.

As we saw in chapter 3, some ethicists assert that nonhuman sentient beings and other environmental entities have a right to exist that is not dependent on their use to humans. For this reason, as we explained in chapter 3, biocentric and ecocentric ethical approaches to value have arisen in the past twenty years. From the point of view of these nonanthropocentric theories of value, the fate of environmental entities should not be determined by human subjective economic preferences. Because market-based prices only measure the strength of human desires, they do not reflect values that are not dependent on human desires to consume.[20] According to biocentric and ecocentric ethical theories, putting a market price on something that should be protected because of ethical obligations is to agree to a process that transforms the sacred into the profane. This is another reason why CBA-based decision logic applied to climate change programs is ethically dubious.

Identifying Costs and Benefits in the Face of Uncertainty

To perform CBA calculations for climate change, the person doing the assessment must determine which consequences of global warming will be considered, whose assessments of harms and benefits will be allowed, and what timescale will be used in assessing the consequences. The CBA analysis therefore often rests on imprecise judgments that are prior to the CBA calculus itself. These decisions cannot avoid making value judgments about how conservative the assumptions should be. Yet on the surface, CBA pretends to be "value neutral." CBAs pretend to gather the economic "facts" while hiding the ethical assumptions.

CBA originally was developed as a technique to compare alternative building projects whose costs and benefits would be experienced usually in a time span of no more than fifteen to twenty-five years and whose benefits were relatively easy to quantify because only direct costs and benefits of the project were considered.[21] However, determining the benefits of global warming programs is a much trickier problem because of its technical complexity, the type of things that may be damaged by global warming, and the time in which the damage may occur. Determining the value of climate change impacts is particularly difficult because of the large time spans for which climate damages may be experienced and, as we saw in chapter 6, the great scientific uncertainties that must be faced to determine the actual timing, magnitude, and impact of global warming.

As we also saw in chapter 6, to determine impacts of future global warming, we need to know the amount of emissions that will be released in the future; how much of these emissions will wind up in the atmosphere; how much temperature change can be expected from increases in atmospheric levels of greenhouse gases; whether temperature changes will cause further nonlinear responses to ocean, terrestrial, and atmospheric systems; and what impacts to human health and the environment will be caused by these changes in climate. Although we know that human activity is changing the climate, we do not know for sure the magnitude and timing of future warming. As was explained in chapter 6, because of some feedback mechanisms in the climate system, such as clouds, whose climate impacts are not well understood, it is impossible to know for sure the amount of damage that will be caused by human-induced global warming. Yet CBA calculations must make assumptions about which damages from global warming will occur and then make assumptions about the value of these impacts.

Many of the CBAs that have been performed for global warming assume that the climate will respond to increased greenhouse gases in a smooth, mostly linear fashion and that the damages will be similar to those described by the IPCC in its 1995 report.[22] For this reason, the global CBAs that have been performed have assumed that the only negative impacts that will be experienced from human-induced climate change are those that come from smooth, mostly linear responses to a doubling of carbon.[23] Yet many scientists believe that much more catastrophic consequences are possible. These catastrophic impacts of global warming are sometimes referred to as "climate surprises," as discussed in chapter 5. They include rapid changes in ocean circulation patterns, rapid increases in sea level due to the breakup of the Antarctic ice shelf, nonlinear increases in atmospheric greenhouse gas concentrations caused by sudden releases in carbon from permafrost melting and forest dieback, and unexpected saturation of carbon "sinks" that will rapidly increase atmospheric levels of carbon. The scientific disputes about potential catastrophic impacts of global warming have been focused largely on the probability of climate surprises, not on the possibility that they will occur. That is, these surprises are plausible because it is well known that the climate system is capable of rapid nonlinear responses that could create much greater and more rapid global warming impacts than those identified in the IPCC's reports that assume that the climate system will respond gradually and smoothly. Although the scientific community agrees that these rapid nonlinear climate responses could occur, the CBAs that have been calculated for global warming have not assumed that any catastrophic impacts will occur.[24]

In fact, the most influential CBAs relied on by climate change program critics assume that no large sudden nonlinear changes will take place.[25] Yet because rapid nonlinear responses are possible, any CBA that does not include identification of potential catastrophic global warming damages is making a value judgment that is hidden in the CBA calculations and biases these calculations in a way that underestimates the potential benefits of global warming programs.

CBAs of global warming calculations must also rely on unproven and hidden assumptions about what costs will be entailed by global warming programs. To determine the costs of global warming programs, the assessor must make an assumption on which mitigation strategies and programs will be implemented and what the costs of each program will be. Along this line, according to one observer of global warming CBAs, "most of the analysis of costs in national studies of the impact of the Kyoto Protocol on the United States assume that the country will rely primarily on a narrow range of legal instruments, especially emissions trading and taxes on CO_2 emissions."[26] That is, the cost analyses in CBAs that have looked at the acceptability of the Kyoto Protocol assume that there will be significant costs from a very limited number of reduction strategies, all of which rely on economic instruments that use higher costs to reduce demand for polluting energy. Yet greenhouse gas reduction strategies and programs could be implemented that have much lower costs than those assumed in the Kyoto-focused CBAs. In fact, it is well known that some global warming programs could be implemented with savings to those who invest in them.[27] For example, every dollar spent in California's electrical demand-side management program in recent years has saved more than $2.[28] For this reason, there is no way of calculating the actual costs of most global warming programs without making assumptions about which method will be employed to achieve the reductions and what the cost will be of the reduction method assumed. For this reason, industry and government analyses of the costs of global warming programs have diverged greatly. The choice of which cost assumptions to make in a CBA must be understood to entail a value judgment about how optimistic or pessimistic the assumption should be. Yet the values assumptions about how much any method will cost are usually hidden in CBA, and the CBAs pretend to be value neutral.

In performing its CBA of the Kyoto Protocol, the Clinton administration itself acknowledged the following major uncertainties in its methods for determining costs:[29]

- The uncertainties that remain over the operational aspects of the Kyoto Protocol

- The inherent limitations of available models to analyze the costs of abating emissions
- The difficulty in quantifying the long-term economic benefits of climate change

In the face of such uncertainty about global warming impacts and their costs, every CBA that does not display a range of benefits that will be avoided or costs entailed by climate change programs is making hidden value assumptions that most likely are ethically dubious.

Ethical Problems with Discounting Future Benefits

Standard CBA methods are also ethically troublesome because of how they assign values to environmental benefits that will be experienced in the future, especially the distant future.[30] Economic theory urges that the value of future environmental benefits be determined in the same way that the market applies value to future events, that is, by understanding the present value of future benefits. The transformation of future benefits into present values through discounting is viewed by economists to be a rational way of thinking about future benefits because if someone waits a year for another person to pay them $1,000 that is now owed, it means that the lender will have to forgo the interest that the money could earn if it were invested now. Therefore, the same amount of money is worth less in the future than it is now to an investor. Accordingly, economists urge that CBA discount future benefits so that investors can know which alternatives will provide a better payback. Because persons will pay less now for something that will be received in the future than for the same thing in the present, economists typically encourage the discounting of the value of future benefits. It should be noticed that this technique makes current investors' interests, not future generations' welfare, the focus of concern in legitimating CBA discounting.

In addition to the justification of discounting practices, the amount of discount rate is also a matter of considerable ethical controversy. The present value of $100 twenty years from now is $37.70 at a 5 percent rate, or $14.90 at a 10 percent rate. The higher the discount rate and the further in the future the benefits will be experienced, the lower the present value of future benefits. Because global warming decisions based on CBA must consider benefits that occur several hundred years in the future, particularly if the discount rate is much above zero, the present value of future benefits for global warming programs is often very, very small. In fact, for benefits that will be experienced 100 years in the future, climate damages in the long term appear acceptable at almost any level. Discounting global warming benefits in this way is ethically problematic because such discounting procedures ignore the rights of future generations and violate principles of distributive justice.

Discounting Benefits Ignores Rights of Future Generations

Discounting benefits in CBA assumes that only contemporary investor-individuals' interests count in determining worth. In this way, discounting ignores the rights or interests of future generations to have a global climate system that has not been degraded by human activities. As a recent observer of discounting practices in CBAs has observed,

> In technical terms, this approach is implemented by assuming that the economy behaves as if decisions regarding economy-environment trade-offs were made by a single generation of human beings whose lives stretched from the present into the long-term distant future. The single generation employs conventional discounting, which gives very little weight to the very long term. While this approach may be sensible for analyzing problems with relatively short time horizons, it obscures the ways in which climate change policies will affect the distinct interests and welfare of present and future generations.[31]

A study prepared by the Pew Center for Global Climate Change attempted to determine what additional costs would be imposed on future generations through discounting.[32] The Pew report found that normal discounting procedures would impose $2.4 trillion per year of uncompensated environmental costs on those who would be living in 2420.[33] This study also found that if one takes strong action to stabilize greenhouse gases now and ignores policy options that would be followed if normal discounting procedures are included in policy analysis, the overall economy in future generations would be much healthier.[34] This analysis makes it clear that although discounting future benefits of climate programs might lead to less immediate costs for present generations than those that would be entailed by climate programs that attempted to stabilize greenhouse gases, such an approach would seriously harm the interests of future generations. For this reason, discounting the benefits of global warming programs in CBAs is ethically troublesome.

Discounting Ignores Distributive Justice

As was the case with CBA procedures in general, discounting procedures used to calculate the present value of future benefits are indifferent to how costs and benefits will be allocated among subgroups. For instance, the future benefit of a global warming program in the United States may be experienced by the citizens of small island developing nations in the Pacific, among others, while the costs that might be avoided by following discounting logic might primarily be costs to U.S. fossil fuel interests. The fact that there are different people who will experience costs and benefits is ignored in discounting procedures. If, for instance, the costs to U.S. fossil fuel interests exceed the discounted value of the environmental benefits to the residents of the small island nations, conventional CBA-based decision-making logic compels that the damage to the residents of the small island state be tolerated. However, discounting procedures applied to environmental protection controversies make sense, if they make sense at all, only if the person receiving the benefit is the same as the person who will pay the cost. This is so because the justification for the discounting process rests on the notion that a single decision maker is attempting to maximize an investment opportunity. Yet this is not the case for CBAs prepared for global warming programs in the United States. That is, the benefits of U.S. global warming programs will accrue to people around the world, not just the United States, while the monies saved in the United States by failing to implement global warming programs will benefit the United States alone. For this reason, the failure of CBAs to consider questions of distributive justice in discounting is not only ethically troublesome but also undermines the very justification for discounting in the first place. That is, discounting practices are justified on the basis that this approach allows a single investor to make a decision knowing whether a project or an alternative has a greater payback. This assumes that either the project under consideration or its alternative will make the investor better off. Yet this is not the case when nations decide whether to invest in global warming programs because if the alternative of no global warming action is selected, the entity that gains from the decision is not the person who will be harmed by the decision. For this reason, discounting benefits of global warming programs makes neither ethical nor logical sense.

CONCLUSION

The most obvious ethically troublesome use of recent CBA-based arguments made in opposition to U.S. programs is that they have often considered costs and benefits to the United States alone as determining the rationality of U.S. policy on global warming. This is particularly troubling because many of the poorest nations around the world will likely be hurt the most by global warming, yet the suffering of these people and their environment appears to be irrelevant to U.S. policymakers. However, even for those CBAs that extend analyses beyond the United States, there are numerous serious ethical problems that remain hidden in standard CBA methods. For these reasons, the recent use of CBA-based arguments in opposition to U.S. programs on global warming does not withstand minimum ethical scrutiny.

Some economists have recognized the many limitations of CBAs when applied to global warming policy and found the criticisms devastating because of the ethical concerns discussed previously.[35] In recognition of the fundamental flaws of CBAs when applied to global warming, some of these economists have concluded that CBAs should not be used to determine whether governments should reduce greenhouse gas emissions.[36] Instead, target reductions should be determined on the basis of ethical considerations and cost analysis should then be used to determine which policy responses will minimize costs. Such an approach would allow cost considerations of global warming policy options to be seriously considered without violating ethical principles. Other economists insist on a role for CBAs in setting basic global warming policy despite these limitations.[37] To deal with the ethical limitations of CBAs, a variety of adjustments to conventional CBAs have been proposed by these economists. Yet because these adjustments also raise ethical considerations, it is imperative that ethical analysis be integrated into CBAs that are used in global warming policy analysis and ethical assumptions of CBAs be made so crystal clear that noneconomists can understand the ethical assumptions adopted in the economic analysis. This is an ethical imperative.

NOTES

1. Jason Shogren and Michael Toman, "How Much Climate Change Is Too Much? An Economics Perspective," *Resources for the Future,* September 2000, 14 (available at <www/rff.org/disc_papers/PDF_files/0022.pdf>, March 22, 2001).

2. See chapter 2.

3. White House, *The Kyoto Protocol and the President's Policies to Address Climate Change: An Economic Analysis,* 1998, 58. (available at <www.epa.gov/globalwarming/publications/actions/wh_kyoto/wh_full_rpt.pdf>, March 22, 2001).

4. White House, *The Kyoto Protocol and the President's Policies to Address Climate Change,* 56–58.

5. White House, *The Kyoto Protocol and the President's Policies to Address Climate Change,* 39–70.

6. White House, *The Kyoto Protocol and the President's Policies to Address Climate Change,* 52.

7. Jim Labe, "Environment: U.S. Economy Comes First, Says Bush," International Press Service, World News (available at <www.oneworld.net/anydoc2.cgi?url=http%3A%2F%2Fwww%2Eoneworld%2Enet%2Fips2%2Fmar01%2F22%5F46%5F082%2Ehtml>, June 6, 2001).

8. For a discussion of worldwide climate change costs, see D. Pierce, W. Cline, A. Achanta, S. Fankhuaser, R. Pachauri, R. Tol, and P. Vellinga, "The Social Costs of Climate Change: Greenhouse Damage and the Benefits of Control," in James Bruce, Hoesung Lee, and Eric Haites, eds., *The Economic and Social Dimensions of Climate Change: Contribution of Working Group III to the Second Assessment Report of the Intergovernmental Panel on Climate Change* (New York: Cambridge University Press, 1996), 179–225.

9. White House, *The Kyoto Protocol and the President's Policies to Address Climate Change*, 39–70.

10. For a discussion of the limits of preference utilitarianism, see Mark Sagoff, "At the Shrine of Our Lady of Fatima or Why Political Questions Are Not All Economic," *Arizona Law Review* 23 (1982): 1281–98.

11. Ernest Partridge, "An Askance Glance at Environmental Policy Making" (paper presented at the Rocky Mountain Biological Laboratories, Crested Butte, Colorado, July 13, 1995).

12. Mark Sagoff, *The Economy of the Earth* (New York: Cambridge University Press, 1988), 8.

13. Sagoff, *The Economy of the Earth*, 52–53.

14. For a discussion of the recognized limitations of CBA applied to global warming, see Stephen Schneider, ed., *Climate Change*, vol. (1999). This volume reviews the state of the art of CBAs applied to climate change. Many of the articles acknowledge the limitations of CBA applied to global warming discussed in this chapter, and a few recommend alternatives to the classical use of CBAs.

15. A few utilitarians have attempted to extend moral consideration to animals. See Peter Singer, "Animal Liberation," in Donald VanDeVeer and Christine Pierce, eds., *The Environmental Ethics and Policy Book* (Belmont, Calif.: Wadsworth, 1997), 95–101.

16. Not all proponents of CBA advocate for such a use of CBA. For a discussion of alternative uses of CBA, see Kristen Shrader-Frechette, "A Defense of Risk-Cost-Benefit Analysis," in Louis P. Pojman, ed., *Environmental Ethics* (Belmont Calif.: Wadsworth, 1997), 500–14.

17. Pierce et al., "The Social Costs of Climate Change," 83.

18. For a good discussion of the global-scale CBAs that have been prepared for global warming, see Scott Barrett, "The Montreal versus Kyoto: International Cooperation and the Global Environment," in Inge Kaul, Isabelle Grunberg, and Marc Stern, eds., *Global Public Goods* (New York: Oxford University Press, 1999), 192–219.

19. Barrett, "The Montreal versus Kyoto," 203.

20. For a good discussion of the ethical limits of markets, see Sagoff, *The Economy of the Earth*.

21. M. Munasinge, M. P. Meier, M. Hodel, S. W. Hong, and A. A. Heim, "Applicability of Cost-Benefit Analysis Techniques to Climate Change," in Bruce, Lee, and Haites, eds., *The Economic and Social Dimensions of Climate Change*, 145–78.

22. Shogren and Toman, *How Much Climate Change Is Too Much?*, 26.

23. Pierce et al., "The Social Costs of Climate Change," 183.

24. Stephen Schneider and Stanley Thompson, "A Simple Model Used in Economic Studies of Global Change," in *New Directions in the Economics of Climate Change*, Pew Center on Global Climate Change, October 2000, 59 (available at <www/pewclimate.org/projects/directions.cfm>, March 22, 2001).

25. Schneider and Thompson, "A Simple Model Used in Economic Studies of Global Change," 60.

26. John Dernbach, "Moving the Climate Change Debate from Models to Proposed Legislation: Lessons from State Experience," *Environmental Law Reporter* 30 (November 2000): 10934.

27. Dernbach, "Moving the Climate Change Debate from Models to Proposed Legislation," 10948.

28. Dernbach, "Moving the Climate Change Debate from Models to Proposed Legislation," 10975.

29. White House, *The Kyoto Protocol and the President's Policies to Address Climate Change*, 39–71.

30. For a discussion of the ethical problems of discounting employed in CBA, see Clive Spash, "Economics, Ethics, and Long Term Environmental Damages," *Environmental Ethics* 15, no. 2 (1993): 117–32.

31. Richard Horworth, "Climate Change and Intergenerational Fairness," in *New Directions in the Economics of Climate Change*, Pew Center for Global Climate Change, October 2000, 43–57 (available at <www/pewclimate.org/projects/directions.pdf>, March 22, 2001).

32. Horworth, "Climate Change and Intergenerational Fairness," 51.

33. Horworth, "Climate Change and Intergenerational Fairness," 51.

34. Horworth, "Climate Change and Intergenerational Fairness," 54.

35. For a summary of some of the economists' criticisms of CBAs, see K. Hasselmann, "Intertemporal Accounting of Climate Change: Harmonizing Economic Efficiency and Climate Stewardship," *Climate Change* 41 (1999): 333–50.

36. Hasselmann, "Intertemporal Accounting of Climate Change."

37. Hasselmann, "Intertemporal Accounting of Climate Change."

Chapter Ten

Ethical Problems with the U.S. Insistence on Its View of the Kyoto Flexibility Mechanisms

Figure 10.1   The rich nations seek to own part of the atmosphere

Reprinted with permission of the Centre for Science and Environment, New Delhi, India, Rustam Vania/CSE.

The fourth argument frequently made against U.S. agreement to the climate change proposals of other nations is premised on the idea that the United States could significantly reduce its costs of lowering emissions if it were allowed to invest in emission reduction projects anywhere in the world where low-cost projects could be found. Such an approach to global warming remediation is feasible because reductions of greenhouse gas emissions from anywhere in the world will help lessen the global problem. In other words, to help reduce atmospheric carbon levels, it makes little difference where carbon emissions are reduced because no matter where greenhouse gases are emitted, they contribute to global atmospheric levels.

Because of the desire to achieve greenhouse gas reductions at the lowest possible cost, the Clinton administration, at Kyoto in 1997 and The Hague in 2000, refused to agree to proposals made by other nations until they accepted the views of the United States on a worldwide system for trading carbon emission rights. A worldwide carbon-trading system would allow the United States to fund carbon reduction projects or buy emission reduction credits or allowances outside the United States and thereby obtain credit against any U.S. carbon reduction target. The Clinton administration took the position from 1997 until it left office that it would agree to reduce U.S. greenhouse gas emissions 7 percent below 1990 levels provided that the world agreed to its version of several carbon-trading mechanisms. Initial pronouncements of the George W. Bush administration have indicated that trading and other market mechanisms would be a cornerstone of its approach to international global warming negotiations even though it has repudiated the Kyoto Protocol. Yet it is not clear at this time how the Bush administration will approach the flexibility mechanism issues if it eventually participates in an international global warming regime. Yet it is likely that it will continue some of the Clinton administration positions on trading. In recent international negotiations that have proceeded without the United States, the international community has retained many of the Kyoto flexibility mechanisms.

In the 1997 lead-up to the Kyoto negotiations, the United States was under great pressure from much of the rest of the world to make a significant binding commitment to reduce greenhouse gas emissions. As we saw in chapter 2, the United States entered the Kyoto negotiations willing to make the smallest commitment among major developed countries to reduce greenhouse gas emissions. The United States pushed the idea that the developed countries should agree to reduce emissions of six major greenhouse gases to 1990 levels by 2008–12. On the other hand, the European Union proposed that developed countries make a commitment to reduce three major greenhouse gas emissions 15 percent below 1990 levels by 2010, with an interim target of 7.5 percent by 2005. Other nations wanted even greater reductions.

During the first week and a half in Kyoto, negotiators were deadlocked largely over the unwillingness of the United States to make the kind of reduction commitments being proposed by other nations. Under great pressure from most of the rest of the world to make a larger commitment than what it had proposed, the United States agreed to a deal at the very end of the negotiations. This bargain was struck when the United States agreed to commit to a 7 percent reduction in greenhouse gas emissions in exchange for the world's accepting what have come to be known as the Kyoto "flexibility mechanisms." Some of these flexibility mechanisms had been initially proposed by other nations, yet they quickly became U.S.-led initiatives. Joint implementation had been originally proposed by Norway, and the "clean development" mechanism originally was an idea of Brazil; however, the United States pushed for their versions of these flexibility mechanisms toward the conclusion of the negotiations. Included in the final Kyoto agreement were three trading mechanisms that would allow the United States to achieve over 80 percent of its greenhouse reduction targets not through actual emission reductions in the United States but through paying for greenhouse reduction projects or buying carbon reduction allowances in other countries.[1] At the last moment, the developing countries agreed to these trading mechanisms, although some of them had previously opposed them as immoral. The developing countries agreed because many of the details of how the trading mechanism would work would have to be worked out in future negotiations. The details about how the Kyoto flexibility mechanisms should work would prove to plague future negotiations from 1997 to the end of the Clinton administration in January 2001.

As a result of its dogged determination, the United States was successful in getting the Kyoto Protocol to include these trading mechanisms that would allow the United States to find "least-cost" projects to achieve its national target. These mechanisms included the following:

- *Emissions trading.* An international trading mechanism that would allow developed nations with Kyoto targets to purchase emissions allowances from developed countries that have more permits than they need
- *Joint implementation.* An international trading mechanism that allows developed nations with emissions targets to obtain credit toward the target by funding emission reduction projects in other developed nations that have targets
- *The clean development mechanism.* An international trading mechanism that allows developed nations with Kyoto targets to obtain credit by paying for carbon reduction projects in developing nations[2]

And so the United States was successful in creating three different trading mechanisms in the Kyoto Protocol. Two allowed trading between the developed nations. Of these, the first allowed a developed nation to obtain credit for projects in other developed nations. The second allowed trading of national allowances among developed nations. The third allowed the rich nations to get credit for carbon reduction projects in developing nations. Under this option, the United States could potentially pay to replace an oil-powered electric generation plant with a solar power plant in Africa and get credit against the 7 percent reduction target of the United States in the amount of carbon emissions avoided by the African solar plant.

Another Kyoto flexibility mechanism pushed by the United States and agreed to in the Kyoto Protocol was the inclusion of provisions that allowed nations to use some carbon sinks to get credit against their Kyoto reduction targets. A sink is an element of the natural world that will remove carbon from the atmosphere and store it for some time. Trees and vegetation of all types act as carbon sinks. Under the Kyoto Protocol, when reporting progress in making their reduction targets, nations may include reductions achieved through changes in forests' sinks since 1990.[3] Therefore, if the United States planted new forests after 1990, it could get credit for the amount of carbon stored in the new forest against the Kyoto target.

Although the general framework of these flexibility mechanisms were agreed to in Kyoto, many of the details of their implementation have been very contentious in negotiations since then. Nevertheless, the Clinton administration continued to insist on the resolution of issues needed to take advantage of the flexibility mechanisms as a precondition for any U.S. fulfillment of its Kyoto promise to reduce U.S. emissions by 7 percent below 1990 emissions level. Although presently the George W. Bush administration has rejected Kyoto entirely, the administration has indicated that it will look to Kyoto-like trading mechanisms as a way of getting credit for reducing the impacts of U.S. greenhouse gas emissions. It is not clear at this time what will be the response of the Bush administration to the Kyoto trading mechanisms that were largely pushed by the Clinton administration. Yet it is likely that if the Kyoto Protocol is ratified by other nations, the United States, although it is presently rejecting the Kyoto Protocol, will insist on taking advantage, one way or another, of the Kyoto trading mechanisms while pushing U.S. positions that were advanced by the Clinton administration.

To achieve full implementation of the Kyoto flexibility mechanisms, negotiators must face a large number of very thorny issues, including the following:

- *How to avoid giving credits to projects that do not actually reduce greenhouse gases.* One way this cheating could occur under emissions trading is sometimes referred to as the "hot-air" problem. One serious hot-air problem arises because several countries of the former Soviet Union are projected to have sizable amounts of credits available for sale because of current economic difficulties. Because some of these countries' economies are depressed, they likely will have between 92 and 350 million tons of allowances to sell that have come not from emissions reductions but simply because of economic downturn. Under the emissions trading mechanism, these countries will be able to sell allowances that they no longer need while taking no steps to actually reduce emissions. And so, for instance, the United States could buy one million tons from Russia that it does need because of Russia's depressed economy and thereby increase the U.S. emission allowance by one million tons.

- *How to avoid giving credit for projects under the clean development mechanism that would have been implemented anyway in absence of trading.* This concern about giving credits to developed countries for projects that do not actually reduce greenhouse gases beyond what would have occurred anyway is sometime referred to as the "additionality" problem. The concern about additionality arises because of the difficulty determining what carbon emission projects or approaches would take place in the future without financing from the developed nations seeking to obtain credit for them against the developed nation's Kyoto target. That is, even in absence of developed-world participation, developing nations are likely to install more efficient technologies for financial reasons. For these projects, the developed world could obtain credits under the clean development mechanism despite the fact that the projects have not actually reduced emissions beyond what they would have been anyway. To deal with this problem, complicated methods for developing future baselines for the developing world projects have been the subject of intense discussions in climate negotiations.
- *How to make sure that real carbon reductions have occurred from projects for which trading credits have been given.* There are many ways in which projects for which credits are given could create no net emissions levels, including through what is usually referred to as the "leakage" problem. Leakage occurs when production from a project for which credit is given is simply moved from the site that is being monitored to another site at which emissions continue.
- *How to measure credit for carbon sequestration projects in forests and agriculture.* This is important because (1) it is not clear what carbon reductions will actually be achieved from such projects; (2) carbon sequestration in plants and trees is only temporary because when the vegetation dies, it will release the stored carbon; and (3) very high temperatures could kill trees and plants that have been earmarked for carbon storage and cause the rapid release of carbon being stored.
- *Whether a rich country like the United States should be able to achieve all its legally required reductions by obtaining credits from poor nations.* It is clear that the United States intended to rely on a large amount of trading rather than domestic emission reductions because the Clinton administration's cost-benefit analysis stated that the United States would achieve 82 to 88 percent of the U.S. reduction requirement from foreign sources.[4]

During the sixth Conference of Parties (COP-6) to the UN Framework Convention on Climate Change held in The Hague in November 2000, the

United States pushed for maximum use of the Kyoto flexibility mechanisms. Of particular concern to the rest of the world, the United States wanted to be able to obtain credit against its 7 percent Kyoto reduction target for forests that were already growing in the United States, thus obtaining credit for doing nothing. The United States also pushed for an unlimited amount of trading to achieve its 7 percent Kyoto target rather than lowering domestic emissions. Much of the rest of the world was opposed to this approach and accused the United States of attempting to create loopholes from its obligations rather than achieve real reductions in greenhouse gas emissions. In large part because of the U.S. positions on these issues, COP-6 concluded without reaching any agreement.

Thus far, this book has described why three arguments that frequently are made in opposition to global warming programs in the United States are ethically indefensible on their face. These arguments are that the United States should not initiate serious global warming programs because of scientific uncertainty about human causation until the developing world makes commitments to reduce emissions and because of cost-benefit consequences to the United States. We have demonstrated that these arguments fail to withstand minimum ethical scrutiny no matter the ethical approach. Unlike these three arguments, which obviously are ethically problematic, the ethical problems with the U.S. position on trading are for the most part contingent on U.S. positions on several of the details of these trading mechanisms. Most observers believe that the goal of seeking "least-cost" solutions is ethically laudatory, yet, as we will see, the ethically benign ends of obtaining least-cost solutions do not justify the ethically dubious means entailed by some of the U.S. positions on these trading mechanisms.

ETHICAL PROBLEMS WITH THE U.S. INSISTENCE ON THE KYOTO FLEXIBILITY MECHANISMS

Because of both the complexities and the inequities entailed by some elements of the flexibility mechanisms, the U.S. insistence that the details of the flexibility mechanisms be fully agreed to as a precondition for the U.S. reductions of its greenhouse gas emissions has been ethically problematic. Given the fact that the United States is the worst greenhouse gas polluter, it was ethically dubious for the United States to make implementation of its version of the flexibility mechanisms a precondition for its commitment to reduce its greenhouse gas emissions, particularly if there are difficult scientific and equity issues that are raised by U.S. positions on the flexibility mechanisms.

For the past three years, trading issues have proven to be an immense barrier to progress on global warming because of the following:

- The technical difficulty and institutional complexity of the issues that need to be resolved to make the trading mechanisms work
- The inherent tension between the need to lower the costs of trading by creating rather simple procedures that will minimize transaction costs, that is, the costs of actually securing the trade and the need to design a set of rules that are not just a grab bag of loopholes that will not lead to real atmospheric reductions
- The developing world's suspicion about how the trading rules may affect their interests

Some economists and industry representatives from the United States have pushed for simplicity in the trading rules to keep transaction costs down, that is, the costs of implementing a trade. They take this position because if the costs of implementing a trade become too high, the economic advantage of trading for carbon reductions rather than making actual emissions reductions becomes less attractive. For this reason, the United States has continued to advocate for very simple rules because complex rules would increase the costs of trading. Yet the simpler the rules, the greater potential there is to create loopholes that could undermine the ability to get real reductions of emissions. Along this line, one observer of the international flexibility mechanisms debate has concluded that "these [flexibility] provisions may lead to the perverse result that global carbon emissions will continue to grow at much the same rate for years to come, Kyoto notwithstanding."[5] Although carbon trading is, in theory, a way of achieving low-cost solutions that are carbon neutral, greenhouse gas emissions might increase under liberal trading regimes if the following occur:

- Carbon credits go mostly to projects that do not create real reductions, such as the potential hot-air credits discussed previously, that would be created by purchasing allowances from Russia and the Ukraine, which have credits to sell despite the fact that they have not taken steps to actually reduce emissions
- Monitoring and enforcement of project success is ineffective and credits are given for projects that do not actually achieve the carbon reductions promised
- Carbon sequestration projects become the dominant method of obtaining credit for the United States and these sequestration projects ultimately release large amounts of stored carbon into the atmosphere

- International carbon baselines used in establishing the amount of credit for clean development mechanism projects fail to identify trends in carbon reductions that would have happened in the absence of targets

The U.S. insistence that the trading rules be designed to minimize transaction costs may very well create a trading system that perversely leads to increases in greenhouse gas emissions. Therefore, the first reason why prior U.S. insistence on implementation of the flexibility mechanisms has been ethically problematic is because it could lead to an international climate regime that fails to significantly reverse the growing global warming problem.

The U.S. position on trading values efficiency over responsibility for reducing emissions. Because the savings that will be achieved through efficiency gains will benefit mainly the developed nations and the harms that may be caused by a focus on efficiency over environmental protection may be most harshly felt by the developing world, there are serious problems of distributive justice entailed by some of the U.S. positions on the trading mechanisms. The second ethical concern, therefore, entailed by the U.S. position on the Kyoto flexibility mechanisms is one that allows questions of efficiency to trump principles of distributive justice.

The United States has a duty to reduce its greenhouse gas emissions because, among other reasons, its emissions will harm nations and people that have not consented to U.S. emission levels. This ethical duty is not contingent on the victims' prior agreement to accept the harming party's lowest-cost solution, particularly when the harming party's preferred solution may harm the victims' interests, as we will see may be the case because of some elements of the U.S. positions on trading. Those seriously harming others have no right to demand, as a precondition for their stopping their injurious behavior, that the victim agrees to a solution designed to minimize the assaulter's cost. Although the goal of driving down the costs of reduction programs through trading may be laudable from an efficiency standpoint, the U.S. position that conditions its promise to reduce domestic greenhouse gas emissions on the rest of the world's agreement to the U.S. approach to trading is also ethically problematic. This is so because the United States has a duty to refrain from doing harm, a responsibility that is independent of and prior to the right of the United States to negotiate an agreement that will reduce its costs. That is, the fact that there exist potential trading mechanisms that could greatly reduce the U.S. costs of complying with Kyoto does not trump the ethical obligations of the United States to desist from harmful behavior as quickly as possible. For example, someone who destroys a neighbor's house by digging under it may not hide behind an excuse for continuing the digging that the victim did not agree to in the digger's proposal to buy the property. Such a position would be seen quite rightly as unethical intimidation. As we will see in this chapter, the developing nations have legitimate concerns with how trading rules proposed by the United States may affect their interests. Because it is ethically troublesome for the party doing the damage to demand that its least-cost solution be accepted by those being harmed, a third ethical concern with the U.S. position on trading is that it can be construed as raising illegitimate conditions for stopping harmful behavior of the United States. If the United States is right that it is in everyone's interest to set up an international trading regime on carbon, this idea should be sold on its own merits while the United States goes about the business of beginning to reduce its emissions.

A CARBON TRADING SCHEME IS JUST ONLY IF THE ALLOCATION OF RIGHTS TO EMIT CARBON IS JUST

According to mainstream economic theory, if nations can achieve their carbon reductions at the lowest cost through trading, they can invest limited resources that would be expended on higher-cost solutions on projects that could produce additional benefits for their citizens. For this reason, according to this economic theory, maximizing efficiency in global warming programs is ethically laudable. However, if national allocation of carbon reduction targets is unjust, a trading scheme to implement these national allocations will be unjust. That is, if a nation receives an unjustly low national carbon reduction target, a trading program becomes a means of further reducing the nation's costs that justice would demand that the nation assume. Therefore, as one commentator on the ethics of trading has observed, a trading scheme can be "ethically benign [only] if the allocation among parties that establishes the reduction targets is just."[6]

Because the United States has less than 5 percent of the world's population but emits 24 percent of the greenhouse gases, its final share of allowable emissions must take into consideration its disproportionate responsibility for the problem. (The next chapter considers the ethical questions entailed by allocation schemes of national carbon targets.) So far, the United States has been unwilling to discuss its equitable share of the worldwide ultimate carbon reduction needs. At Kyoto, the United States agreed to reduce greenhouse gas emissions 7 percent below 1990 levels, a first step to reducing greenhouse gases but only a drop in the bucket compared to levels of reduction that will be needed. The Kyoto commitment of the United States has been based not on its equitable responsibilities but instead on the notion that it should only have to do what is economically reasonable given its historical emissions use.

The unwillingness of the United States to discuss an equitable basis for establishing its reduction target, such as the per capita allocation of greenhouse gas reductions pushed by many developing nations (discussed in the next chapter), has created great resistance and suspicion among some developing nations. China and India, for instance, have expressed concern that the United States has showed no desire to accept an equitable allocation of its reduction responsibilities and for that reason have expressed concern over the trading mechanisms. If the United States eventually accepts an equitable carbon reduction target, the trading mechanisms may be equitably benign. Yet for as long as the United States refuses to acknowledge its ethical responsibilities to emit only those amounts of greenhouse gases as consistent with principles of distributive justice, the trading mechanisms being pushed by the United States are ethically tainted. By insisting that issues of efficiency be resolved before issues of ethical responsibility, the United States has deflected attention from its ethical responsibility. Because the trading mechanisms are methods for finding lowest-cost solutions to the reduction of greenhouse gas emissions, they are of most interest to nations such as the United States that will be required to achieve the greatest reductions from status quo emissions. However, those developing nations that have little responsibility for the current problem have a legitimate interest in making sure that the large polluters accept their just responsibility. For this reason, issues of justice are of greater interest to many of the poorer nations than maximizing efficiency. If the nations concerned mostly about justice agree to trading mechanisms before an equitable national allocation is agreed to, they give away their leverage to achieve a just national allocation. For this reason, it may not be in the developing nations' interest to immediately agree to trading rules that are not implementing a fair allocation of emissions responsibilities. Therefore, a fourth ethical concern about the U.S. position on trading is that the trading mechanisms are not tied to equitable national allocations.

A TRADING SCHEME IS UNJUST IF IT ALLOWS RICH NATIONS TO PURCHASE THE CHEAPEST REDUCTIONS WHILE LEAVING THE POORER NATIONS WITH MORE EXPENSIVE REDUCTIONS

The clean development mechanism will allow the United States to fund cheap reduction projects in the developing world and obtain a credit toward its Kyoto target, bank the credit toward future U.S. carbon reductions, or sell the credit. The United States and other developed nations will no doubt attempt to find and fund the projects that will reduce the greatest amount of greenhouse gas emissions at the lowest possible price. For instance, because the capital and labor for planting trees are very inexpensive in the developing world, it is expected that the United States, along with other developed

Figure 10.2   Rich nations buy the atmosphere at a "fair" price

Reprinted with the permission of the Centre for Science and Environment, New Delhi, India, Rustam Vania/CSE.

nations, will fund inexpensive reforestation projects before funding capital-intensive electrical generation projects if the option is allowable under the trading rules. In deciding which projects to fund in the developing world, the United States and the developed nations will attempt to determine which projects provide the best ratio of carbon reduction credit to project cost. Along this line, to help buyers of carbon reduction projects find the projects that will create the least ratio of cost to carbon reduction, the World Bank is developing a portfolio of potential clean development mechanism projects. Once the United States or other developed nation funds such low-cost, high-credit projects, the credit for the amount of carbon reduced will go to the funding nation. Under the trading mechanisms, the developed nations may find low-cost projects and bank credits for future use. If, in the future, developing nations are allocated reduction targets, they may find that only more expensive carbon reduction projects are available because the cheapest ones have been appropriated by the developed nations. For this reason, the clean development mechanism may mean that the poorer nations are burdened with more expensive strategies to meet global warming obligations than the richer developed nations. Such a result would be unjust and is also a classic example of practices employed by colonial powers that sought to expropriate the resources of subjugated nations while not paying the true value. And so, some developing nations have demanded that the international allocations be negotiated before the rules to the clean development mechanism are finally agreed to. They are following this strategy because unless they know how much they can emit, they cannot know how much they can sell. A fourth ethical concern about the U.S. position on trading is that trading must be tied eventually, if not initially, to an equitable allocations scheme. A fifth reason why the U.S. position on the Kyoto trading mechanisms is ethically suspect is that it asks the developing nations to agree to a set of rules before the implications of these rules to the poor nations' interests are fully understood.

A TRADING SCHEME IS UNJUST IF IT LEADS TO GREATLY DIFFERENT RIGHTS OF PARTIES TO USE THE ATMOSPHERE AS A SINK

Many countries are arguing that it would be unjust to allow the developed countries to meet their entire reduction commitments through trading. The European Union and many of the developing nations assert that there should be some limitations on any nation's ability to use trading so that at least part of the domestic commitments are met through domestic emission reductions. The United States, Canada, Australia, Norway, and Japan, among others, want to be allowed to be able to meet their entire reduction commitments through trading. The ethical basis of an argument that trading should be a limited tool for meeting a national allocation is as follows:

• *A trade allows a nation like the United States to keep emitting a certain amount of pollution domestically, provided that it pays for equivalent reductions somewhere else.* Under the trading schemes created by the Kyoto Protocol, the amount of entitlements the United States gets through trading schemes to continue emitting greenhouse gases is equal to the amount of carbon emissions reduced outside the United States. Without a limit on the amount of pollution rights it could obtain, the United States could purchase the rights to keep polluting at very high levels domestically. For instance, under the Kyoto Protocol the United States would have to reduce emissions by 31 percent below its expected emissions in 2008. If the United States chooses to fund foreign projects to achieve this 31 percent reduction, it could wind up with credits to continue to be used against reduction goals of up to 552 million metric tons.[7] This is the amount of reduction from business as usual that is believed the United States must achieve to meet its 7 percent Kyoto target.[8] Under some versions of trading rules, the right to use these credits includes the right to bank credits for indefinite future use. For this reason, the United States could not only meet its target through trading but could also obtain unlimited reduction credits through trading that could be applied against future allowances. Yet future emission reduction targets will have to be much greater than those agreed to in the Kyoto Protocol to stabilize greenhouse gases in the atmosphere at safe levels. For instance, scientists believe that the world will need to reduce global emissions by as much as 60 to 80 percent below 1990 levels to stabilize greenhouse gases at safe levels. To implement such reductions, the world will need to negotiate an allocation for each nation. If this allocation is based on equitable principles, the U.S. share of a final reduction would be even greater than the 60 to 80 percent global reductions needed to achieve safe atmospheric stabilization levels because the United States is already emitting almost a quarter of the world's emissions. But if the United States purchases rights to offset any target by an indefinite amount of existing reductions, the United States may own a very large share of safe future global allowable emission rights. If a U.S. citizen's right to use the atmosphere as a carbon sink turns out to be much larger than the rights of citizens of other nations, the trading mechanisms that led to this result may lead to an unjust use of the global commons. This is so because justice demands a fair sharing of a problem's burdens and benefits. If the United States winds up with much larger rights to use the atmosphere as a sink than other nations and if carbon fuels remain cheaper than other fuels, trading may lock into place U.S. rights to use much cheaper fuels per capita than many other people worldwide. Trading may therefore lead to both higher benefits and lower burdens for Americans than others. Although trading may have generated the least-cost solutions to the global warming problems, it may also in this way lead to problems of distributive justice. For this reason, some believe that any nation should have only limited rights to use trading to meet national obligations.

- *By allowing the United States to buy its way out of making domestic reductions, the Kyoto Protocol trading mechanisms take the pressure off the United States to use alternative energy and more efficient energy and transportation and to fund alternatives to greenhouse emitting activities.* Yet the 7 percent reduction target is most likely less than 10 percent of a reduction target that the United States will need to meet to do its fair share to stabilize greenhouse gases at a safe level in the atmosphere. Therefore, if the United States is allowed to use unrestrained trading to achieve its entire Kyoto reduction, the United States will have little incentive to begin the major transformation away from activities that produce greenhouse gas emissions. The longer the world waits to reduce greenhouse gas emissions by adopting alternative energy systems, the more difficult it will be to stabilize greenhouse gases in the atmosphere at safe levels. Therefore, by allowing the United States to postpone serious domestic reduction of greenhouse gas emissions, full use of the trading mechanisms to achieve its Kyoto Protocol target may make it more difficult to stabilize greenhouse gases at safe levels in the future.

THE KYOTO TRADING MECHANISMS CREATE PROPERTY RIGHTS IN THE GLOBAL COMMONS

Under some versions of rules pushed by the United States, the Kyoto Protocol trading mechanisms can be understood to create property rights in the use of the global commons. This is so because credits received by those financing carbon reduction projects in other nations are classified as "entitlements" by the Kyoto Protocol and apparently create rights that extend indefinitely in the future. The United States has also pushed that any credits be "bankable," that is, usable at any future time. For instance, if the United States finances a carbon sequestration project in Africa that prevents 200,000 tons of carbon from being emitted into the atmosphere, under the U.S. preferred version of the trading rules, the United States is entitled to a credit for 200,000 tons of carbon that can be used against any future reduction target, or the credit can be sold by the United States at any time. In this way, rights to use the atmosphere as a sink become a commodity that can be bought or sold while the owner of the right has an expectation that it can cash that right in at any time it feels appropriate as any holder of valuable property would. Yet many feel that the atmosphere should be common trust property and should not be commodified.[9] That is, the atmosphere, along with other global commons resources such as the oceans, should be treated as public trust resources that should be protected by the government for the benefit of all citizens worldwide and future generations.

The recognition that certain natural resources should be protected as "public trust" resources has a long tradition in Roman, English, and American law.[10] Resources held in public trust are entrusted to government to be protected for the benefit of all people, including future generations. A central premise of what is usually referred to as the "public trust doctrine" is the notion that governments have no power to sell these resources but have an absolute duty to protect them for the benefit of all citizens, including future generations. If the atmosphere is a public trust resource, therefore, its use should not become the property of individuals or nations. The trustee must retain the right to do whatever is necessary to protect the public trust resource, yet property rights vest control not in the trustee but in the property holder.

If, for instance, it became necessary fifty years from now to limit all additional emissions of greenhouse gases because of threats to human health and the environment, the trustees' options should not be constrained by property rights that allow nations or individuals to continue emitting carbon. The practical implication of the public trust approach is that no nation or person should hold property rights to use the commons resources in ways that are not always subject to revision by those who are responsible for managing the resource for the benefit of all. Therefore, granting property rights in public commons resources conflicts with the idea that the public's interest should always be superior to private interests in the resource.

Among theories in environmental ethics discussed in chapter 3, biocentric and ecocentric ethical theories would be particularly opposed to treating the atmosphere as human property, for such an approach would make human interests superior to duty to protect plants, animals, and ecosystems.

One way in which trading could go forward without transforming the atmosphere into a commodity is to implement trading rules that give only temporary rights to use the atmosphere as a sink, provided that the temporary rights could be rescinded for cause. To implement such an approach, the rules on trading must expressly provide that carbon credits achieved through the trading mechanisms have only temporary significance and may at any time be rescinded by act of the trustee for cause. This temporary use would be understood to be subject to whatever revisions are necessary to protect the global commons for the benefit of all.

CONCLUSION

As we have seen, the flexibility mechanisms pushed by the United States designed to achieve the lowest-cost solutions to its obligations to reduce greenhouse gas emissions have raised serious ethical questions. Because the United States has a prior existing duty to reduce its greenhouse gas emissions to an equitable level, the U.S. insistence on global acceptance of its view of how the trading mechanisms should be structured is ethically troublesome. As one observer has said, if the United States gets its way on trading, "it will ensure inequitable and unjust trading, which will make the developing world poorer and the developed world richer."[11]

The U.S. approach to the trading rules also creates particularly disturbing precedents in regard to creating property rights to what many believe should be construed as global commons resources. At minimum, an intense global debate about the wisdom of creating property rights in the atmosphere is needed. The rush to adopt the trading rules pushed by the United States has not provided near enough time for full exploration of the wisdom of this approach.

There may be ways to create trading rules that avoid some of the ethical questions raised in this chapter. However, until a fair national allocation of greenhouse gas emissions levels are agreed to that will protect the global environment, any trading scheme will remain under an ethical cloud. The issue of what is a fair national share of environmentally acceptable global carbon emissions is the subject of the next chapter.

NOTES

1. White House, *The Kyoto Protocol and the President's Policies to Address Climate Change: An Economic Analysis,* 1998, 58 (available at <www.epa.gov/globalwarming/publications/actions/wh_kyoto/wh_full_rpt.pdf>, March 22, 2001).

2. Kyoto Protocol to the United Nations Framework Convention on Climate Change, December 10, 1997, UN Document FCCC/CP/197L.7/Add.1, Articles 4, 12, 17.

3. Kyoto Protocol to the United Nations Framework Convention on Climate Change, Article 3.3.

4. White House, *The Kyoto Protocol and the President's Policies to Address Climate Change,* 58.

5. Herman Ott and Wolfgang Sachs, *Ethical Aspects of Emissions Trading* (Wuppertal, Germany: Wuppertal Institute for Climate, Environment, and Energy, 2000) (available at <www.wupperinst.org/Publikationen/wp.html>, March 23, 2001).

6. Mark Sagoff, "Controlling Global Climate: The Debate over Pollution Trading," *Philosophy and Public Policy* 19 (1999): 1–6.

7. United States Energy Information Agency, *Carbon Emissions in Annex 1 Countries, 1990 to 2010, and Effects of the Kyoto Protocol in 2010* (available at <www.eia.doe.gov>, February 15, 2001).

8. United States Energy Information Agency, *Carbon Emissions in Annex 1 Countries, 1990 to 2010, and Effects of the Kyoto Protocol in 2010.*

9. For a discussion of private ownership issues to the atmosphere, see Peter Barnes, "Who Shall Inherit the Sky," Corporation for Enterprise Development, September 2000 (available at <www.cfed.org>, March 13, 2001).

10. For a discussion of public trust resources, see Helen Wyatt, "Common Assets: Asserting Rights to Our Shared Inheritance," Corporation for Enterprise Development, September 2000 (available at <www.cfed.org>, March 10, 2001).

11. Ross Gelbspan, "Rx for a Planetary Fever," *The American Prospect,* May 8, 2000 (available at <www.heatisonline.org/contentserver/objecthandlers/index.cfm?id=3477&method=full>, March 23, 2001).

Part III

OTHER GLOBAL
WARMING ETHICAL ISSUES

Chapter Eleven

An Equitable Allocation of Greenhouse Gas Emissions among Nations

Figure 11.1 Equity is left out of climate negotiations

EQUITY   CLIMATE NEGOTIATIONS

Reprinted with the permission of the Centre for Science and Environment, New Delhi, India, Rustam Vania/CSE.

THE IMPORTANCE OF EQUITABLE NATIONAL ALLOCATIONS IN INTERNATIONAL GLOBAL WARMING NEGOTIATIONS

The past four chapters examined the ethical dimensions of four arguments frequently made in opposition to global warming programs in the United States. However, the most important ethical question entailed by global warming that the United States needs to face is most probably the issue of what is its fair share of total global emissions that will maintain atmospheric levels of greenhouse gases at safe levels. The reason why this question is so

203

consequential is that this unresolved issue is the largest barrier currently blocking an international consensus on how to approach global warming. This is so because the question of what is a fair share of greenhouse gas emissions for each nation—although it has not been directly on the negotiation table—is at the very center of a number of recent impasses in climate negotiations. For instance, the developing nations have strongly resisted making commitments to reduce emissions pushed by the United States until the developed nations, and the United States in particular, agree to reduce emissions to an equitable level. The poorer nations are afraid that if they agree to cut back on carbon emissions now, the developed nations will demand that the poorer nations cut back further in the future rather than agree to a fair allocation for all nations. Because those rich nations that are most responsible for the greenhouse emergency have shown little interest in acknowledging their proportional responsibility for the existing problem, the poorer nations are often refusing to compromise on other issues.

The developed nations' failure to reduce their emissions to an equitable levels is, of course, also at the very center of the issue discussed in chapter 8, namely, whether the developing nations should make commitments to reduce greenhouse emissions at the same time the developed nations agree to implement their Kyoto reduction targets. This chapter takes up the issue of what equity requires of the developed and the developing nations if international negotiations turn to the issue of national allocations of greenhouse gases.

To get global warming under control, all nations will need to limit their greenhouse gas emissions to a specific amount in such a way that the total from all nations will stabilize atmospheric levels at safe concentrations. Because the richer nations emit more greenhouse gases than the poorer nations and because of the enormous magnitude of reductions that will be necessary to stabilize greenhouse gases in the atmosphere at safe levels, the issue of what is a fair allocation among nations raises enormously important but difficult political questions. This issue of equitable emissions allocations among nations is also of profound historical importance because it will force the international community to come to terms with how it will approach vital global commons questions. In coming to terms with the questions of emissions equity, for instance, the international community will have to decide such questions as whether the rich and powerful nations will be given greater rights than poorer nations to use the atmosphere as a sink for greenhouse gases. For this reason, the richer and more powerful nations will not be able to duck the question of whether they will come down on the side of global fairness or narrow national interest. Unfortunately, thus far, few of the more powerful richer nations, including the United States, have shown little interest in global fairness.

This chapter examines the question of global fairness in determining national allocations of greenhouse gas emissions. We already saw in chapter 5 that damages from global warming will affect the poorer nations more than developed ones.

To understand the enormous challenge to the international community posed by the issue of fair and equitable national allocations of greenhouse gas emissions, it is necessary to understand the enormous magnitude of emissions reductions that will be required to keep global warming from causing catastrophic damages. Because the cuts by the international community from existing emission levels need to be very steep to stabilize atmospheric greenhouse gas concentrations at safe levels, there is a lot at stake for nations in the magnitude of their national allocation.

The U.S. government understands that the reductions agreed to by nations in the Kyoto Protocol are only a first step toward reductions that will be necessary to achieve safe atmospheric levels of greenhouse gases. The Kyoto Protocol originally required that the United States reduce its greenhouse gases emissions by 7 percent below 1990 levels and that other developed nations collectively reduce emissions by 5.2 percent below 1990 emissions. This is only a first step because, as was explained in chapter 5, global emissions will need to be reduced between 50 and 80 percent below present emissions levels in order to achieve the goal of the UN Framework Convention on Climate Change (UNFCCC) of stabilizing atmospheric concentrations at safe levels. Eventually, nations will need to agree on what level of atmospheric greenhouse gases should be the stabilization target and then to an allocation among nations that will achieve this atmospheric goal. If, for instance, the world chooses to attempt to stabilize carbon dioxide at 500 parts per million (ppm), the total number of tons of carbon dioxide emissions that will maintain this level in the atmosphere can be calculated. However, the actual emissions reductions that will be necessary to achieve this atmospheric target will depend on the atmospheric levels that exist at the time of the calculation. The later the atmospheric target is agreed to, the greater the reductions will be needed to achieve the safe atmospheric level unless steep interim targets have been achieved. After calculating the total number of tons of carbon reductions needed to achieve the atmospheric target, nations will need to agree on their fair share of total allowable emissions. It is this question of a fair share of global emissions that raises extraordinarily important questions for the United States and for all members of the international community.

The principles of the UNFCCC provide some relevant guidance to nations on how they should think about their allocations. The principles provide that each nation should "protect the climate system for the benefit of present and future generations of humankind, on the basis of *equity* and in accordance with their *common but differentiated responsibilities* and respective capabilities"[1] (italics added). Therefore, the United States has already agreed in the UNFCCC that it should reduce its emissions to an equitable level. Yet one may ask, What does equity require of the United States?

Many have asserted that equity simply means the quality of being fair with others.[2] Yet if equity simply means "fairness" and because different parties have claimed that their approaches to emissions reductions are fair, an understanding of equity as simple fairness without criteria for determining what is fair provides no way of resolving disputes among contending parties who claim that their approach is fair. Along this line, at an April 2001 conference on equity and climate change organized by the Pew Center for Climate Change, a few speakers asserted that various positions that have been advanced as fair by nations should be given equal respect as fair because there was no way of deciding what constitutes fairness.[3] If there are no principles for deciding among claims about the fairness of various national proposals for the right to future use of the atmosphere to absorb greenhouse emissions, as some assert, the only way of resolving disputes about fairness is through negotiation. Without principles to use in negotiation, raw power will likely determine outcomes. Yet because so much is at stake for nations in the quantity of greenhouse gases that they will be allowed to emit pursuant to an allocation, no global consensus is likely to emerge on national allocations unless nations perceive that global allocations are fair. For this reason and because many philosophers, theologians, and other interested people hold that there are principles that can help illuminate the concepts of equity and fairness, the next few sections of this chapter examine principles for a just and fair allocation of national emissions.

Under the UNFCCC, several nations have made specific proposals on criteria to define what principles constitute equitable reductions. The Intergovernmental Panel on Climate Change (IPCC) has grouped these proposals into the following categories:[4]

- *Ad hoc proposals.* These include various approaches to equitable allocations, including those that divide total global emissions into equal shares between developed and developing nations and those that make allocations follow some proportional relationship to a nation's gross domestic product (GDP).
- *Equal per capita entitlements.* Many developing nations have suggested that national allocations should be based on the idea that all human beings should be entitled to an equal share of the atmospheric resource.
- *Status quo.* Several developed nations have argued that current rates of emissions should be entitled to "status quo" entitlements. Because the United States has only been willing thus far to negotiate emissions reduc-

tions from current levels, the U.S. position in negotiations on national allocations has sometimes been interpreted as a version of status quo entitlements or even as a version of "squatter's rights," the idea that whoever used the commons first has a legal right to continue to use it at levels that are based on past use.

- *Mixed systems.* Several nations have proposed rules for equitable allocations based on mixes of per capita, equal percentage cuts, status quo, and historical responsibility and entitlements.

In addition to these criteria to define "equitable" allocations contained in national proposals, others have identified a host of additional principles that they have argued could or should be followed to make equitable allocations of greenhouse gas emissions among nations. These include the following:[5]

- *Basic needs and Rawlsian criteria.* These principles urge that allocations would follow the presumptions on just allocations advocated by John Rawls (discussed in chapter 3) that provide that the poorest nations should be first in line to receive allocations needed to meet their basic needs to participate in the world as full citizens and that in no case should the poorest nations be made worse off through any allocation scheme.
- *Proportionality and the polluter-pays principle.* This principle would make allocations on the basis of each nation's historical and existing contribution to the damage caused by global warming.
- *Comparable burdens.* This principle would make allocations on the basis that each nation should share the effort equally of reducing emissions to safe levels. Such a rule could be implemented if each nation would allocate an equal percentage of its GDP to greenhouse gas emissions.
- *Ability to pay.* This principle would make the richer nations more responsible than the poorer ones because of their greater ability to absorb costs of reducing emissions.
- *Principles of narrow welfare economics.* Many, although not all, welfare economists argue that distributions should be made on the basis of which option maximizes utility. As we saw in chapter 3, such claims often are based on utilitarian ethical theories.

What sense can be made of these competing criteria to determine the equity of national greenhouse gas emissions reduction allocations? Are all definitions of equity entitled to equal respect as asserted by some? The following analysis demonstrates that as a matter of ethics or justice, many proposed criteria for determining equitable national allocations of greenhouse gases are quite dubious and must be rejected.

CONSIDERATIONS FOR JUDGING PROPOSED EQUITABLE NATIONAL ALLOCATIONS OF GREENHOUSE GAS EMISSIONS

This section identifies a few principles that can be used to judge the acceptability of proposals to establish national greenhouse gas emissions allocation schemes.

Efficiency Claims versus Justice Claims

A number of economists have recommended that greenhouse gas allocations among nations be set to maximize global utility or efficiency.[6] The idea is that the allocation scheme to reduce greenhouse gas emissions should be chosen that maximizes global GDP or some other measure of global economic activity. It would make no difference under such proposals if the U.S. economy would prosper more than other nations that might shoulder more of the burden of reducing greenhouse gas emissions, provided that total global economic activity is maximized in the chosen option compared to alternative allocation schemes for reducing greenhouse gas emissions. The ethical basis for such proposals is, as discussed in chapter 3, the utilitarian notion that public policy decisions should choose the option that maximizes happiness or utility as measured by market preferences.

Such utilitarian prescriptions are often indifferent to how burdens are distributed. That is, according to some often-followed economic theories, distribution inequalities in assigning burdens to implement public policy can be ignored, provided that aggregate utility is maximized. If such an approach were followed in determining national allocations for greenhouse gas emissions, it could lead to the result that some people would have vastly different rights than others to use the atmosphere as a sink. In other words, such approaches often ignore distributional equity.

Not all economists, of course, argue that distributional inequities should be ignored. Some economists actually urge that compensation should be provided to those who are harmed by public policy decisions that seek to achieve international welfare maximization or that such decisions should avoid disproportionate harm altogether.[7] Yet many narrow welfare maximization schemes ignore distributional effects.[8] Because distributional equity is ignored in these schemes, proposals to define equitable criteria on the basis of welfare maximization without compensation to losers must be rejected out of hand as fundamentally inconsistent with the idea of equitable and just distributions. Although some economists and others argue that public policy options be chosen that maximize utility without regard to distributional effects, it is disingenuous of proponents of this approach to argue that this approach is "equitable" for so long as distributional equity is ignored. Equity and justice demand that policymakers examine whether those who are harmed by public policy decisions are being treated fairly. If these questions are ignored in the prescriptions recommended by some, they cannot claim that their prescriptions are equitable.

In addition to the ethical concern with the use of welfare maximization strategies to assign national greenhouse gas emission rights, there are large practical problems with such approaches in an international setting that are not present in domestic policymaking. Any nation could choose to follow welfare maximization strategies domestically because sovereign governments have the ability to choose such strategies on behalf of their citizens. Yet if some nations are asked to shoulder proportionally larger burdens of protecting the atmosphere than other nations, it is highly unlikely that they would agree to a strategy that would make them poorer while others gained simply on the basis that total aggregate global welfare would be increased. This is particularly the case where some nations have been benefiting from irresponsible energy use. In an international system, nations are likely to prefer options that are viewed as just over those that maximize global utility. For this reason, narrow welfare maximization strategies are not only inconsistent with theories of equity but are also less likely to achieve widespread international support. Particularly the poorest countries that do not receive the benefits of high levels of global economic activity will likely strongly oppose proposed allocations that ask them to bear disproportionate burdens.

"Status Quo" or "Grandfathering" as a Basis for National Allocations

So far, the United States has not been willing to discuss its equitable share of the worldwide carbon reduction needs, although its position in negotiations could also be understood to stand for the proposition that "grandfathering" its high rate of emissions is fair. The term "grandfathering" in this context is usually understood to connote certain rights to use resources based on prior use levels.

The United States understood that Kyoto was only a first step toward much larger reductions that would be needed to be made to stabilize greenhouse gases at safe levels. The United States has never denied that eventually it must reduce its emissions based on equity; it simply has fought to keep commonly understood equitable considerations from becoming the basis for its early commitments.[9]

At Kyoto, the United States agreed to reduce greenhouse gas emissions 7 percent below 1990 levels. This Kyoto commitment was based neither on what reductions were necessary to achieve safe atmospheric greenhouse gas levels nor on what the United States thought were equitable shares for each nation of needed global reduction goals. Instead, the commitments of the United States and other developed nations were based on what were reasonable reductions from historical emissions. The United States, along with some other developed nations, has strongly resisted basing reductions on equity in the early commitment periods. Whether the United States would agree to equity as a basis for future commitments is an open question because of how strenuously the United States has resisted considerations of equity thus far. Because of this resistance to discuss equity, some have interpreted the U.S. position as a claim that those who have used the atmosphere as a sink for the absorption of emissions have a right to continue using the atmosphere in an amount that is linked to historical use reduced only by economically feasible reductions. In other words, the U.S. position on allocations could be understood as a call to accept grandfathering of its high level of emissions. However, if the United States continues to argue that its emissions should be limited to economically feasible reductions from historical use, it will have both ignored the previously mentioned UNFCCC provision requiring all parties to reduce emissions on the basis of equity and offended principles of distributive justice that require a fair sharing of benefits and burdens of a problem, as we will see in this chapter.

Acknowledging rights in existing uses of natural resources is an approach that has been recognized as valid by some nations under some circumstances, including many western states in the United States, under the legal theory of "prior appropriation" of water rights.[10] This legal theory holds that those who first appropriate water resources for personal use have prior rights over others who come later. The legal maxim that is often used to explain the law of prior appropriation is, "First in time, first in right." The notion that people who first appropriate natural resources for their own use should be understood to have acquired rights to continued use is also a theory often attributed to the philosopher Robert Nozick, who was influenced by John Locke.[11]

Yet rights to the continued use of international natural resources based on prior use levels have not been recognized by the international community. Such rights would also be inconsistent with: the UNFCCC's provision that nations should reduce their emissions to equitable levels, the polluter-pays principle, and principles of distributive justice discussed in this chapter. In addition, in the case of global warming, the activity that some seek to grandfather is not simply some benign use of a natural resource but also levels of polluting activities. Even the law of prior appropriation does not create prescriptive rights to pollute at historical levels.

One form that a claim for grandfathering prior use levels takes is in proposals that call for all nations to be given uniform reductions from existing emissions levels. Yet clearly, the drafters of the UNFCCC had something else in mind when they provided in the UNFCCC that nations should reduce their emissions on the basis of "equity." This is clear because, as we have seen, the UNFCCC also provides that *equity* should be determined in "*accordance with common but differentiated responsibilities*" (italics added). This clause makes it clear that equity must turn on responsibility for the problem under the climate change treaty. But if responsibility for the global warming problem is to be a criteria for reducing emissions to an equitable level, a nation that asserts that its high rate of emissions should be grandfathered and that such grandfathering is consistent with equity is advancing a position fundamentally inconsistent with the UNFCCC. For this reason, all national proposals, including recent positions of the United States, that attempt to define equitable reductions as uniform reductions from existing emissions levels should be rejected as inconsistent with the UNFCCC's call for equitable reductions.

Distributive Justice

As we saw in chapter 3, how benefits and burdens of public policy should be distributed among societies is a classic problem of distributive justice. Distributive justice demands that the benefits and burdens of public policy to society be distributed according to concepts of equality or merit or some combination of these two. Principles of distributive justice attempt to resolve tensions between treating people equally and making distributions on the basis of merit or deservedness. Not all claims to be treated differently in public policy are entitled to respect as a matter of distributive justice. For instance, a person's claim that she should be paid more because she has green eyes would not be recognized by principles of distributive justice as valid. This is so because having green eyes is an accident of birth, not something that is based on merit. On the other hand, if two children are given equal amounts of money and one invests the money while the other wastes it, justice would acknowledge that the child who invests the money is entitled to have more than the child who wastes the money because the child who invested the money acted meritoriously. The difference in outcomes, in this case, is supported by principles of distributive justice because the difference in result has been caused by a meritorious act.

Distributive justice puts the burden on those who want to be treated differently than others to show that the basis for being treated differently is a relevant distinction based on merit or deservedness. For this reason, as a matter of distributive justice, those who propose criteria for defining equity that is different than giving all people equal rights to use the atmosphere have the burden of proving that differences in treatment are based on merit or deservedness of such a kind that should be recognized by distributive justice. And so contrary to the notion discussed previously that because fairness cannot be defined all claims of fairness are entitled to equal respect, concepts of distributive justice start from the notion that equal treatment should be the starting presumption and that no claim for differential treatment should be acknowledged unless it is based on relevant merit or deservedness considerations.

One exception to the rule that only distinctions based on merit or deservedness should be considered just are rules of justice proposed by the philosopher John Rawls (see chapter 3) that would justify differential treatment if an option increases the well-being of the least well off. Yet whether one follows more traditional principles of distributive justice or Rawlsian rules that would make distributions benefit the poor, the proponent of any distributive scheme that deviates from treating equally should have the burden of demonstrating why the proposed distribution scheme is just.

One distinction based on deservedness that distributive justice would acknowledge as a relevant basis for treating people differently in greenhouse gas emission allocations is differences among people in responsibility for the existing problem. Responsibility for a harm is a type of deservedness that principles of distributive justice will recognize. Therefore, the polluter-pays principle discussed in earlier chapters is not inconsistent with theories of distributive justice because polluters deserve to have greater responsibilities for the problem because they caused the problem.

Prior Agreements Relating to National Responsibility for Emissions

As we saw in chapter 4, the United States agreed to the polluter-pays principle as well as the idea that nations have a duty to prevent transboundary environmental damage to other nations in the Rio Declaration at Principles 2 and 16.[12] These principles make the United States responsible for its proportionate share of greenhouse gases in the atmosphere beyond naturally occurring levels. As we saw previously, in the UNFCCC the United States also agreed to the notion that equity should be interpreted in *"accordance with common but differentiated responsibilities"* (italics added). Because the United States and other nations have already agreed to these principles and because in determining the meaning of a term in dispute such as "equity" in the UNFCCC it is appropriate as a matter of international law to look to the terms used in existing customs and prior agreements, any national allocation scheme must be consistent with these principles that tie responsibility to reduce emissions to causation of the greenhouse problem. For this reason, in examining national proposals to establish criteria for national allocations of greenhouse gas emissions, any proposal that fails to assign responsibility for emissions on the basis of proportional causation of the problem can be rejected as inconsistent with prior international agreements.

REVIEW OF THREE METHODS FOR ALLOCATING GREENHOUSE EMISSIONS AMONG NATIONS

As we have seen, there have been a number of proposals that have been floated by nations on how nations should implement reductions to an equitable level. For the most part, these proposals have been designed to secure advantage for the nation making the proposal. This section examines the ethical dimensions of three prominent proposals on equitable sharing of global emissions by applying the previously discussed principles. The proposals on making national greenhouse gas emissions allocations reviewed here include per capita allocations, proposals on emissions-to-GDP ratios, and a hybrid proposal by the Pew Center for Climate Change.

Per Capita National Allocations

In 1991, the Indian government, in global warming negotiations held at Geneva, introduced the idea that equity demands that national emission caps be based on a global per capita calculation. At this meeting, the Indian representative said,

> The problem of global warming is caused by excessive levels of per capita emissions of these [GHG] gases . . . an equitable solution can only be found on the basis of significant reductions in levels of per capita emissions in industrial countries, so that, over a period of years, these converge with rising per capita emissions in developing countries.[13]

In the aftermath of Kyoto, many of the developing nations have continued to argue that equity demands that national allocations be based on equal per capita shares of global targets. These per capita–based allocations could be calculated by first deciding on a safe concentration of greenhouse gases in the atmosphere and then dividing the total number of tons of emissions that will achieve the atmospheric goal by the world's population. For instance, the IPCC suggested 450 ppm as a safe concentration level (though even at this level there will be a temperature increase of 0.7°C and a sea-level rise of 10 to 65 centimeters).[14] In this case, the worldwide per capita entitlement in 1990 would have been 1.1 metric tons of carbon (tC) per capita.[15] The European Union has advocated a 550-ppm atmospheric target for carbon dioxide. The

1990 per capita entitlement would then have been 1.5 tC for a stabilization goal of 550 ppm.[16] The U.S. per capita emission level in 1990 was 5.41 tC.[17] Therefore, if the United States were to accept a per capita allocation to stabilize greenhouse gases at either 450 or 550 ppm, it would have to reduce its emissions by 70 to 80 percent below 1990 levels. For this reason, the United States has strongly resisted greenhouse targets derived through per capita calculations.

Of course, it would be physically impossible for the United States to implement a per capita–based allocation in the short term, for such an allocation would require almost immediate abandoning of fossil fuel–derived energy, a practical impossibility. Given that even under a very aggressive U.S. global warming prevention strategy it will take decades to replace power plants that burn fossil fuel and most of the transportation sector that runs on gasoline, it would be impossible for the United States to implement a per capita–based greenhouse gas national allocation in the short to medium term unless the United States were allowed to trade for credits as discussed in chapter 10.

Because of the long phase-in time that would be required to move toward per capita allocations in the developed nations, those developing nations pushing for per capita allocation have proposed an approach usually referred to as "contraction and convergence." Contraction and convergence means an allocation that would allow the large emitter nations long enough time, perhaps thirty or forty years, to contract their emissions through the replacement of greenhouse gas–emitting capital and infrastructure and eventually converge on a uniform per capita allocation.[18] Support for contraction and convergence has been building around the world with the European Parliament in 1998 recently calling for its adoption with a 90 percent majority.[19]

A per capita allocation would be just for the following reasons:

- It treats all individuals as equals and therefore is consistent with theories of distributive justice.
- It would implement the ethical maxim that all people should have equal rights to use a global commons.
- It would implement the widely accepted polluter-pays principle.

A per capita allocation would implement the polluter-pays principle because, through implementation of this approach, no nation would be polluting at a level greater than its fair share of pollution loading.

A per capita–based national carbon allocation, of course, would have the greatest impact on those nations that have the highest per capita emissions rates, such as the United States. A per capita allocation would require some nations, including the United States, to deeply reduce per capita emissions while others are allowed to expand to per capita amounts. Particularly for this reason, a per capita–based allocation is a particularly tough sell in the United States because it is feared that it would create incentives for domestic carbon-intensive industries to go offshore or require huge transfer payments to developing nations.[20] The only way that a per capita allocation approach is politically feasible in the United States is to make the target effective at a long enough time in the future to allow domestic industries time to adjust and adopt new technologies that produce less carbon.

As a result of the intense political opposition to the per capita approach to carbon targets, a few alternative approaches to equitable allocations have been pushed in the United States, including the "emissions/GDP" allocation formula and the Pew Center for Climate Change proposal discussed in this chapter.

Because of the burden that a per capita–based allocation scheme would have on the developed countries to dramatically reduce their emissions, opposition in some of the rich nations, and particularly in the United States, has been strong. Yet some have argued, and a strong case could be made, that a per capita–based allocation would not be fair enough to the poorest nations because such an approach fails to consider the cumulative contribution of the rich nations to the existing problem. The factual basis of this argument is, as we have seen in earlier chapters, that most of the existing global warming problem has been caused by the developed nations. Therefore, it can be argued that the poorer nations should be given larger emission rights than purely per capita–based allowances. This amount would be determined by adjusting per capita–based amounts by amounts that take into account the historical responsibility of nations that have caused the existing problem.

Others oppose a per capita–based national emissions allocation scheme on the basis that it would reward irresponsible population growth. However, several schemes have arisen for dealing with this potential problem, including proposals to set a population baseline at 1990 population levels.[21]

Allocations Based on the Emissions-to-GDP Ratio

Some have argued that in determining an equitable national share of a global greenhouse gas emission limitation, it would also be fair to consider a ratio of emissions per unit of GDP.[22] This should be a relevant "equitable" consideration, according to the argument made by some, because those who produce less greenhouse gases per unit of GDP should be rewarded for more efficient carbon reductions per unit of economic activity and, at the same time, not be penalized for having achieved higher levels of economic activity. Yet using efficiency as the sole determinate of an equitable allocation does not withstand ethical scrutiny for the following reasons:

- *A national greenhouse gas allocation will determine how much of the global commons (i.e., the atmosphere) each person on the planet is entitled to use in the future.* Principles of distributive justice make us ask whether more efficient use of the atmosphere should be recognized as a relevant basis for deviating from the expectation that people should have equal rights to use the atmosphere. As a matter of distributive justice, efficiency is a relevant basis for allowing the efficient to obtain greater benefit from their use of the atmosphere due to the increased economic activity that efficiency will allow. This greater economic benefit will be experienced by the efficient even if an initial allocation is based on per capita considerations. However, efficiency is not a relevant consideration for determining a just initial allocation because efficiency is not relevant to how the initial distribution should be made. That is, although efficiency could be classified as something deserving recognition for "merit" or "deservedness" that should be recognized under the concept of distributive justice as a basis for justifying differences in economic outcomes, it cannot be shown that efficiency is a relevant consideration for justifying differences in initial distributions of how much of the atmosphere each person should be entitled to use. Where no good ground can be shown for treating people differently, they clearly ought to be treated alike according to principles of distributive justice.[23] Therefore, although the more efficient will be able to generate greater wealth from the same amount of absorptive capacity of the atmosphere assigned to them as others, the efficient should not be able to argue that they should be entitled to use more of the absorptive capacity of the atmosphere according to principles of distributive justice. That is, efficiency is not a morally relevant category for the initial distribution of the atmosphere's absorptive capacity.
- *An efficiency-based allocation would mean that members of future generations who had ancestors who were less efficient than others' ancestors would be given less access to the use of the atmosphere than those who had more efficient ancestors.* Therefore, through no fault of their own, if fossil fuels remain cheaper than other sources of energy, some members of future generations would be asked to share a greater burden to protect the global commons than others who happened to have ancestors who had access to more efficient technology. Because such a distribution would not be based on equality or other considerations relevant to just distributions, it would not be just in regard to future generations.
- *An efficiency-based allocation does not implement the polluter-pays principle discussed previously.* If efficiency alone were the basis of national al-

locations, those nations that were adding the most carbon to the atmosphere would have no responsibility to reduce emissions in proportion to their pollution levels.

- *An efficiency-based allocation might unfairly freeze the rights of the richer nations at levels much higher than those of the poorer nations, thus cementing into place inequities in the international economic system.* This is so because the richer nations might be able to afford more costly but more efficient technology, thereby reducing carbon emissions per unit of GDP and giving them a leg up against those poorer nations that could not afford the less polluting technology. This result would be particularly ethically troublesome, as some of the industrial countries have reached a high level of development because they have failed to pay the full cost of their use of natural resources.[24] In other words, some of the rich nations became rich by exploiting the environment.

The Pew Climate Change Formula for Equity

In 1998, the Pew Center for Climate Change issued a report on equity and climate change that is likely to be adopted by the United States in future negotiations because its results are roughly consistent with prior U.S. positions.[25] Although an analysis of the equity of the Pew position requires elaboration of a number of very technical considerations, it is included here because it is likely to be supported by many in the United States if and when the United States finally faces equitable allocation issues.

The Pew Center proposal on equity divides nations into three categories through an analysis of three variables that Pew has chosen to define equity: responsibility, standard of living, and opportunity to reduce emissions more cheaply than others. The first of these (responsibility) and perhaps the second (standard of living) are not inconsistent with concepts of distributive justice per se, yet problems of distributive justice arise in the Pew scheme in some of the details of how these criteria are used, as we will see. The Pew proposal identifies all three of these categories as constituting an equitable approach without explaining why these categories are entitled to respect as equitable. Therefore, one must speculate on why various distinctions have been made in the Pew approach to equity.

The Pew Use of "Responsibility" to Determine Equity

Under the concept of "responsibility," Pew categorized all nations into low, medium, and high levels of responsibility for historical climate change emissions from 1950 to 1995.[26] In calculating the credit that any nations obtained for responsibility for emissions, the Pew allocation used per capita emissions in 1995 and future responsibility for carbon dioxide emissions measured by an average annual rate of growth in carbon dioxide emissions between 1992 and 1995.

The Pew Use of "Standard of Living" to Determine Equity

Under the concept of "standard of living," Pew categorized all nations into low, medium, and high standards of living using GDP per capita as the measure of the nation's standard of living. Those nations that had GDP per capita above the average were ranked as high, those that had GDP per capita amounts between the median and the average were classified as medium, and all countries below the median were ranked as low.

The Pew Use of "Opportunity to Reduce Emissions Cheaply" to Determine Equity

Under the concept of "opportunity to reduce emissions," Pew categorized nations into low-, medium-, and high-energy intensity, where energy intensity was determined by dividing the amount of a nation's energy use by its GDP. Those nations that had energy intensity ratios above the average were ranked as high, those that had energy intensity ratios between the median and the average were classified as medium, and all countries below the median were ranked as low.

How Pew Integrated Responsibility, Standard of Living, and Opportunity to Reduce Emissions Cheaply to Determine Equitable Responsibilities

Nations that ranked high in responsibility and standard of living regardless of their ranking in opportunity to reduce emissions were ranked in the category "must act now." Nations were classified in the "should act now but differently" category if they ranked in the middle of any two classifications (responsibility, opportunity, and standard of living) or if they did not qualify for the "could act now" category. Any nation that ranked low in two classifications of responsibility, opportunity, and standard of living were ranked in the "could act now" category.

Using these methods, Pew ranked these nations as follows:

- *Must act now:* Argentina, Australia, Austria, Belgium, Canada, Chile, Czech Republic, Denmark, France, Germany, Greece, Israel, Italy, Japan, Kuwait, Malaysia, Mexico, the Netherlands, Norway, Portugal, Saudi Arabia, Singapore, Slovenia, South Korea, Spain, Thailand, United Arab Emirates, United Kingdom, United States, and Venezuela

- *Should act now but differently:* Algeria, Azerbaijan, Belarus, Brazil, Bulgaria, China, Columbia, Ecuador, Egypt, Estonia, Finland, Gabon, Georgia, Hungary, Iceland, India, Iran, Ireland, Jamaica, Jordan, Kazakhstan, Kyrgyz Republic, Latvia, Lithuania, Mauritius, Moldavia, New Zealand, Oman, Panama, Papua New Guinea, Paraguay, Peru, the Philippines, Poland, Romania, Russia, Slovak Republic, South Africa, Suriname, Sweden, Switzerland, Syria, Tajikistan, Trinidad and Tobago, Tunisia, Turkey, Turkmenistan, Ukraine, Uruguay, Uzbekistan, and Yugoslavia
- *Could act now:* Albania, Angola, Armenia, Bangladesh, Barbados, Benin, Bhutan, Bolivia, Botswana, Burkina Faso, Cambodia, Cameroon, Cape Verde Islands, Central African Republic, Chad, Comoros, Democratic Republic of Congo, Republic of Congo, Cook Islands, Costa Rica, Cote d'Ivoire, Djibouti, Dominica, Dominican Republic, El Salvador, Eritrea, Ethiopia, Fiji, Gambia, Ghana, Grenada, Guatemala, Guinea, Guinea-Bissau, Guyana, Haiti, Honduras, Indonesia, Kenya, Kiribati, Laos, Madagascar, Malawi, Maldives, Mali, Mauritania, Mongolia, Morocco, Mozambique, Myanmar, Nepal, Nicaragua, Niger, Nigeria, Niue, North Korea, Pakistan, Samoa, Senegal, Sierra Leone, Solomon Islands, Sri Lanka, Sudan, Swaziland, Tanzania, Togo, Uganda, Vanuatu, Vietnam, Yemen, Zambia, and Zimbabwe

Some of the ethical problems with the Pew approach to an equitable carbon allocation include the following:

- *The Pew equity scheme does not answer the question of how much any country needs to act to meet its equitably based obligations.* That is, the categories of "must act now," "should act now but differently," and "could act now" give no indication of what amount of action or reductions any nation needs to achieve. Under the "must act now" category, for instance, the United States could continue to implement its Climate Action Plan, which has made little progress in decreasing U.S. greenhouse gas emissions, and argue that it is acting and therefore has fulfilled its equitable duty to "act now." For this reason, the Pew categories not only do not establish what levels of reduction a nation needs to achieve but also allow a nation to argue that any action fulfills its national responsibility.
- *The Pew equity scheme puts nations with very different levels of historic responsibility in the same category and thereby assigns to them the same responsibility to act.* For instance, the United States emits 19.4 tons of carbon dioxide per capita, while Thailand emits 2.9 tons of carbon dioxide per capita, and they both have the same responsibility that they "must act now."[27] The Pew scheme also puts nations with similar levels of responsibility in different categories. For instance, Ireland emits 9.2 tons of carbon

dioxide per capita but is ranked in the category "should act now but differently," while Thailand, with 2.9 tons per capita of carbon dioxide emissions, is ranked in the "must act now" category. The Pew scheme does not explain why such a result is just. In fact, the Pew scheme does not explain why its categories satisfy principles of distributive justice or why the classifications of nations into the groups within categories are just. By putting nations with similar historical responsibility in different categories, the Pew scheme ignores the polluter-pays principle.

- *The ethical basis for using "standard of living" and "opportunity for making reductions" categories is not clear from the Pew explanation.* The Pew Center appears to assume that nations with high standards of living or the opportunity to make reductions have an ethical obligation to make reductions regardless of the amount of responsibility they have to act because of their past and current contributions in causing the problem. Although the notion that those with the most resources to help suffering around the world have the greatest ethical obligation to reduce the suffering might be noble, it is not a norm that has been recognized in the international community, nor does it follow from principles of distributive justice. Under such an approach, the United States would have the greatest responsibility for foreign aid, yet the United States is last in foreign aid as a percentage of GDP among the developed nations. In addition, it is not clear how the financial ability or technical opportunity to reduce greenhouse gases should be considered in relation to responsibility.
- *Under the Pew scheme, nations that achieved a high standard of living and had high responsibility had the same ethical responsibility.* That is, they "must act now" even though some nations that would be ranked high in these categories had done much more to lower greenhouse gas emissions than others. For instance, although most of Europe and the United States are ranked high in both standard of living and responsibility, some of the European nations have done much more than the United States to reduce greenhouse gas emissions. Yet under the Pew scheme, no recognition for prior responsible behavior is recognized.
- *In assigning responsibility to nations, the Pew scheme considers "potential future use" as well as historical use to determine existing responsibility.* Yet the very purpose of an equitable allocation is to guide future use. Why future use would be relevant to an equitable allocation is not obvious and appears to be a device to find greater responsibility for developing nations that have been growing rapidly. As we have seen, distributive justice requires that any consideration different from equal treatment of people that is to be used to calculate how much of burden a nation must accept for a problem must be shown to be based on merit or deservedness.[28] Yet it is not

clear why potential future use is in any way a morally relevant consideration for establishing obligations that exist now.

CONCLUSION

As we have seen, agreement on equitable greenhouse gas national allocations that maintain atmospheric concentrations of greenhouse gases at safe levels may be the most important ethical question that the United States needs to face in the future. Yet thus far, the United States has demonstrated no interest in facing this issue. The failure to face this issue has been and is likely to continue to be a barrier to a much-needed international solution to global warming. That is, as argued in chapter 4, only if the developing world believes that it is being treated fairly is it likely to support a global agreement.

The U.S. position on equity should be consistent with principles of distributive justice. Distributive justice requires that any criterion that is to be used to justify deviations from giving people equal rights to use the atmosphere must be based on considerations of merit or deservedness or other morally relevant factors. There may be other morally relevant considerations not discussed in this chapter that could serve as a basis for adjusting national allocations from per capita–based calculations. Yet the proponents of those criteria must demonstrate why these considerations are entitled to ethical respect.

Rather than giving any proposal to define equity equal respect, distributive justice demands that criteria to establish deviations from equality be shown to be ethically compelling. For this reason, any proponent of criteria to define equity that is different from an approach that would give all humans equal rights to use the atmosphere should have the burden of proof to make compelling ethical arguments why their alternative is entitled to ethical respect. For this reason, if the United States desires to propose an alternative to a per capita allocation, it must demonstrate why its proposed alternative is ethically compelling.

Those opposing allocations that give people equitable rights to use the atmosphere will argue that all claims of fairness are entitled to equal respect; therefore, there is no alternative to negotiating alternative proposals. Yet this chapter has demonstrated that there are a number of well-established principles to judge equitable approaches to sharing the benefits and burdens of public policy. Those who assert that all claims to fairness are entitled to equal respect rob moral reasoning of its rational basis and deny time-honored approaches to determining fairness of public policy.

An enormous historical challenge is facing the United States. The question is whether the world's greatest power will be willing to abide by ethical and moral considerations in accepting its fair share of use of the global commons. That is, will the United States be willing to abide by an equitable rule relating to carbon emissions that requires the United States to put global interests ahead of narrow national interest? The world desperately needs the United States to answer this question in the affirmative. Although it is not alone, so far the United States has been leading the parade of those nations that want to make the rules on greenhouse emissions allocations protect the national interests of the richest nations. The United States is now called on to show historically profound ethical leadership. The way to protect its national interest ethically is to negotiate a reasonable amount of time to come into compliance with an equitable international allocation. Given the tremendous innovative creativity of the United States, it could likely achieve a just national allocation by the middle of this century. It would, however, require a tremendous act of political courage for any American politician to entertain this approach unless the American public understands its ethical responsibility and demands that the United States accept its just obligations.

NOTES

1. United Nations Framework Convention on Climate Change (UNFCCC), New York, May 9, 1992, UN Document A/CONF.151/26, Article 3.

2. See, for example, Paul Harris, "Is the United States Sharing the Burden?" in Paul Harris, ed., *Climate Change and American Foreign Policy* (New York: St. Martin's Press, 2000), 32. For another example of the claim that equity means only "fairness," see T. Banuri, K. Goran-Maler, M. Grubb, H. K. Jacobson, and F. Yamin, "Equity and Social Considerations," in *Economic and Social Dimensions of Climate Change: Contribution of Working Group III to the Second Assessment Report of the Intergovernmental Panel on Climate Change* (Cambridge: Cambridge University Press, 1996), 85.

3. For copies of presentations made on equity and climate made at the Pew Center for Climate Change conference held on April 16–17, 2000, on equity and climate change, see <www.pewcenter.org>, April 22, 2001.

4. Banuri et al., "Equity and Social Considerations," 106.

5. This list is a synthesis of equitable criteria to be considered in making allocations identified by Banuri et al., "Equity and Social Considerations," and Adam Rose, "Equitable Considerations of Tradable Carbon Emission Entitlements" in United Nations Conference on Trade and Environment, *Combating Global Warming: Study on a Global System of Tradable Carbon Emission Entitlements* (New York: United Nations, 1992), 55. For a discussion of the national proposals on criteria to determine equitable allocations, see also David M. Reiner and Henry D. Jacoby, "Annex I Differentiation Proposals: Implications for Welfare, Equity and Policy," in *Joint Program on Science and Policy of Global Change* (Cambridge: MIT Press, 1997).

6. Not all economists argue that efficiency alone should be the criteria on which to base public policy decisions relating to distributions of the benefits and burdens. A growing group of economists concerned with equity argue in support of both efficiency and equity as criteria to be considered in attempting to maximize human welfare.

7. For instance, Adam Rose, in "Equitable Considerations of Tradable Carbon Emission Entitlements," 62, acknowledges that Pareto optimality, an economic prescription dealing with distribution concerns advocated as a decision rule by some economists, requires that policy options should be chosen only if they do not make someone worse off.

8. For example, Adam Rose, Brandt Stevens, Jae Edmonds, and Marshall Wise, "International Equity and Differentiation in Global Warming Policy," *Environmental and Resource Economics* 12 (1998): 25–51.

9. Paul Beer, "Equity and Climate Change" (paper to be published by the Climate Equity Project).

10. For a discussion of prior appropriation law, see Anne J. Castle, "Water Rights Law—Prior Appropriation" (available at <www.profs.lp.findlaw.com/water/castle .html>, April 30, 2001).

11. For a discussion of Nozick's theory, see R. J. Kilcullen, "Robert Nozick: Against Distributive Justice" (available at <www.humanities.mq.edu.au/Ockham/ y64117.html>, April 30, 2001).

12. United Nations, *Rio Declaration on Environment and Development,* UN Document A/CONF.151/5, June 16, 1992, Principles 2 and 16.

13. Anonymous, "India Throws Down the Gauntlet," in *ECO, an NGO Newsletter,* issue 2, June 20, p. 2, cited in Makund Govind Rajan, *Global Environmental Politics: India and the North-South Politics of Global Environmental Issues* (New Delhi: Oxford University Press, 1991), 122.

14. "Equal Rights to the Atmosphere," in *Equity Watch,* Centre for Science and the Environment, New Delhi, November 22, 2000 (available at<www.cseindia.org/html/ cmp/climate/ew/art20001122_4.htm>, March 25, 2001).

15. Equity Watch, *Equal Rights to the Atmosphere.*

16. Equity Watch, *Equal Rights to the Atmosphere.*

17. Emission data from National Communication (FCCC/AGBM/1996/7), cited in Anil Agarwal, S. Narain, and A. Sharma, eds., *Global Environmental Negotiations in Green Politics* (New Delhi: Centre for Science and the Environment, 1999), 86.

18. For a discussion of contraction and convergence, see Aubery Meyer, *Contraction and Convergence: The Global Solution to Climate Change,* Scumacher Briefing No 5. (Devon, U.K.: Green Books, 2000).

19. Meyer, *Contraction and Convergence.*

20. For one attempted calculation of the costs to the United States entailed by a per capita allocation, see Rose et al., "International Equity and Differentiation in Global Warming Policy." These calculations do not, however, provide for large-scale reductions in technical innovation that might provide for much-reduced costs if the per capita allocation requirement would be effective thirty to forty years from now as assumed by the "contraction and convergence" proposal.

21. For a discussion of ways of not rewarding irresponsible population with a per capita national allocation, see Michael Grubb, "Seeking Fair Weather: Ethics and the International Debate on Climate Change," *International Affairs* 71, no. 3 (1995): 463–96.

22. Eileen Clausen et al., *Equity and Global Climate Change: The Complex Elements of Global Fairness* (Arlington, Va.: Pew Center for Global Climate Change, 1998), 8.

23. Stanley Benn, "Justice," in *Encyclopedia of Philosophy* (New York: Macmillan, 1967), 301.

24. Snorre Kverndokk, "Tradable CO_2 Emission Permits: Initial Distribution as a Justice Problem," *Environmental Ethics* 4 (1995): 138.

25. Clausen et al., *Equity and Global Climate Change,* 8.

26. Clausen et al., *Equity and Global Climate Change,* 15.

27. Clausen et al., *Equity and Global Climate Change,* 28.

28. Kverndokk, "Tradable CO_2 Emission Permits," 139.

Chapter Twelve

Ethical Dimensions of a Greenhouse Gas Atmospheric Stabilization Target

As we saw in previous chapters, humans have already changed the climate system in ways that make return to preindustrial atmospheric concentrations of greenhouse gases in the atmosphere impossible for hundreds of years. Given that business-as-usual greenhouse emission trends threaten to create catastrophic climate change, it will be necessary for the international community to agree on a stabilization target for atmospheric greenhouse gases. In other words, the international community will need to decide whether they will stabilize greenhouse gases in the atmosphere at, for instance, 450, 550, or 600 parts per million (ppm) of carbon dioxide equivalent. The international community must make this decision because unless an atmospheric target is agreed on, no nation will know what are its emission reduction obligations. National reduction obligations make sense only in terms of global atmospheric carbon goals.

The objective of the 1992 UN Framework Convention on Climate Change (UNFCCC) in this regard is

> stabilization of greenhouse gas concentrations in the atmosphere at a level that would prevent *dangerous anthropogenic interference with the climate system.* Such a level should be achieved within a time-frame sufficient to allow ecosystems to adapt naturally to climate change, to ensure that food production is not threatened and to enable economic development to proceed in a sustainable manner.[1] (italics added)

Although nations have already agreed to stabilize greenhouse gases in the atmosphere, there is some ambiguity about what they have promised to do. Because the UNFCCC does not specify what is meant by "dangerous anthropocentric interference," international negotiations will need to determine what this phrase means in future negotiations. Different levels of stabilization will create different levels of protection for human health and flora and fauna. In addition, final stabilization levels may greatly threaten some nations much more than others. For these reasons, the issue of an atmospheric carbon stabilization level must be understood to raise a host of ethical concerns.

Although it will be scientifically difficult to determine precisely which levels of atmospheric carbon will create what amount of damage to human health and the environment, it can be said without fear of contradiction that the higher the levels of atmospheric greenhouse gases, the more human health and species of plants and animals will be threatened. Since we know that humans are already affecting the climate system in a way that will harm some humans, plants, and animals, every day that the international community fails to achieve stabilization creates additional damages to humans, plants, and animals. For this reason, the issue of the atmospheric stabilization level raises serious ethical questions about what our duties are to protect future generations and plants and animals from global warming.

Although the United States approach to other global warming issues discussed in this book have been shown to be ethically problematic as a matter of mainstream anthropocentric consequentialist, deontological, and theories-of-justice ethical approaches discussed in chapter 3, the greenhouse atmospheric stabilization level issue also raises fundamental ethical questions about human duties to nonhuman species. This is so because the issue of what is the appropriate level of greenhouse gas atmospheric stabilization directly raises the question of what degree of protection we should give to nonhuman species or ecosystems from climate change damage.

Humans must wake up to the reality that we must now decide who and what will live or die because of global warming. We no longer have time in negotiations to prevent all damages: the oceans are rising, glaciers are melting, local climate patterns are changing, the range of disease-carrying mosquitoes and vectors is increasing, soils are drying up more quickly, and heat is increasing. All this will harm some people and areas more than others. People and plants and animals have always suffered because of natural climate changes, and now, for the first time in history, climate change will be at least in part human caused.

As the international community negotiates climate change issues, the unavoidable damage that we will experience from global warming is surely increasing. Thus far, international negotiations have not been focused on establishing atmospheric concentration stabilization levels, although the European Union once proposed attempting to stabilize carbon dioxide at 560 ppm.[2] As we saw in chapter 5, many scientists and policymakers believe that a doubling of carbon dioxide from preindustrial levels to 560 ppm may be unavoidable during this century.[3] This is so because the world's political and economic

Figure 12.1   Waiting until it's too late to protect the atmosphere

Reprinted with the permission of the Centre for Science and Environment, New Delhi, India, Rustam Vania/CSE.

system cannot respond rapidly enough to make faster changes in polluting sources, such as gasoline-powered automobiles and coal-fired power plants.

As we have seen, the national reduction targets agreed to in the Kyoto Protocol were arrived at in negotiations that considered economically reasonable reductions from existing emission levels for each nation; they were not based on levels necessary to protect human health and the environment. Nor have the post-Kyoto negotiations taken up the issue of what is an appropriate atmospheric stabilization level. Yet this issue must soon be faced if the world desires to protect human health and plants and animals from significant global warming damage.

In fact, a strong ethical argument can be made that this issue should be faced in international negotiations as soon as possible because the longer the international community waits to act on an atmospheric climate target, the steeper will be the amount of reductions needed to meet a desirable target. If the international community does not set an atmospheric stabilization target soon, it may turn out to be too late to set a target at ethically acceptable levels. In fact, arguments can be made that the minimum likely level for carbon dioxide stabilization of 560 ppm is already very ethically troublesome because this amount of carbon in the atmosphere will likely mean significant levels of climate change damage, particularly to the poorest people around the world.

For all these reasons, the atmospheric stabilization level is an extraordinarily important matter that needs to be faced soon for both practical and ethical reasons. However, once the international community turns to the subject of atmospheric stabilization, they will need to face a host of other ethical issues entailed by this question. At the top of the list of these issues is the question of whether the nations that will be less directly harmed by climate are willing to take the dramatic action that is necessary for the sake of those nations that are most harmed. This is so because not all people, plants, and animals are equally vulnerable to climate change. As we have seen in chapter 5, climate models show that the poorest people around the world are most vulnerable to climate change. This is so for the following reasons:

- The ecological systems of many of the poorest nations are most at risk.
- The poorest nations are the most vulnerable to storms, flooding, and sea-level rise.
- The health of the poorest people worldwide is at greatest risk from global warming.
- The food supplies of the poor are at risk from global warming.
- The poorest nations have the least financial and institutional ability to adapt to climate change.

Other obvious ethical questions entailed by the issue of the need to select a stabilization atmospheric target level include the following:

- Given the scientific uncertainties in determining exactly what levels of atmospheric greenhouse gases will create specific risks to humans, plants, and animals, to what extent will the international community be willing to follow the precautionary principle discussed in chapter 7 in agreeing on an atmospheric target of carbon?
- In thinking about the costs of reaching a national target that has been allocated to achieve a safe atmospheric concentration level, will nations look only at costs and benefits to themselves, as has been the tendency of policymakers in the United States as discussed in chapter 9?
- Will the developed nations be willing to accept an equitable share of a global reduction target as discussed in chapters 8 and 11?
- Who should pay for unavoidable damages that will occur anyway?

The rest of this chapter examines the ethical questions entailed by selecting an atmospheric stabilization level.

THE ETHICAL DIMENSIONS OF SETTING
THE ATMOSPHERIC TARGET TO PROTECT
HUMANS, PLANTS, ANIMALS, OR ECOSYSTEMS

As we saw in chapter 3, environmental ethicists are comprised of utilitarians, deontologists, those concerned about justice, biocentrists, ecocentrists, deep ecologists, and ecofeminists, among others. At one end of this continuum are some anthropocentrists who hold that human interests alone should be the focus of ethical concern, while at the other end are those who see strong ethical duties to protect all of nature from human interference. In reality, these categories of ethical approaches are not discrete. For instance, among the utilitarians interested in environmental issues are some who extend utilitarian concepts to the protection of all beings that could suffer pain. In addition, there are rights-based theorists who believe that rights should be extended to at least some animals. Despite the continuum of views (rather than the neat categories suggested by ethical labeling), for the purposes of examining the issues entailed by the entire continuum, this section examines what practical difference would be made in setting greenhouse gas stabilization levels in the atmosphere if the atmospheric level were set at levels implementing a more anthropocentric, biocentric, or ecocentric ethic.

Setting the Atmospheric Greenhouse Target to Protect Human Interests

Although some anthropocentric ethical approaches have been extended to nonhumans by some ethical theorists, there are many ethicists who believe that ethics make sense only when applied to human interests and concerns. If the UNFCCC's stabilization target was interpreted to require only protection of human interests, the atmospheric stabilization level should be determined by examining what atmospheric carbon level will harm human health or well-being, including the human dependence on ecological systems for such ecological services as food production.

Some assume that greenhouse gas emissions might rise to a doubling of carbon dioxide from preindustrial levels, from 280 to 560 ppm, without seriously endangering human health and the food supply. If this is the case, policy should be directed at stabilizing greenhouse gases in the atmosphere so as not to exceed this level. This conventional wisdom, however, is not without controversy. For instance, even small rises in sea levels will harm those people already threatened by ocean storms. Increasing the range of disease-carrying mosquitoes, a phenomenon that is already happening, will surely put some people at risk. In other words, any additional levels of greenhouse gases in the atmosphere are likely to harm some humans. Yet many argue that these adverse human impacts can be anticipated and responded to by such adaptive responses as moving people away from rising oceans or initiating public health measures to wipe out vectors. That is, some argue that humans can adapt to the type of climate change that we will be seeing with a doubling of greenhouse gases. However, it is also generally recognized that the climate system is capable of surprises, that is, nonlinear responses of the climate system. These climate surprises could mean that if we allow carbon dioxide to double, we could have much more rapid and larger temperature changes than the 1.4°C to 5.8°C predicted most recently by the Intergovernmental Panel on Climate Change (IPCC) for this century. As we saw in chapter 5, these rapid changes could be caused by, among other events, sudden changes in ocean circulation patterns, large instantaneous releases of carbon stored in permafrost, or large melting of the Antarctic ice cap. Most scientists believe that these surprises are plausible but low-probability events that could happen in this century even with only a doubling of carbon dioxide. Of course, if a climate surprise were triggered, human interests would be threatened much more than generally assumed, and adaptation would be more difficult. Yet humans might still be able to adapt to such rapid climate changes, although some of the poorest people undoubtedly would be hurt even in the absence of climate surprises.

Because great harm could come to some humans and particularly the poorest, even anthropocentric ethical systems would condemn the status quo on global warming. For this reason, the world does not need to agree on more environmentally protective ethical approaches, such as the biocentric or ecocentric views discussed in chapter 3, to find the status quo on climate change ethically reprehensible. Yet for as long as human interests alone are at the center of concern, given that many humans could adapt to a warmer planet, there is a surprising lack of the urgent need to radically change course on greenhouse gas emissions.

In arriving at the conclusion that there is no urgency to protect human interests, many policymakers often are influenced by cost-benefit analysis of the type discussed in chapter 9. These cost-benefit analyses also rely on techniques for calculating the value of what will be damaged by global warming as if only human interests count. That is, as we have seen, the cost-benefit analyses use "willingness to pay" in markets as the measure of value of environmental entities that could be harmed by global warming. Yet as we have seen in chapter 9, these cost-benefit analyses also often fail to respect the rights of future generations of humans in preparing such analyses through the use of standard discounting techniques. For this reason, even from a human interest point of view alone, these cost-benefit analyses are usually ethically deficient.

The only conceivable way of squaring a strict anthropocentric ethic with allowing greenhouse gases to continue to grow to some level in the atmosphere above where they are now would be to deal with the limitations of standard cost-benefit analyses discussed in chapter 9 and to have those that have caused unavoidable damages to some humans pay for the damages. Yet if this approach were seriously followed so that those nations that are causing unavoidable damage would have to pay for it, in all probability it would be much less expensive for them to reduce emissions as rapidly as possible. In other words, even if a very limited anthropocentric ethic were applied to the question of greenhouse gas stabilization level, the potential liability of those nations causing the problem would lead them to stabilize the atmospheric levels at the lowest level possible.

Setting the Atmospheric Greenhouse Target to Protect All Living Beings

A biocentric interpretation of the UNFCCC's atmospheric target would mean that climate change policy should be implemented in such a way either to allow individual plants and animals to flourish or to ensure that species are preserved. This is so because among the biocentrists are those who are concerned with individuals and others interested in protecting species preservation. Yet the conventional scientific wisdom about global warming includes the notion not only that humans have already caused some warming but also that, even if the international community were able to stabilize greenhouse gases at current levels (370 ppm of carbon dioxide), the earth would continue to warm for a least a 100 years because of thermal lags in oceans. Without doubt, these changes will continue to adversely affect individual animals and plants from flourishing and create grave threats to some species of plants and animals. It is therefore already impossible to implement greenhouse gas stabilization objectives in such a way as to accomplish what a biocentric ethic would demand. Therefore, if the UNFCCC's stabilization goal were to be interpreted as a duty to all living beings, it would require immediate and maximum reduction of greenhouse gas emissions. This is so because irreversible damage from global warming to some plants and animals is already unavoidable, and a biocentric ethic would require that we protect plants and animals to the extent that we are able to do so.

Setting the Atmospheric Greenhouse Target to Protect Ecosystems

An ecocentric interpretation of the UNFCCC's stabilization goal would require that atmospheric greenhouse gas targets be set at levels that would protect ecosystems. However, as was the case for the biocentric goal, it is already very likely too late to prevent damage to many ecosystems around the world. For instance, expected unavoidable rising sea levels will undoubtedly destroy some wetlands and marshes and threaten many estuarine ecosystems because of increasing salinity entailed by rising ocean levels. It is also already too late to prevent damage to many terrestrial ecosystems, including forests.

However, if climate change is gradual enough, some scientists believe that many ecosystems will have time to adapt without massive dieback. Yet it is virtually impossible to predict what level of environmental stresses will exceed the ecosystem's natural resiliency and ability to adapt, that is, to exceed its ecological integrity.[4] For this reason, assumptions that the world's ecosystems will go through a smooth transition while adapting to a warmer climate constitute at best a dangerous bet about the natural world's ability to respond smoothly. This bet is particularly risky in light of the potential climate surprises discussed in chapter 5. In fact, some climate models now predict that massive forest dieback in the later part of this century is likely.[5] It therefore can be said that an ecocentric ethic would require, just as a biocentric ethic would, setting the greenhouse gas atmospheric stabilization target at the lowest possible level in the quickest time.

CONCLUSION

As we have seen, even if policymakers were to take only human interests into account in setting an atmospheric greenhouse gas stabilization target, that target would be set at the lowest possible level. Under biocentric- and ecocentric-based ethical approaches to setting such a target, there is little doubt that the target would have to be set at the lowest achievable level and that this level should be agreed to as quickly as possible. The reason for urgency is that the longer the international community waits to agree on the target, the higher the target will need to be set because of the impossibility of achieving lower levels.

A more anthropocentric interpretation of the UNFCCC's stabilization goal might perhaps require a little less urgency, yet because it is already too late to prevent damage to the poorest people, setting atmospheric stabilization targets at any level higher than the lowest level possible means that those responsible for greenhouse emissions should pay for all climate damages and particularly those damages that could have been avoided if nations refusing to make the maximum reductions possible had followed the most aggressive approaches to domestic greenhouse gas emissions reductions. Of course, no matter which ethical rule is followed in deciding on an atmospheric stabilization goal, the status quo on global warming emissions is ethically reprehensible.

NOTES

1. United Nations, United Nations Framework Convention on Climate Change, 1992, Rio de Janeiro, Article 2.
2. For a discussion of the unavoidability of some greenhouse damages, see chapter 5.

3. William Stevens, "Experts Doubt a Greenhouse Gas Can Be Curbed," *New York Times,* November 3, 1997, A1.

4. For a discussion of the state of the art on ecological integrity, see David Pimentel, Laura Westra, and Reed Noss, eds., *Ecological Integrity: Integrating Environment, Conservation and Health* (Washington, D.C.: Island Press, 2000), and Phillipe Crabbe, Alan Holland, Lech Ryszkowski, and Laura Westra, *Implementing Ecological Integrity: Restoring Regional, Environmental, and Human Health* (Dordrecht: Kluwer Academic Publishers, 2000).

5. The Hadley Center, "Climate Change: An Update of Research for the Hadley Center," November 2000 (available at <www.meto.govt.uk/research/hadleycentre/pubs/brochures/B2000/summary.html>, March 28, 2001).

Chapter Thirteen

Conclusion: Some Additional Issues

This book has reviewed the ethical dimensions of the U.S. role in the global warming problem. It has concluded that the excuses of the United States for its failure to seriously reduce greenhouse gas emissions do not pass the most minimum ethical scrutiny. That is, the often-stated justifications of the United States for not implementing a strong global warming policy because of uncertainty in global warming science, cost-benefit to the U.S. economy, and the failure of the developing world to make binding commitments are all ethically bankrupt. The book has also considered ethical problems with previous U.S. positions on the Kyoto flexibility mechanisms. Ethical considerations demand that the United States urgently and comprehensively reduce its greenhouse gas emissions to an equitable level.

The book has also identified other key global warming issues that the United States needs to face in the years ahead that raise important ethical questions. Two of these issues have been discussed in some detail: the need to agree to an equitable national allocation of greenhouse gas reduction targets and the need to agree on a stabilization target for atmospheric greenhouse gases. There are several other ethical issues that need to be faced soon by the United States that are mentioned here only in passing because they are not believed to be as urgent as the issues discussed in chapters 11 and 12. These include the following:

- What is a fair allocation of costs among nations for damages caused by global warming that cannot reasonably be avoided, given differences among nations in responsibility for the problem?
- To what extent should any nation be allowed to rely on carbon sinks, such as forests, to reduce its national responsibility to reduce greenhouse gas

Figure 13.1   Fair trades for carbon sinks

Reprinted with the permission of the Centre for Science and Environment, New Delhi, India, Rustam Vania/CSE.

emissions given that (1) many sinks store carbon only temporarily and may release stored carbon in large nonlinear amounts in response to large temperature changes[1] and that (2) any nation's ability to maintain forests is in part an accident of geographic and climatic setting that provides the right temperatures and amounts of rainfall to support the growth of sinks? As a result, some arid nations and those whose climate will become more arid because of global warming will not be able to use sinks as an offset against national reduction obligations, while others will get large credits for doing little because they are blessed with the right temperatures and adequate rainfall.

These are among the most important ethical questions entailed by global warming that the United States needs to face in the years ahead, yet others are sure to arise. It is the goal of this book to place the ethical dimensions of these and other global warming issues at the very center of public policy debate because, as we have seen, the ethical dimensions of global warming policy are often hidden in the policy languages of science and economics.

THE ENORMOUS ETHICAL CHALLENGE TO THE UNITED STATES ENTAILED BY GLOBAL WARMING

This book has argued that there are both ethical and practical reasons why the United States needs to face the ethical dimensions of global warming controversies. That is, if the United States fails to approach several global warming issues on the basis of equity, justice, and ethics, not only will the U.S. response to global warming be unethical, unjust, and unfair, but the much-needed global consensus to climate change will not likely emerge.

As President Clinton acknowledged at the United Nations in 1997, the United States has a special responsibility for global warming. This unique American obligation exists for the following reasons:

- The United States releases a disproportionate share of the greenhouse gases.
- The United States, among the developed nations, has most consistently continued to resist proposed international solutions that, if agreed to at the time they were proposed, would have made the existing problem less serious.
- In comparison to many developed nations, the United States has most failed to take global warming seriously.
- The United States has significant technical and financial resources to attack global warming.

The world desperately needs the United States to accept its clear responsibility on global warming and act accordingly. However, probably not until Americans understand the ethical dimensions of global warming will a strong political cry emerge that demands serious action to reduce global warming's immense threat.

This book has argued that one of the reasons U.S. citizens have failed to see the ethical dimensions of global warming is because some economic interests have been successful in leading Americans to focus on the nonethical dimensions of the global warming problem. For this reason, the global warming problem is a powerful example of why the United States needs to make the ethical questions entailed by important global environmental problems a clearly visible concern in public discourse and decision making. That is, the United States needs to more consciously and openly integrate environmental ethical considerations into day-to-day environmental policymaking. However, the global warming experience thus far also makes it clear that those interested in environmental ethics must be more knowledgeable about the scientific, economic, and factual context in which environmental controversies arise if they are going to make relevant contributions to policymaking. Only by following the scientific and economic controversies created by global warming can one identify the critical ethical issues that need attention. As was stated in the preface to this book, identifying the ethical questions embedded in science and economics is a first-order challenge. Unless such questions and economic disputes are identified as ethical questions, they will escape ethical scrutiny.

It is lamentable that this book has been harshly critical of the U.S. role in global warming policy. It has been written in the belief, however, that once Americans see the ethical dimensions of the global warming problem, they will demand change. That is, when Americans understand their ethical obligations, they will rally behind strong global warming programs forged with an eye toward international distributive justice. Americans will again demand justice as they did on civil rights reform legislation once they saw the dogs and the policemen on the Selma, Alabama, bridge attack the peaceful civil rights marchers. When the American people finally and clearly see that the positions taken by their politicians on global warming have had potentially disastrous consequences to innocent people around the world and the precious legacy of plants and animals that we share the planet with, they, as they have before, will insist on justice and equity in national policy. Although the United States has too often let narrow economic interests control political discourse, once the American people see the full ethical dimensions of this problem, they will scorn the resistance of these economic interests and their political spokespersons to anything less than an all-out response to lower carbon emissions. With this belief, this book has been written in an effort to help Americans understand how the U.S. responses to global warming thus far has been ethically equivalent to the dogs attacking the civil rights marchers in Selma mentioned by Bill McKibben in the *New York Times* op-ed quote that began this book.[2]

However, when U.S. citizens inevitably begin to demand that the United States change its approach to global warming, almost certainly the economic interests that so far have been successfully resisting government programs on global warming will continue to fight by trying to make the debate focus on issues of scientific certainty and cost-benefit analysis, that is, on the technical details and arguments that both hide the ethical questions and diffuse the potential energy created by ethical concern. For this reason, those who feel an obligation to speak out on global warming will need to be prepared to show how important ethical issues are hidden in the scientific and economic arguments. This will prove quite challenging because it will require that those who are energized by the ethical dimensions of this problem are capable of untangling the ethical issues from the scientific and economic discourses that economic interests will try to position at the center of global warming policy discussions.

Concerned citizens will need to be able to say that the amount of scientific information that one needs to trigger an ethical responsibility is both a scientific and an ethical question. They will also need to argue that it is an ethical question whether cost-benefit analyses on global warming policy options identify who is harmed and who will benefit, that is, whether cost-benefit analyses expressly consider questions of distributive justice. They must be willing to show why a cost-benefit analysis use of a discount rate and willingness-to-pay methods to determine the vale of environmental entities harmed by global warming is an ethical question, not an economic question alone. They must be willing to help people see that if the United States is unwilling to make policy to reduce greenhouse gas emissions, that is, to act to prevent damage to other people without their consent, such decisions are ethical matters, not simply matters of domestic economic concern. They must be willing to explain why procedural justice demands that in such matters the United States must consult with and attempt to achieve consensus with those who may be damaged by U.S. decisions on global warming before the United States forges final policy.

In summary, Americans will need to learn to identify the ethical dimensions of arguments made in the policy languages of science and economics because it is through the use of these languages that narrow economic interests distract us as they put the rabbit in the hat when influencing U.S. policy on global warming.

Concerned philosophers and theologians who are beginning to be engaged in global warming have an important role to play in helping citizens understand the ethical dimensions of these issues, but they will need to engage these issues as they unfold in negotiations, for the important issues are usually hidden in what purports to be value-neutral policy languages but that are ethically laden at their very core. For this reason, identifying where the ethical issues are hidden in the policy languages is often a step logically prior to applying an ethical principle. This is so because for as long as the ethical questions remain hidden, they cannot be openly considered and understood. In the global warming debate thus far, the dogs are not on the bridge for all to see; they are in the dense linguistic thickets of scientific and economic discourse manipulated by narrow economic interests.

Maurice Strong, the former UN undersecretary-general responsible for the 1972 Stockholm and the 1992 Rio Earth Summit conferences, said that the rhetoric recently surrounding climate change reminded him "of the clamor surrounding earlier fundamental changes in the way business was done—that is the movements to abolish the slave trade and later child labor. Then as well, the dominant economic ethos of the times clashed with a new moral and ethical responsibility."[3]

At the time this book was written, short-term and short-sighted economic interests are prevailing over what should be seen as obvious ethical obligations to do something significant about global warming. For the most part, the ethical obligations of the United States for global warming are still invisible in the national debate.

Global warming is shaping up to be a problem of profound historical consequence for the United States. It is a huge environmental, economic, social, and foreign policy challenge. Global warming is likely to force us to think more deeply about international equity than any previous international challenge. It has many, if not all, of the issues embedded in civil rights controversies because it raises the question of whether some people will be allowed to gain at other people's expense, including their very life. Global warming will force us to think more deeply about human duties to plants and animals than any other environmental crises because the decision on atmospheric greenhouse gas stabilization levels will make us decide which plants and animals will survive. Global warming will also make the United States come to terms with the question of whether it desires to build a just international order or pursue narrow national self-interest.

Given the immensity of this problem, the current lack of ethical focus on global warming in the United States is truly astonishing. As this book goes to press, the United States is waking up to an energy problem that started to be noticed as an inadequate electricity supply problem in California, coupled with rapidly increasing gasoline prices around the nation. That these problems, like global warming, have been caused in part by an unquestioned assumption that the United States has a right to consume as much fossil fuel as necessary to meet domestic energy demand no matter how wasteful or necessary is curiously escaping public attention. Although President George W. Bush's recent rejection of Kyoto has also put global warming on the front page of many American newspapers for the first time because of the international firestorm it created, when the energy problem is discussed in the media, it is rarely linked to the global warming problem despite the fact that President Bush's initial response to the emerging energy problem has been to propose large increases in fossil fuel–generated energy that will surely exacerbate the global warming problem. Quite amazingly, the U.S. media have yet to focus on the fact that large increases in the use of fossil fuel in response to an energy problem will only make the country's inequitable share of global greenhouse gas emissions larger. Although there has been some discussion in the media of the proposed Bush energy policy in terms of the potential adverse environmental impacts of drilling in the Arctic National Refuge in Alaska, there has been comparatively little media focus on the relationship between Bush's proposed energy policy and the U.S. rejection of Kyoto. As a result, President Bush has been able to claim that his energy strategy is environmentally benign because drilling in Alaska can be done with miniscule environmental impact. So few people apparently see the enormous contradiction between an energy plan that will create 1,300 new fossil fuel–fired power plants and the need to implement serious global warming policies that the current president can claim his energy policy is environmentally harmless if oil exploration and production does not create adverse environmental impacts at the production site.

In a speech on energy policy that advocated large increases in coal consumption, Vice President Dick Cheney said, "Conservation may be a sign of personal virtue, but it is not a sufficient basis for a sound, comprehensive energy policy."[4] The ethical deafness of such a position is startling if one understands that increases in U.S. fossil fuel emissions will more than likely hurt people, plants, and animals, and for that reason, even if there is no reasonable alternative to using some fossil fuel to meet increased demand, there is clearly an ethical duty to achieve as much energy conservation in the use of greenhouse gas–producing sources as the nation can possibly accomplish. For that reason, energy conservation is not only a noble personal sentiment but also a moral imperative for U.S. energy policy.

Nothing could be clearer: Those concerned about the ethical dimensions of U.S. policy on global warming have their work cut out for them. Yet it will not be enough to talk in the abstract about the ethical duties of the United States on global warming. Concerned persons will need to demand that ethics be at the very center of U.S. public policy debates on energy, foreign policy, economic policy, and social justice. It is an ethical imperative that economic and scientific discussions of U.S. global warming policy be examined through an ethical lens.

On a more positive note, as this book goes to press, an increasing number of American corporations are acknowledging the responsibility of the United States to curb greenhouse gas emissions. Many of the most responsible companies have joined the Pew Center for Climate Change, an organization supporting responsible business approaches to global warming.[5] Yet, although a growing number of U.S. corporations acknowledge global warming responsibility, many of the most powerful industry trade associations appear to be geared up for a continuing scuffle over global warming programs.

In addition to the powerful resistance to global warming programs generated by narrow economic interests are the forces of the extreme ideological right. This group seems to be energized not by economic considerations but by the belief that the problem of global warming is a subterfuge created by those who desire to establish a world government that will eventually eradicate individual freedoms. This more ideologically motivated resistance to global warming programs is currently flooding the Internet and the letters-to-the-editor pages of local newspapers with misleading or shallow scientific analyses of the global warming problem along with unsubstantiated claims that global warming programs will rapidly impoverish American society. In my local newspaper, numerous letters have recently appeared claiming that there is no credible scientific evidence that global warming is a threat at all. These letters, when coherent, often uncritically quote out of context the scientific skeptics' views discussed in earlier parts of this book. In fact, when the global warming skeptics' views are relied on in these letters, they are often not even representative of the most recent views of the skeptics who now, for the most part, acknowledge that the earth's surface is warming and that the warming is proportional to human use of fossil fuels. There is no doubt that the writers of these letters are honestly stating their views, yet their ability to confuse American citizens in a way that might lead to the continued refusal of the United States to accept its ethical responsibility for global warming is very troubling development. Those who understand the enormous ethical responsibility of the United States to reduce greenhouse gas emissions will need to understand enough of the science and economics of global warming to engage this group in public debate. They will need to encourage this group to publicly examine their assumptions, that is, to expose the scientific and economic bases for their positions and to examine these in light of their ethical dimensions. This is likely to be one of the most important challenges for the United States in the twenty-first century.

The global warming questions before us include how much of nature's endowment we are willing to sacrifice for cheap energy and what responsibility the United States is willing to assume to reduce greenhouse gas emissions to ensure that millions of present and future inhabitants of our blue planet do not suffer from global warming. We need to make the ethical dimensions of these questions an American preoccupation.

NOTES

1. For a discussion of the scientific basis for concern with the ability of carbon sinks to sequester carbon, see Andrew Revkin, "Studies Challenge Role of Trees in Curbing Greenhouse Gases," *New York Times*, May 21, 2001, A17.

2. Bill McKibben, "Indifferent to the Pain," *New York Times*, September 4, 1999, op-ed.

3. Maurice Strong, *Where on Earth Are We Going?* (New York: Texere, 2001), 43.

4. Joseph Kahn, "Cheney Promotes Increasing Supply as Energy Policy," *New York Times*, May 1, 2001, A1.

5. For identification of companies that have joined the Pew Center, see Pew Center for Climate Change (<www.pewclimate.org/about/index.cfm>, July 3, 2001).

Glossary

Adaptation—A concept that refers to decisions to modify natural or human systems in response to actual or expected global warming that cannot be avoided by emissions reductions.

Additionality—A term used in relation to the Kyoto Protocol trading rules. According to the Kyoto Protocols rules on two of the trading mechanisms—joint implementation and the clean development mechanism—credits will be awarded to project-based activities provided that the projects achieve reductions that are additional to those that otherwise would occur. Therefore, a challenge that must be faced in implementing the Kyoto trading mechanisms is to set up a workable implementation scheme to determine whether proposed projects for which a credit has been applied for to reduce a national reduction target will result in real carbon reductions that would not be achieved except for the project. This is a challenging problem because it requires an understanding of what would happen in a country without the project.

Alliance of Small Island States (AOSIS)—A coalition of small island and low-lying coastal countries that share vulnerability to the adverse effects of global climate change. The AOSIS has a membership of forty-three states and observers, drawn from all oceans and regions of the world: Africa, the Caribbean, the Indian Ocean, the Mediterranean, the Pacific, and the South China Sea.

Anthropocentric ethics—Ethical theories that limit ethical concern to human interests and matters of value to humans alone.

Banking—Parties to the Kyoto Protocol may save excess emissions allowances or credits from the first commitment period for use in subsequent commitment periods (post-2012).

Biocentric ethics—Ethical theories that make all life the center of value rather than human interests alone.

BTU tax—An energy tax levied at a rate based on the BTU (British Thermal Unit) energy content of a fuel.

Carbon cycle—The natural processes that govern the exchange of carbon among the atmospheric, ocean, and terrestrial systems. Major components include photosynthesis, respiration, and decay between atmospheric and terrestrial systems; thermodynamic invasion and evasion between the ocean and the atmosphere; and operation of the carbon pump and mixing in the deep ocean. Deforestation and fossil fuel burning also are now part of the carbon cycle.

Carbon dioxide (CO_2)—A naturally occurring gas; also a by-product of burning fossil fuels and biomass as well as land-use changes and other industrial processes. It is the principal anthropogenic greenhouse gas that affects the earth's temperature.

Carbon sequestration—The long-term storage of carbon or carbon dioxide in the forests, soils, ocean, or underground in depleted oil and gas reservoirs, coal seams, and saline aquifers.

Carbon sinks—Natural or man-made systems that absorb carbon dioxide from the atmosphere and store them. Trees, plants, and the oceans all absorb carbon dioxide and therefore are carbon sinks.

Clean development mechanism (CDM)—One of three trading mechanisms created by Kyoto Protocol. CDM projects allow developed countries to obtain credits against their national targets for projects undertaken in developing countries.

Climate feedbacks—A feedback is a change in one variable that changes another variable. Some feedback variables increase the variable under concern, while others decrease it. Climate feedbacks are interactions between greenhouse gas–produced warming and physical mechanisms or processes that will tend to magnify or decrease the amount of warming due to their reaction to the initial increases in radiation. Important climate feedbacks include vegetation, water vapor, ice cover, clouds, and the ocean. Such interactions can increase, decrease, or neutralize the warming produced by increased concentrations of greenhouse gases.

Climate models—Large and complex computer programs used to mathematically simulate global climate. They are based on mathematical equations that seek to represent the physical processes that govern the earth–atmosphere system.

Climate surprises—Rapid nonlinear unexpected and relatively sudden changes in the climate system. These could include events such as the shutting down of the North Atlantic oscillation or the rapid release of sedimentary methane hydrates, triggering even greater changes in climate.

Conference of the Parties (COP)—The supreme body of the UN Framework Convention on Climate Change (UNFCCC) comprised of countries that have ratified or acceded to the UNFCCC. The first session of the COP (COP-1) was held in Berlin in 1995; COP-2 in Geneva, 1996; COP-3 in Kyoto, 1997; COP-4 in Buenos Aires, 1998; COP-5 in Bonn, 1999; and COP-6, held initially in The Hague and continued in Bonn, 2000.

Contraction and convergence—A term that denotes a method for implementing the UNFCCC's requirement that nations reduce emissions to an equitable level. Under contraction and convergence, each nations would receive an emission cap that is based on per capita emissions. To allow each nation sufficient amount of time to meet the per capita allocation, each nation would be given enough time to converge over time toward equal per capita emission rights for all countries so that total emissions allowances to countries are proportional to population.

Ecocentric ethics—Ethical theories that make the natural world itself the focus of ethical concern rather than human interests alone.

Emissions trading—Allows nations with targets to achieve credits against those targets by trading with other nations that have trading targets. This is one of the Kyoto flexibility mechanisms.

Ethics—As used in this book, connotes the domain of inquiry that attempts to answer the question "What is good?" Ethical statements are propositions of the form that such and such is good or bad, right or wrong, obligatory or nonobligatory.

Flexibility mechanisms—Procedures that allow countries with Kyoto Protocol targets to meet their commitments under the Kyoto Protocol based on actions outside their own borders. As potentially market-based mechanisms, they have the potential to reduce the economic impacts of greenhouse gas emission reduction requirements. They include joint implementation, clean development mechanisms, and emissions trading. Although this term usually applies to the trading mechanisms, sometimes the Kyoto flexibility mechanisms also are understood to include the flexibility that nations have to (1) meet reductions targets through carbon sequestration, (2) use the basket of six Kyoto greenhouse gases to meet reduction targets, and (3) meet reduction targets in a flexible commitment period that extends from 2008 to 2012.

Fossil fuels—Carbon-based fuels formed in the ground over very long periods, including coal, oil, and natural gas.

Global Environment Facility (GEF)—A joint funding program established by developed countries to meet their obligations under various international environmental treaties. GEF was established to forge international cooperation and to finance actions to address four critical threats to the global environment: loss of biodiversity, climate change, degradation of international waters, and ozone depletion. Launched in 1991 as an experimental facility, GEF was restructured after the Earth Summit in Rio de Janeiro to serve the environmental interests of people in all parts of the world. In 1994, thirty-four nations pledged $2 billion in support of GEF's mission; in 1998, thirty-six nations pledged $2.75 billion to protect the global environment and promote sustainable development. GEF is jointly administered by the World Bank, UN Environment Program (UNEP), and the UN Development Program (UNDP).

Global warming—The view that the earth's temperature is being increased in part because of emissions of greenhouse gases associated with human activities, such as burning fossil fuels, burning biomass, manufacturing cement, rearing cows and sheep, deforestation, and other land-use changes.

Greenhouse gases (GHGs)—Gases in the earth's atmosphere that absorb and reemit infrared radiation. These gases occur through both natural and human-influenced processes. The major GHG is water vapor. Other primary human-produced GHGs include carbon dioxide, nitrous oxide, methane, ozone, and chlorofluorocarbons.

Group of 77 and China (G-77)—Originally seventy-seven, now more than 130 developing countries that act as a major negotiating bloc. The G-77 and China include the poorest nations as well as other developing countries.

Intergovernmental Negotiating Committee (INC)—The body created by the United Nations in 1990 responsible for negotiating a global warming convention, the UNFCCC. After the UNFCCC came into effect, the INC was supplanted by the COP under the UNFCCC.

Intergovernmental Panel on Climate Change (IPCC)—A panel established in 1988 by governments under the auspices of the World Meteorological Organization (WMO) and the UNEP. It prepares assessments, reports, and guidelines on the science of climate change and its potential environmental, economic, and social impacts; technological developments; possible national and international responses to climate change; and cross-cutting issues. It provides advice to the UNFCCC's COP. It is currently organized into three working groups that address science; impacts, adaptation, and vulnerability; and mitigation. There is also a working group to address GHG inventories.

Joint implementation (JI)—One of three Kyoto trading mechanisms. Jointly implemented projects that limit or reduce emissions or that enhance sinks are permitted among developed countries under Article 6 of the Kyoto Protocol.

Kyoto basket (or Kyoto GHGs)—Under the Kyoto Protocol, parties have committed to control emissions of a "basket" of six GHGs. This basket includes carbon dioxide, methane, nitrous oxide, hydrofluorocarbons, per-fluorocarbons, and sulfur hexafluoride. The arrangement gives the flexibility that would enable a party to increase emissions of any gas in the basket provided that commensurate reductions were made in another gas in the basket.

Kyoto Protocol—The protocol drafted during the Berlin Mandate process that, on entry into force, would require countries listed in its Annex B (developed nations) to meet differentiated reduction targets for their emissions of a basket of GHGs relative to 1990 levels by 2008–12. It was adopted by all parties to the Climate Convention in Kyoto in December 1997.

Methane (CH_4)—One of the basket of six GHGs to be controlled under the Kyoto Protocol. It has a relatively short atmospheric lifetime of 10 ∀_2 years. Primary sources of methane are landfills, coal mines, paddy fields, natural gas systems, and livestock.

Natural greenhouse effect—The trapping of heat by naturally occurring heat-retaining atmospheric gases (water vapor, carbon dioxide, nitrous oxide, methane, and ozone) that keeps the earth about 30°C (60°F) warmer than if these gases did not exist.

Nitrous oxide (N_2O)—One of the basket of six GHGs to be controlled under the Kyoto Protocol. It is generated by burning fossil fuels and the manufacture of fertilizer.

Nongovernmental organization (NGO)—NGOs can include registered nonprofit organizations and associations from business and industry, environmental groups, cities and municipalities, academics, and social and activist organizations. Under the United Nations, NGOs must be accredited to observe its activities and to do so must meet certain qualifications.

Precautionary principle—From the UNFCCC Framework (Article 3), parties should take precautionary measures to anticipate, prevent, or minimize the causes of climate change and mitigate its adverse effects. Where there are threats of serious or irreversible damage, lack of full scientific certainty should not be used as a reason for postponing such measures taking into account that policies and measures to deal with climate change should be cost-effective so as to ensure global benefits at the lowest possible cost.

Supplementarity—The Kyoto Protocol states that emissions trading and joint implementation activities are to be supplemental to domestic actions, that is, actions taken in countries with Kyoto targets to reduce GHG emissions. (e.g., domestic emissions limitations, energy taxes, and fuel efficiency standards). Under some proposed definitions of supplementarity (e.g., a concrete ceiling on level of use), developed countries could be restricted in their use of the Kyoto mechanisms to achieve their reduction targets. This is a subject of great contention in negotiations.

UN Environment Program (UNEP)—The UN agency established in 1972 to coordinate the environmental activities of the United Nations. It provides technical advice, coordinates scientific research, and disseminates environmental information in the UN system. UNEP played a key role in the development of the UNFCCC and other international environmental treaties.

UN Framework Convention on Climate Change (UNFCCC)—A treaty signed at the 1992 Earth Summit in Rio de Janeiro by more than 150 countries. Its ultimate objective is the "stabilization of greenhouse gas concentrations in the atmospheric at a level that would prevent dangerous anthropogenic [human-induced] interference with the climate system." While no legally binding level of emissions is set, the treaty includes a goal that developed countries should reduce emissions to 1990 levels by the 2000. The treaty took effect in March 1994 on the ratification of more than fifty countries; a total of over 180 nations have now ratified. The UNFCCC is a framework convention that is intended to be added onto by protocols. The Kyoto Protocol was agreed to in 1997. Its secretariat is based in Bonn, Germany. In the biennium 2000–01, its approved budget and staffing level are approximately $12 million annually with approximately eighty personnel.

World Health Organization (WHO)—An international agency created in 1946 to promote and coordinate research and programs that advance the cause of disease prevention and primary health care.

World Meteorological Organization (WMO)—An international agency created in 1951 to promote the exchange of weather information and science.

Bibliography

Agarwal, Anil, Sunita Narrain, and Anju Sharma. *Green Politics, Global Environmental Negotiations*. New Delhi: Centre for Science and the Environment, 1999.

Agrarwala, Shardul, and Stiener Anderson. "Indispensability and Indefensibility? The United States in Climate Treaty Negotiations." *Global Governance* 5, no. 4 (December 1999).

Arrhenius, Svante. "On the Influence of Carbonic Acid in the Air upon Temperature of the Ground." *The London, Edinburg, and Dublin Philosophical Magazine and Journal of Science,* 5th series (April 1896): 237–76.

Baer, Paul. "Equity and Climate Change." Paper to be published by the Climate Equity Project.

Banuri, K., K. Goran-Maler, M. Grubb, H. K. Jacobson, and F. Yamin. "Equity and Social Considerations." In *Economic and Social Dimensions of Climate Change: Contribution of Working Group III to the Second Assessment Report of the Intergovernmental Panel on Climate Change,* edited by James Bruce, Hoesung Lee, and Eric Haites. New York: Cambridge University Press, 1996.

Barione, Delphne, and Jean Ripert. "Exercising Common but Differentiated Responsibility." In *Negotiating Climate Change: The Inside Story of the Rio Convention,* edited by I. M. Mitzner and J. A. Leonard. Cambridge: Cambridge University Press and Stockholm Environment Institute, 1994.

Barrett, Scott. "Montreal versus Kyoto: International Cooperation and the Global Environment." In *Global Public Goods,* edited by Inge Kaul, Isabelle Grunberg, and Marc Stern. New York: Oxford University Press, 1999.

Benn, Stanley. "Justice." *Encyclopedia of Philosophy.* New York: Macmillan, 1967.

Bodansky, David. "Prologue to the Climate Change Convention." In *Negotiating Climate Change: The Inside Story of the Rio Convention,* edited by I. M. Mitzner and J. A. Leonard. Cambridge: Cambridge University Press and Stockholm Environment Institute, 1994.

Bradsher, Keith. "Fuel Economy for New Cars Is at Lowest Level since '80." *New York Times,* May 18, 2001.

Brown, Donald A. "Ethics, Science, and Environmental Regulation." *Environmental Ethics* 9 (1987): 331–49.

———. "Making the United Nations Commission on Sustainable Development Work." *Earth Negotiations Bulletin,* April 1998.

———, and John Lemons. "The Role of Science in Sustainable Development and Environmental Decisionmaking." In *Sustainable Development: Science, Ethics, and Public Policy.* Dordrecht: Kluwer Academic Publishers, 1995.

Brown, Peter, G. *Ethics, Economics, and International Relations.* Edinburgh: Edinburgh University Press, 2000.

———. *Restoring the Public Trust.* Boston: Beacon Press, 1994.

Bruce, J. P., H. Lee, and E. F. Haites, eds. *Economic and Social Dimensions of Climate Change Contribution of Working Group III to the Second Assessment of the Intergovernmental Panel on Climate Change.* Cambridge: Cambridge University Press, 1995.

Callendar, G. S. "An Attempt to Frame a Working Hypothesis on the Cause of the Glacial Periods on an Atmospheric Basis." *Journal of Geology* 64 (February 1938): 223–40.

Callicott, J. Baird. *Companion to a Sand County Almanac.* Madison: University of Wisconsin Press, 1987.

———. "Hume's Is-Ought Dichotomy and the Relation of Ecology to Leopold's Land Ethic." *Environmental Ethics* 4 (1982): 46–74.

Centre for Science and the Environment. "Equal Rights to the Atmosphere." *Equity Watch.* New Delhi, November 22, 2000. <www.cseindia.org/html/cmp/climate/ew/art20001122_4.htm>, March 25, 2001.

Christianson, Gale E. *Greenhouse: The 200-Year Story of Global Warming.* New York: Walker, 1999.

Clausen, Eileen, et al. *Equity and Global Climate Change: The Complex Elements of Global Fairness.* Arlington, Va.: Pew Center for Global Climate Change, 1998.

Congressional Research Service. *Global Climate Change Briefing Book.* <www.cnie.org/nle/clim-7/index.html>, June 11, 2001.

Crabbe, Phillipe, Alan Holland, Lech Ryszkowski, and Laura Westra. *Implementing Ecological Integrity: Restoring Regional, Environmental, and Human Health.* Dordrecht: Kluwer Academic Publishers, 2000.

Dasgupta, Chandrashekner. "The Climate Negotiations." In *Negotiating Climate Change: The Inside Story of the Rio Convention,* edited by I. M. Mitzner and J. A. Leonard. Cambridge: Cambridge University Press and Stockholm Environment Institute, 1994.

Dernbach, John. "Moving the Climate Change Debate from Models to Proprosed Legislation: Lessons from State Experience." *Environmental Law Reporter* 30 (November 2000): 10934, 10948, 10975.

Engle, J. Ronald. *Ethics of Environment and Development, Global Challenge, International Response.* Tucson: University of Arizona Press, 1990.

Environmental Defense Fund. *Global Warming: The History of an International Scientific Consensus.* <www.edf.org/pubs/factSheets/d_GWFact.html>, December 20, 2000.

Environmental Ethics. *A Brief History of Environmental Ethics for the Novice.* <www.cep.unt.edu/novice.html>.

Falk, Jim, and Andrew Brownlow. *The Greenhouse Challenge: What's to Be Done?* New York: Penguin Books, 1989.

Forum for Religion and Ecology. <www.environment.harvard.edu/religion/research/home.html>, May 4, 2001.

Fourier, Joseph. "Remarques Generales sur la Temperatures du Globe Terrestre et des Espaces Planetaires." *Annales de Chimie et de Physique* 27 (1824): 136–67.

Friedman, Thomas. *The Lexus and the Olive Tree: Understanding Globalization.* New York: Farrar, Strauss & Giroux, 1999.

Gates, K. L., A. Henderson-Sellers, G. J. Boer, C. K. Folland, A. Kitoh, B. J. McAveney, F. Semazzi, N. Smith, A. J. Weaver, and Q. C. Zeng. "Climate Models—Evaluation." In *The Science of Climate Change: Contribution of Working Group II to Working Group II,* edited by John T. Houghton, L. G. Meira Filo, B. A. Callander, N. Harris, A. Kattenbverg, and K. Maskell. Cambridge: Cambridge University Press, 1995.

Gelbspan, Ross. *The Heat Is On.* Reading, Mass.: Perseus Books, 1998.

Goldemberg, Jose. "The Road to Rio." In *Negotiating Climate Change: The Inside Story of the Rio Convention,* edited by I. M. Mitzner and J. A. Leonard. Cambridge: Cambridge University Press and Stockholm Environment Institute, 1994.

Gore, Albert. *Earth in the Balance.* New York: Houghton Mifflin, 1992.

Grubb, Michael. "Seeking Fair Weather: Ethics and the International Debate on Climate Change." *International Affairs* 71, no. 3 (1995): 463–96.

Guha, Ramachandra. "Radical American Environmentalism and Wilderness Preservation: A Third World Critique." In *The Great New Wilderness Debate,* edited by J. Baird Callicott and M. P. Nelson. Athens: University of Georgia Press, 1996.

Hadley Center. "Climate Change: An Update of Research for The Hadley Center," November 2000. <www.meto.govt.uk/research/hadleycentre/pubs/brochures/B2000/summary.html>, March 28, 2001.

Hapka, Gerald. "Climate Change: The Policy and the Political Process." Unpublished paper by for the Pew Climate Change Program.

Harris, Paul. "Climate Change: Is the United States Sharing the Burden?" In *Climate Change and American Foreign Policy,* edited by Paul Harris. New York: St. Martin's Press, 2000.

——. "Considerations of Equity and International Institutions." *Environmental Politics* 5, no. 2 (1996): 274–301.

——. "Defining International Distributive Justice: Environmental Considerations." *International Relations* 15, no. 2 (August 2000).

—— "Environmental Security and International Equity: Burdens of American and Other Great Powers." *Pacifica Review* 11, no. 1 (1999): 25–42.

——. "Sharing the Costs of Climate Change: An Assessment of American Foreign Policy." *Cambridge Review of International Affairs* 12, no. 2 (1999).

——. "Understanding America's Climate Change Policy: Realpolitik, Pluralism, and Ethical Norms." Oxford Center for the Environment Ethics and Society Research Paper No. 15 (June 1998).

——, ed. *Climate Change and American Foreign Policy.* New York: St. Martin's Press, 2000.

Hasselmann, K. "Intertemporal Accounting of Climate Change: Harmonizing Economic Efficiency and Climate Stewardship." *Climate Change* 41 (1999): 333–50.

Hidore, John, and John Oliver. *Climatology: An Atmospheric Science.* New York: Macmillan, 1993.

Horworth, Richard. "Climate Change and Intergenerational Fairness." In *New Directions in the Economics of Climate Change.* Pew Center for Global Climate Change, October 2000. <www.pewclimate.org/projects/directions.pdf>, March 22, 2001.

Houghton, John, G. Jenkins, and J. Ephraums, eds. *Scientific Assessment of Climate Change.* Boston: Cambridge University Press, 1990.

———, Filho, B. A. Callender, N. Harris, A. Kattenberg, and K. Maskell, eds. *The Science of Climate Change: Contribution of Working Group I to the Second Assessment of the Intergovernmental Panel on Climate Change.* Cambridge: Cambridge University Press, 1995.

———. *Global Warming: The Complete Briefing.* Cambridge: Cambridge University Press, 1997.

Hydar, Tariq Osman. "Looking Back to See Forward." In *Negotiating Climate Change: The Inside Story of the Rio Convention,* edited by I. M. Mitzner and J. A. Leonard. Cambridge: Cambridge University Press and Stockholm Environment Institute, 1994.

Intergovernmental Panel on Climate Change. *About IPCC.* <www.ipcc.ch/about/about .htm>, February 10, 2001.

———. *An Introduction to Simple Climate Models used in the Second Assessment Report,* 1997. <www.ipcc.ch/pub/IPCCTP.II(E).pdf>, March 17, 2001.

———. *Report of Working Group L, Technical Synthesis,* 1995. <www.ipcc.ch/pub/ sarsyn.htm>, March 18, 2001.

———. *Synthesis of Technical and Scientific Information.* <www.ipcc.ch/pub/sarsyn .htm>, March 17, 2001.

———. *Third Assessment Report: Summary for Policy Makers—Contribution of Working Group I,* January, 2001. <www.usgcrp.gov/ipcc/wg1spm/pdf>, March 17, 2001.

———. *Third Assessment Report: Summary for Policy Makers—Contribution of Working Group I,* January, 2001. <www.ipcc.ch>, March 18, 2001.

Jamieson, Dale. "Ethics and Intentional Climate Change." *Climatic Change* 33 (1996): 323–36.

———. "Ethics, Public Policy, and Global Warming." *Science, Technology, and Human Values* 17 (1992): 139–53.

Jonas, Hans. *The Imperative of Responsibility.* Chicago: University of Chicago Press, 1984.

Kegley, Charles W., and Eugene R. Wittkoph. *World Politics: Trend and Transformation.* New York: St. Martin's Press, 1997.

Kilcullen, R. J. "Robert Nozick: Against Distributive Justice." <www.humanities.mq .edu.au/Ockham/y64117.html>, April 30, 2001.

Kverndokk, Snorre. "Tradable CO_2 Emission Permits: Initial Distribution as a Justice Problem." *Environmental Ethics* 4 (1995): 138.

Labe, Jim. "Environment: U.S. Economy Comes First, Says Bush." International Press Service, World News. <www.oneworld.net/anydoc2.cgi?url=http%3A%2F% 2Fwww%2Eoneworld%2Enet%2Fips2%2Fmar01%2F225F46%5F082%2Ehtml>, June 6, 2001.

Landes, David. *The Wealth and Poverty of Nations: Why Some Are So Rich and Some So Poor.* New York: W. W. Norton, 1998.

Lemons, John. *Scientific Uncertainty and Environmental Problem Solving.* Cambridge, Mass.: Blackwell Science, 1996.

——, and Donald Brown. "The Role of Science in Sustainable Development and Environmental Decisionmaking." In *Sustainable Development: Science, Ethics, and Public Policy.* Dordrecht: Kluwer Academic Publishers, 1995.

Lemons, John, Rudolph Heridia, Dale Jamieson, and Clive Splash. "Climate Change and Sustainable Development." In *Sustainable Development: Science, Ethics, and Public Policy,* edited by John Lemons and Donald Brown. Dordrecht: Kluwer Academic Publishers, 1995.

Lumsdaine, David H. *Moral Vision in International Politics.* Princeton, N.J.: Princeton University Press, 1993.

MacIntyre, Alasdair. "Utilitarianism and Cost/Benefit Analysis: An Essay on the Relevance of Moral Philosophy to Bureaucratic Theory." In *Values in the Electric Power Industry,* edited by K. M. Sayre. South Bend, Ind.: University of Notre Dame Press, 1983.

Malman, J. D. "Uncertainties in Projections of Human-Caused Climate Warming." *Science,* November 1997.

McElroy, Robert W. *Morality and American Foreign Policy.* Princeton, N.J.: Princeton University Press, 1992.

McKibben, Bill. *The End Of Nature.* New York: Anchor Books, 1990.

——. "Indifferent to the Pain." *New York Times,* September 4, 1999, op-ed.

——. "Some Like It Hot." *New York Review of Books* 43, no. 11, July 5, 2001.

McMichael, A. J. *Planetary Overload.* Cambridge: Cambridge University Press, 1993.

Meyer, Aubery. *Contraction and Convergence: The Global Solution to Climate Change.* Schumacher Briefing No 5. Devon, U.K.: Green Books, 2000.

More, Thomas G. *Climate of Fear.* Washington, D.C.: Cato Institute, 1998.

Morrissey, Wayne. *Global Climate Change: A Concise History of Negotiations and Chronology of Major Activities Preceding the 1992 U.N. Framework Convention.* Congressional Research Service, Report for Congress, 1998. <www.cnie.org/nle/clim-6.html>, March 9, 2001.

Naess, Arne. "The Shallow and the Deep, Long-Range Ecological Movement." *Inquiry* 16 (spring 1973).

National Academy of Sciences. *Climate Change Science: An Analysis of Some Key Questions.* Washington, D.C.: National Academy of Sciences. <www.books.nap.edu/html/climatechange/ >, June 21, 2001.

National Resource Council. *Reconciling Observations of Global Temperature Change.* Washington, D.C.: National Academy Press, 2000.

Nizte, William A. "A Failure of United States Leadership." In *Negotiating Climate Change: The Inside Story of the Rio Convention,* edited by I. M. Mitzner and J. A. Leonard. Cambridge: Cambridge University Press and Stockholm Environment Institute, 1994.

Nordhouse, W. D. *Managing the Global Commons.* Cambridge: MIT Press, 1994.

Oberthur, Sebastian, and Herman Ott. *The Kyoto Protocol: International Climate Policy for the 21st Century.* Berlin: Springer Publishing, 1999.

Ott, Herman. "Climate Change: An Important Foreign Policy Issue." *International Affairs* 2 (2001): 277–96.

Partridge, Ernest. "An Askance Glance at Environmental Policy Making." Unpublished paper presented at Rocky Mountain Biological Laboratories, Crested Butte, Colorado, July 13, 1955.

Pew Center for Climate Change. <www.pewclimate.org/about/index.cfm>, July 3, 2001.

Pierce, D., W. Cline, A. Achanta, S. Fankhuaser, R. Pachauri, R. Tol, and P. Vellinga. "The Social Costs of Climate Change: Greenhouse Damage and the Benefits of Control." In *The Economic and Social Dimensions of Climate Change: Contribution of Working Group III to the Second Assessment Report of the Intergovernmental Panel on Climate Change,* edited by James Bruce, Hoesung Lee, and Eric Haites. New York: Cambridge University Press, 1996.

Pimentel, David, Laura Westra, and Reed Noss, eds. *Ecological Integrity: Integrating Environment, Conservation and Health.* Washington, D.C.: Island Press, 2000.

Pojman, Louis P., ed. *Environmental Ethics.* Belmont, Calif.: Wadsworth, 1997.

Rajan, Makund Govind. *Global Environmental Politics: India and the North-South Politics of Global Environmental Issues.* New Delhi: Oxford University Press, 1991.

Rawls, John. *A Theory of Justice.* Cambridge: The Belknap Press of Harvard University Press, 1971.

Reiner, David M., and Henry D. Jacoby. "Annex I Differentiation Proposals: Implications for Welfare, Equity and Policy." In *Joint Program on Science and Policy of Global Change.* Cambridge: MIT Press, 1997.

Reuters New Service. "Environmentalists Blast Bush Energy Plan." May 18, 2001. <www.nytimes.com/pages/reuters/world/index.html>, June 1, 2001.

Revkin, Andrew. "Studies Challenge Role of Trees in Curbing Greenhouse Gases." *New York Times,* May 21, 2001.

Rose, Adam. "Equitable Considerations of Tradable Carbon Emission Entitlements." In *Combating Global Warming, Study on a Global System of Tradable Carbon Emission Entitlements.* United Nations Conference on Trade and Environment. New York: United Nations, 1992.

———, Brandt Stevens, Jae Edmonds, and Marshall Wise. "International Equity and Differentiation in Global Warming Policy." *Environmental and Resource Economics* 12 (1998): 25–51.

Sagoff, Mark. "At The Shrine of Our Lady of Fatima or Why Political Questions Are Not All Economic." *Arizona Law Review* 23 (1982): 1281–98.

———. *The Economy of the Earth.* New York: Cambridge University Press, 1988.

Schneider, Stephen, ed. *Climate Change* 41 (April 1999). Special volume devoted to the strengths and weaknesses of integrated assessment applied to global warming.

Seelye, Katherine, and Andrew C. Revkin. "Panel Tells Bush Global Warming Is Getting Worse." *New York Times,* June 7, 2001.

Sharpe, Virginia. "Ethical Theory and the Demands of Sustainability." Paper presented at the American Chemical Society Meeting on Ethics and Society, October 1995.

Shrader-Frechette, Kristen. "A Defense of Risk-Cost-Benefit Analysis." In *Environmental Ethics,* edited by Louis P. Pojman. Belmont, Calif.: Wadsworth, 1997.

———. "Methodological Rules for Four Classes of Scientific Uncertainty." In *Scientific Uncertainty and Environmental Problem Solving,* edited by John Lemons. Cambridge, Mass.: Blackwell Scientific Press, 1996.

———, and Edward D. McCoy. *Methods in Ecology.* Cambridge: Cambridge University Press, 1993.

Shogren, Jason, and Michael Toman. "How Much Climate Change Is Too Much? An Economics Perspective." *Resources for the Future* (September 2000): 14. <www.rff/org/disc_papers/PDF_files/0022/pdf>, March 22, 2001.

Shue, Henry. "After You: May Action by the Rich Be Contingent upon Action by the Poor?" *Indiana University School of Law–Bloomington Law Journal.* <www.law.indiana.edu/glsj/vol1/shue.html>, March 21, 2001.

Singer, Peter. "Animal Liberation." In *The Environmental Ethics and Policy Book,* edited by Donald VanDeVeer and Christine Pierce. Belmont, Calif.: Wadsworth, 1997.

Singer, S. Fred. *The Scientific Case against Global Climate Treaty.* Fairfax Va.: The Science and Environmental Policy Project, 1997.

Spash, Clive. "Economics, Ethics, and Long Term Environmental Damages." *Environmental Ethics* 15, no. 2 (1993): 117–32.

Stevens, William. "At Meeting on Global Warming, U.S. Stands Alone." *New York Times,* September 10, 1991.

———. *The Change in the Weather, People, Weather, and the Science of Climate.* New York: Delacorte Press, 1999.

———. "Cushioning the Shock of Global Warming." *New York Times,* November 30, 1997.

———. "Experts Doubt a Greenhouse Gas Can Be Curbed." *New York Times,* November 3, 1997, A1.

———. "Global Warming: The Contrarian View." *New York Times,* February 29, 2000. <www.nytimes.com/library/national/science/0229000sci-environ-climate>, March 18, 2001.

———. "The Oceans Absorb Much of Global Warming, Study Confirms." *New York Times,* March 24, 2000.

Stocker, Thomas F. "Past and Future Reorganizations in the Climate System." *Quaternary Science Reviews* (2000): 301–19.

Streets, D., and M. Glantz. "Exploring the Concept of Climate Surprises." *Global Climate Change* 10, no. 2 (July 2000).

Strong, Maurice. *Where on Earth Are We Going?* New York: Texere, 2001.

Taylor, Paul. "Ethics of Respect for Nature." *Environmental Ethics* 3 (1981): 261–67.

Tucker, Mary Evelyn, and John A Grim. *Worldviews and Ecology, Religion, Philosophy, and the Environment.* Maryknoll, N.Y.: Orbis Books, 1999.

Turner, R. Kerry, David Pierce, and Ian Bateman. *Environmental Economics: An Elementary Introduction.* Baltimore: The Johns Hopkins University Press, 1993.

United Nations. *Agenda 21.* UN Document A/CONF.151/26, June 16, 1992, Rio de Janeiro. United Nations Framework Convention on Climate Change, May 29, 1992, UN Document A:AC.237/18.

———. *Climate Change Information Kit.* <www.unfccc.de/resource/iuckit/fact07 .html>, March 18, 2001.

———. New York, May 9, 1992, UN Document A/CONF.151/26, Article 3, Paragraph 1. <www.194,95,93/default1.htf>, March 16, 2001.

———. Protocol on Substances That Deplete the Ozone Layer. September 16, 1987, 26 ILM 1541.

———. *Universal Declaration of Human Rights.* G.A. Resolution 217A (III), UN Document A/810 at 71, December 10, 1948, adopted by the General Assembly of the United Nations (without dissent).

United States Department of Energy. *The Climate Change Action Plan of the United States.* United States Government Printing Office, ISBN NO. 0-16-048178-3, 1993.

United States Energy Information Administration. *Annual Energy Outlook 2001 with Projections to 2020.* Report No. DOE/EIA-0383(2001), December 22, 2000.

———. *United States Emissions of Greenhouse Gases.* Report No. EIA/DOE-0573, 1999. <www.eia.doe.gov/oiaf/1605/ggrpt/index/html>, March 15, 2001.

United States Environmental Protection Agency. *Inventory of U.S. Greenhouse Gas Emissions and Sinks: 1990–1997.* EPA 236-R-99-03. Washington, D.C.: U.S. Environmental Protection Agency. <www.epa.gov/globalwarming/publications/emissions/ us1999/index.html>, March 13, 2001.

Utility Commission of Ohio. *Chronology of Climate Change.* <www.puc.state.oh.us/ consumer/gcc/chron.html>, June 6, 2000.

VanDeVeer, David, and Charles Pierce. "An Introduction to Ethical Theory." In *The Environmental Ethics and Policy Book.* Belmont, Calif.: Wadsworth, 1997.

Warick, Joy, and Peter Baker. "Clinton Details Global Warming Plan." *Washington Post,* October 23, 1997, A6.

Warren, Karren. "The Power and Promise of Ecofeminism." In *The Environmental Ethics and Policy Book,* edited by David VanDeVeer and Charles Pierce. Belmont, Calif.: Wadsworth, 1997.

Watson, Robert T., M. C. Zinyowera, and R. H. Moss. *Impacts, Adaptations and Mitigation of Climate Change: Scientific-Technical Analyses—Contribution of Working Group II to the Second Assessment of the Intergovernmental Panel on Climate Change.* Cambridge: Cambridge University Press, 1995.

Wentz, Peter. *Environmental Ethics Today.* New York: Oxford University Press, 2001.

Westra, Laura. *An Environmental Proposal for Ethics.* Lanham, Md.: Rowman & Littlefield, 1974.

———, David Pimentel, and Reed Noss, eds. *Ecological Integrity: Integrating Environment, Conservation and Health.* Washington, D.C.: Island Press, 2000.

Westra, Laura, Phillipe Crabbe, Alan Holland, and Lech Ryszkowski. *Implementing Ecological Integrity: Restoring Regional, Environmental, and Human Health.* Dordrecht: Kluwer Academic Publishers, 2000.

White House. *The Kyoto Protocol and the President's Policies to Address Climate Change: Administration Economic Analysis.* July 1998. WGB-98 0042.

———. *National Energy Policy: Analysis.* May 2001.

Wiegel, George. *American Interests, American Purpose: Moral Reasoning and U.S. Foreign Policy.* Washington, D.C.: Praeger Press, 1989.

Index

About the Author

Donald A. Brown is director of the Pennsylvania Consortium for Interdisciplinary Environmental Policy (PCIEP), an organization comprised of forty-three colleges and universities and state-level environmental decision makers dedicated to improving environmental policy through interdisciplinary analyses of environmental and sustainable development problems and solutions. From 1995 to 1998, Brown served as program manager for UN organizations at the U.S. Environmental Protection Agency, Office of International Environmental Policy. For most of his career, Brown has been employed as an environmental lawyer or in senior management positions with various government agencies. Throughout his career, Brown has been interested in and written extensively on the need to integrate environmental science, economics, and law with ethics in environmental and sustainable development policymaking. The opinions expressed in this book are his alone and in no way represent the positions of present or former employers.